HONOR AND VIOLENCE
IN THE OLD SOUTH

HONOR AND VIOLENCE IN THE OLD SOUTH

BERTRAM WYATT-BROWN

New York   Oxford

OXFORD UNIVERSITY PRESS

Oxford University Press

Oxford   New York   Toronto
Delhi   Bombay   Calcutta   Madras   Karachi
Petaling Jaya   Singapore   Hong Kong   Tokyo
Nairobi   Dar es Salaam   Cape Town
Melbourne   Auckland

and associated companies in
Beirut   Berlin   Ibadan   Nicosia

Published by Oxford University Press, Inc.,
198 Madison Avenue, New York, New York 10016-4314

Oxford is a registered trademark of Oxford University Press

Library of Congress Cataloging-in-Publication Data
Wyatt-Brown, Bertram, 1932–
Honor and violence in the Old South.
Abridged ed. of: Southern honor. 1982.
Bibliography; pp.   Includes index.
1. Southern States—Civilization.
2. Southern States—Moral conditions.
I. Wyatt-Brown, Bertram,
1932–   . Southern honor.   II. Title.
F209.W895   1986   975   86–12884
ISBN 0–19–504241–7 (alk. paper)
ISBN 0–19–504242–5 (pbk. : alk. paper)

The genealogical table of the Foster family is based on a table in *Prince Among Slaves* by Terry Alford, by permission of Harcourt Brace Jovanovich and Professor Alford.

8 10 9
Printed in the United States of America

Dedicated to
Natalie Wyatt-Brown
and
in Memory of Laura Wyatt-Brown

Preface

The concept of honor seems inherently and perversely contradictory: comic and tragic, romantic and shrewd, inhumane and magnanimous, brave and hypocritical, sane and mad, like the famous Don in pursuit of the unresponsive Dulcinea. But for all the perplexities that the elusive concept raises, in many regions, especially in slaveholding societies, honor may be seen as a people's theology, a set of prescriptions endowed with an almost sacred symbolism. Under honor's law those who have power to demand, and to hold, esteem and authority are able to do so because the entire social order has sanctioned their rule and called it moral. Whereas in Christian and humanistic ethical systems distinctions are drawn between moral and physical power, honor places them in close proximity.

In these pages, which are an abridgment of *Southern Honor: Ethics and Behavior in the Old South,* the ethnic of honor takes on larger and more socially active meanings than ordinary parlance tends to convey. Honor in the pre-Civil War slave states was an encoded system, a matter of interchanges between the individual and the community to which he or she belonged. Meaning was imparted not with words alone, but in courtesies, rituals, and even deeds of personal and collective violence. In such a system, words could assume particular, and sometimes dangerous, force, as in the case of communicating a challenge to a duel. Likewise, the language of politics was less devoted to rational explanation than to rituals reconfirming shared values; the style of oratory for which the South was famous served to remind listeners of common principles rather than to challenge existing beliefs. Both deeds and words of this character helped to create structure, hierarchy, race control, and social discourse.

Although we prefer to dwell on the individualistic and open-handed side of honor, we must establish its essentially defensive posture. Whites in the antebellum South were a people of honor who would not subject themselves to the contempt of a ruthless enemy, as the Yankee supporters of Abraham Lincoln and abolitionists were thought to be. As early as 1851, secessionist leader James Jones of South Carolina argued that even if the overwhelming power of the North were to defeat a Southern struggle for independence, the Southerners would have at least "saved our honour *and lost nothing*." The chief aim of this notion of honor was to protect the individual, family, group, or race from the greatest dread that its adherents could imagine. That fear was not death, for dying with honor would bring glory. Neither was it the prospect of damnation in the life hereafter. Judgments of that kind were in the hands of God. Rather, the fear was of public humiliation. This vulnerability was distressing not only in itself, but, and more important, because it forced the humbled party to admit the shame to himself and to accept the full implications. With his loss of autonomy, he had betrayed kinfolk and manhood, in fact, he had betrayed all things held dear.

Thus, honor existed in intimate relation to its opposite: shame. This book describes the fears and projections of ignominy with almost as much attention as it does the usages of honor; one cannot be understood apart from the other. An individual was expected to have a healthy sense of shame, that is, a sense of his own honor. Shamelessness signified a disregard for both honor and disgrace. When shame was imposed by others, honor was stripped away.

In slaveholding cultures, the contrast between the free and the unfree—the autonomy of one, the abjectness of the other—prompts an awareness of moral, as well as political and social stratification. Not all honor societies were slaveholding. Yet no slaveholding culture could casually set aside the strictures of honor. The very debasement of the slave added much to the master's honor, since the latter's claim to self-sufficiency rested upon the prestige, power, and wealth that accrued from the benefits of controlling others.

American planters in the South were far from indifferent to the exigencies of obedience brought about by such a system. While slavery would not have existed without a cash basis, white Southerners spoke more glowingly of the supposed social benefits than they did about the economic advantages of the system. Whatever we may think of their morality, slavery was considered an honorable institution indeed. The assumption of the rightfulness of ownership was a social fact built into the Southern way of life.

Without slavery to sustain the appropriate environment, Southern honor would have died early. But the ethical code that American settlers brought with them from the Old World justified a racial and social bondage that first made temporary chattels of white servants, then made permanent slaves of African imports. From the start, slavery and honor were mutually dependent. After emancipation in 1865, honor, like the labor system that had nourished it, lived on in truncated yet vigorous form, especially with regard to laws and practices that perpetuated the humiliation and subjugation of black people—the imposition of lynch law, Jim Crow, and restrictive education. The most psychologically powerful expression of Southern honor was the sexual dread of black blood in a white womb. In the patriarchal imagination, no humiliation was greater.

For a considerable length of time scholars have concentrated almost exclusively upon the history and meaning of slavery, while the moral underpinnings for the Southern way of life—including slaveholding itself—have received little attention. This book seeks to correct the balance. Honor was neither the romantic fantasy of belles and gallants found in sentimental fiction, nor was it the baseless illusion unworthy of historical notice that some scholars have contended. The ethic cannot be explained as precisely as one can dissect the clauses of a treaty or enumerate the birth and death rates of a New England village. Yet its social force, regardless of how much we admire, loathe, or smile at its manifestations, can be demonstrated as one of the most remarkable features of American cultural history.

May 13, 1986   Bertram Wyatt-Brown

Note

A word should be said about the changes made for this abridgment. By and large I sought to remove redundant material with minimal damage to coherence. To that end, one chapter was excised from each of the three sections. The footnotes have also been eliminated. In addition, I have cut some introductory explanations about honor in the Old World because their presence, in so short a work, would be too prominent and perhaps misleading. For the most part, the analytical, rather than the descriptive sections, have been retained.

More than *Southern Honor,* this abridgment stresses the collective aspect of honor rather than domestic features. Important though honor was as a feature of daily household life, its public function mattered most because of the expediencies of race control. This work, with its opening and closing chapters devoted to the communal aspects of honor and shame, thus emphasizes the role of honor in society. A bibliographical essay to guide the interested reader has been supplied and includes the most significant and most recent materials readily available.

Contents

PART ONE
FOUNDATIONS

1. Honor in Literary Perspective *3*
2. The Nature of Primal Honor *25*
3. Gentility *40*
4. Family *63*
5. Sexual Honor, Expectation, and Shame *85*

PART TWO
PUBLIC ETHICS

6. Hospitality, Gambling, and Personal Combat *121*
7. Policing Slave Society: Insurrectionary Scares *154*
8. Tar and Feathers: Community Disorder *187*
9. Anatomy of a Wife-Killing *214*
   Suggested Readings *249*
   Index *263*

Part One

·

Foundations

1

Honor in Literary Perspective

Paradox, irony, and guilt have been three current words used by historians to describe white Southern life before the Civil War. They are popular terms because it is hard for us to believe that Southerners ever meant what they said of themselves. How could they so glibly reconcile slaveholding with pretensions to virtue? We prefer to assume that their defenses were either lies or self-delusions. If neither of these alternatives meets the complexities of the circumstances, then their mental gymnastics and their habits may be characterized as unintended paradox—a discrepancy between boasted ideals of freedom and a contrary assumption that those values could forever rest upon the enslavement of blacks. Apart from a few lonely dissenters, Southern whites believed (as most people do) that they conducted their lives by the highest ethical standards. They thought that they had made peace with God's natural order. Above all else, white Southerners adhered to a moral code that may be summarized as the rule of honor. Today we would not define as an ethical scheme a code of morality that could legitimate injustice—racial or class. Yet so it was defined in the Old South. The sources of that ethic lay deep in mythology, literature, history, and civilization. It long preceded the slave system in America. Since the

earliest times, honor was inseparable from hierarchy and entitle-
ment, defense of family blood and community needs. All these exigencies required the rejection of the lowly, the alien, and the
shamed. Such unhappy creatures belonged outside the circle of
honor. Fate had so decreed.

For all the many meanings that the word "honor" has been
given, the ethic for centuries was fairly stable. Ages differed on
which aspect should have priority: inner feelings of self-worth, gentility, and high-mindedness, or public repute, valor for family and
country, and conformity to community wishes. Each of these aspects of the ethic might conflict with others, and much of Western
literature is concerned with how and why such opposites have
both helped and hindered men's choices of action. Nevertheless,
honor has retained over centuries a character that most could comprehend. That is no longer true. Our view of honor is so rarefied
that we do not see how it could really coexist with violence and the
complacent subjugation of so-called inferiors. Since paradox, irony,
and guilt tell us more about our modern ethics than about the antebellum Southerners', we need a better strategy to reach the heart of
the past. The most efficacious means is through literature, at least
at first. For introductory purposes, I will not begin by defining
honor, or even by offering specifically Southern examples of it. To
do so might at once resurrect long-standing moral preconceptions,
before we are ready to rediscover the South that once existed. It is
best to look elsewhere.

We will start by observing honor at a moment of crisis. It is one
in which a ritual, tragically common in the American South but at
one time more widespread in the Western world, helped a community to overcome its fears and reassert its primal values.

In 1832 Nathaniel Hawthorne, explorer of the New England soul,
published a short story that well illuminates the role of traditional
honor and shame in human affairs. The setting for "My Kinsman,
Major Molineux" is a colonial New England port (Boston, though
unnamed.) True, the site of the tale bears no physical resemblance
to the agrarian South about which this study is concerned. None-

theless, the principles of conduct that guide Hawthorne's characters were ones quite familiar to white citizens of the slave states. They too knew the exigencies of honor, the horrors of shame. In fact, Southerners saw them as means of holding fast to the social order that they so deeply cherished. It was threat of honor lost, no less than slavery, that led them to secession and war.

At the beginning of the story, Hawthorne assures the reader that the incidents to be described are not conscious foretellings of the coming American Revolution. The message, he implies, lies elsewhere. He is concerned with the relations of individuals to their community, one that had not yet broken the cake of custom. He places the sketch at 1732 or thereabouts. Throughout the early history of the colonies, Hawthorne says, officials of the provincial government displeased both their English masters in London by failing to carry out orders and their American subjects by attempting to do so. The result, Hawthorne concludes by way of dismissing politics from center stage, was "much temporary inflammation of the popular mind."

The narrator then introduces Robin, an eighteen-year-old youth who has walked from his distant forest home to the somnolent port with its wooden buildings, narrow streets, and odors of pitch and the sea beyond. Night has just descended. His mission is to locate a respected first-cousin-once-removed—Major Molineux. "The Major," Robin later tells a kindly gentleman, "having inherited riches, and acquired civil and military rank, had visited his cousin, in great pomp, a year or two before; had manifested much interest in Robin and an elder brother, and, being childless himself, had thrown out hints respecting the future establishment of one of them in life."

According to old and early New England customs, Robin's elder brother was to inherit the family farm. In those days, many American young men would receive less of the patriarchal bounty than the firstborn. Though neither in the North nor South was primogeniture ever popular, inheritances were not always evenly distributed, especially when a father's resources were severely limited. The second son had to settle for unimproved acres or a chance for apprenticeship at a trade. Some, like Robin, relied upon a patron. The prominence and wealth of an uncle or another relation could assist the advance of a kinsman on the threshold of career and adulthood. Reliance upon family connections was not a sign of weakness, but a necessity. Such was the pattern in the South long after these common practices had begun to erode in the antebellum North.[3]

First, Robin encounters a dignified gentleman, jealous of his rank and rude to inferiors, an attitude symbolized by his manner of walking with a long, polished cane and a pompous "hem, hem" punctuating his stately tread. When Robin boldly asks directions to the major's dwelling, the periwigged old man turns in outrage. "I know not the man you speak of! What! I have authority. I have—hem, hem—authority," he shouts. Robin hastens away as two barbers standing nearby roar with laughter at his predicament. Throughout his ill-directed wanderings in the town, those overhearing the exchanges, like a Greek chorus, echo the derision of the barbers. Robin encounters a pretty prostitute, whose blandishments he virtuously rejects, a tavern-keeper and his rowdy guests, a watchman representing the law. All refuse to answer young Robin's simple question. Other townsmen, one and all, eye him with unfeigned suspicion. In exasperation, Robin belligerently halts a stranger who, he perceives, had been among the scornful revelers at the inn. Now, however, the stranger's countenance has been made grotesque, with some black substance smeared down one side of his face and red dye down the other. A violently misshapen nose separates the two colors. The cloaked masquerader gruffly tells him to wait an hour and the major will pass by. The figure vanishes.

While waiting, Robin sees a church standing desolate, faint moonbeams playing over the pulpit and open Bible within. The cold solitude of the church and nearby cemetery remind him of the contrasting warmth of religion at home. He half-dreams that his family is gathering under an ancient oak where his father, a penurious clergyman, customarily holds summer prayer. In the pastoral tableau, his father strains against his emotions for the missing son and the others indicate their grief in stolid but poignantly revealing ways. Then the family enters the house, but in his mind's eye Robin is "excluded from his home." The adventurer knows that he cannot, or at least should not, return in defeat. He must be on his own, however much he misses the innocence and domestic joys of the simple country life that he has left behind.

Another gentleman passes. This time when the request is made, however, the newcomer is cordial, though he urges Robin to wait for the Major just as the previous stranger had commanded. The brief, cheerful interlude ends as a trumpet bleats oddly. Then distant shouts are heard. The people in the imposing houses in front of which Robin and the genial companion linger step out to join the approaching procession with its discordant music. Robin sees "a dense multitude of torches." At the head is a single horseman, the grim figure with the particolored visage. He is "clad in a military dress" and carries a drawn sword, "and, by his fierce and variegated countenance, appeared like war personified; the red of one cheek was an emblem of fire and sword; the blackness of the other betokened the mourning that attends them." Others are dressed as Indians. Some have costumes and faces made up in totally meaningless perversity, as incomprehensible as the passwords that groups of rowdies had earlier whispered to Robin as they passed. Then the leader steps directly in front of Robin, as if the whole pageant were for his edification. The noise diminishes to a low hum deadlier than silence. The torches flicker on the sole occupant of a wooden cart in the midst of the crowd. There sat Major Molineux "in tar-and-feathery dignity."

> He was an elderly man, of large and majestic person, and strong, square features, betokening a steady soul; but steady as it was, his enemies had found means to shake it. His face was pale as death, and far more ghastly; the broad forehead was contracted in his agony, so that his eyebrows formed one grizzled line; his eyes were red and wild, and the foam hung white upon his quivering lip. His whole frame was agitated by a quick and continual tremor, which his pride strove to quell, even in those circumstances of overwhelming humiliation.

A poignant, climactic moment follows: the major's recognition of his kinsman. "The foul disgrace of a head grown gray in honor" was now compounded; the cousins "stared at each other in silence, and Robin's knees shook, and his hair bristled, with a mixture of pity and terror." Robin realizes that all those who had tormented him earlier are nudging each other and leering at him from various points in the immense throng: the watchman, the strumpet in the scarlet dress, the innkeeper, the tavern guests, and the barbers. From underneath the balcony of a mansion that Robin had earlier imagined belonged to the major, there rings out a laugh—"Haw, haw, haw,—hem, hem,—haw, haw, haw." The peal of raucous mockery comes from the first ancient Robin had met. A nightcap has taken the place of the periwig, and his silk hose hang loosely about his legs. But the old man is leaning on his polished cane, scepter of power. Against his will, against all rationality, Robin bursts into uncontrollable laughter, as if in answering bray. All join in, most especially those whom Robin had previously encountered. But Robin's shouts are the loudest of all. The rite ends. The crowd disperses. The cart bears the major away. Drained of all feeling, Robin turns to his companion and says with finality, "Thanks to you, and to my other friends, I have at last met my kinsman, and he will scarce desire to see my face again. . . ." He asks for directions home, but the kind gentleman demurs. Instead he suggests that Robin stay longer; "as you are a shrewd youth, you may rise in the world without the help of your kinsman, Major Molineux."

The story is a fantasy. The masquerading, deceptions, shadowy confusions might be appropriate to a mystery story such as Edgar Allan Poe's "Gold Bug." Colors, and their absence, also suggest the Gothic mode. The writer calls attention to the primary reds of the whore's dress, the crowd's torches, the horseman's half-face, the thrusts of light from the barbers' windows, the harsh glare of lamps and fires at the tavern. These contrast with the blackness of unlighted passageways, the other side of the horseman's visage, the gloom of the mansion opposite the church. The narrator's description of fitful moonbeams upon church and cemetery are also dramatic devices. But myth and reality are curiously conjoined. When people knew only of wooden carts, rude houses, filth-runneled alleys, and meager sources of illumination, the flash of color and the pomp of ceremony were greatly prized. Romance was intended, but it was the romance enlivening a medieval life of grayness, rotting wood, deadly odors, and drab existence. It was a world with little safety or light, one where honors were few but so preciously regarded that cruelty was born of fear for their loss.

The focus of the story is upon Robin's coming of age. The pastoral reverie reveals the disorientation that naturally would arise when a boy far from home meets unexplained rebuff. He is homesick, but also feels somewhat abandoned, even by those who love him. Yet he takes strength from their memory. Loyalty to family, to the father who had sacrificed part of his meager salary to send him thither, was a virtue highly respected, and infidelity was to be greatly condemned. By the time the kind gentleman arrives, Robin is already subdued. He supplicates rather than demands help. Robin is a child still: he even jumps up to show the stranger that he is full grown. The response of Robin's new friend is genial, but the initiation into corporate life is just begun. When the noise of the paraders grows louder, Robin disputes his companion's observation that it is only a handful of ruffians making fun. No, he says, the tumult must come from a "thousand voices." The kind gentleman asks, "May not a man have several voices, Robin, as well as two complexions?" One must learn to accept men as they are, even though their actions belie their outward claims. Just as some men are religious and God-fearing, others pay only lip service. It is only the foolish and the misguided who dare challenge all the ways of the world. Robin is forced to agree. Then the youth replies with spirit, "But Heaven forbid that a woman" should be so deceptive as well. He has in mind the pretty prostitute's "seductive tones" when she pretended to be the major's housekeeper. A woman's honor, he means, is much more circumscribed than a man's. She cannot act shamelessly and yet retain respect. The gentleman does not dispute his observation. It was a universal judgment.

Although the perspective is that of a very young man meeting a cruel world, in a few pages Hawthorne has also described the basic moral theme of early Anglo-American popular culture: the sovereignty of a primeval community in the distribution of honor—and dishonor—and the effects of that coercive spirit upon the subjects of the community's rulings. The author makes it abundantly clear that the ritual saturnalia—the mock crowning of the Scapegoat King—has the acquiescence, if not the connivance, of the local establishment. The constabulary was present, not to repress the cruel merriment but to join the proceedings. The single horseman at the head of the crowd represents the fraternity of the colonial militia, the citizen army by which a semblance of order was maintained. The figure with the cough and cane testifies to the complicity of the highest local authority. For the sake of preserving ordinary governance, he permits, and probably had even instigated, the sacrifice of Major Molineux, one of his own councillors. The townspeople who join the procession just as it reaches Robin and his companion live in fine houses near the church and presumably worship there. They would not have initiated so crude a rite, which had its beginning in the meaner districts. Nonetheless, the upper-class folk were scarcely averse to applauding the show.

The tale has been seen almost exclusively as a classically Freudian rendition of the oedipal myth—Robin laughs because the "son" is celebrating the defeat of the surrogate father, Major Molineux. But it must be remembered that while we see events through Robin's eyes (with occasional authorial departures) there is a veiled drama contained in the action, too. It is the struggle, offstage, between the major and Authority, personified by the old gentleman with the cane. Old age has triumphed over Molineux the councillor, himself a man of graying hair but at the height of his powers, until enemies found his vulnerability. Jealous of rivals, determined to retain the preferments of office, the old man under the balcony has found the means to fend off a challenge, perhaps for the last time before death. At the very least, he has preserved his rapport with the vulgar elements of the town under the strange horseman's control. It is this victory, the success of near dotage, that Authority finds so delicious. Fortuitous circumstances—Providence—had placed a young kinsman of the enemy on the scene to witness the ruin of Authority's victim. Since both the cane-carrying official and Major

Molineux were long in years, we cannot assert unequivocally an oedipal relation between them. But still, there is a hint that whatever the situation was prior to the scapegoating ritual, established authority in the town has won a struggle. Robin, still the innocent, sees the pageant as a child would, with himself the center of adult concern, but clearly the old man under the balcony and the demonic militiaman had more serious business to perform. The oedipal factors, if present, must be considered, at least in part, as the reverse of a son's triumph over a patriarch. The "father" of the community is the victor; he makes Robin the child laugh. We shall discover in the Old South that the refusal of the old to surrender power sometimes led to the frustration and degradation of the young. As the figure of Authority exemplified, men deny death's inevitability even when the effects of age confront them. As it has ever been, the relation of father and son could be corrupting, not solely because the young wished the death of the old but also because the old could not always recognize the ravages of age and relinquish power to the young. Triumphs such as that of Authority in "Major Molineux" were hollow. The son, when his turn finally came, either learned to exercise power with similar ruthlessness or, because of a dependency lasting too long, felt unable to replicate the father's success. Hawthorne's story masterfully gives rise to such thoughts, while permitting other possibilities to seem equally valid.

In any case, the climax of the story demonstrates a social fact of traditional life. When crises arose, Hawthorne implies, rich and poor, high and low, join together in the selection of a person to blame. Someone, anyone, should pay for the collective sense of apprehension and outrage. Through the victim, their anxieties are personified and exorcised for the sake of all. At earlier times in New England, wretched old women and zealous Quakers had served similar purposes. Why Molineux should have been chosen is not important. Hawthorne disdains even to offer a clue. The politics of the moment do not concern him, or us, but rather the inexorable will of the populace, whatever the reason, however guilty or innocent the party selected might be.

It is a literal world that Hawthorne describes, but one not seeking justice so much as the facsimile of it. It is all one could expect in a world of risk and vulnerability to misfortune, human and natural. Justice was only public retribution, not abstract principle. If these inclinations were peculiar to New England in its pre-Revolutionary years, the story would be a curious comment on antique ways and little more. But the ethic that produced Molineux's distress lived on in the slave South. It endured, in fact, long afterwards too. The active participation of one part of a white community and the silence or even hidden manipulations of the rest in such affairs were a means of preserving communal solidarity. The invocation of the Lord of Misrule for the maintenance of order was usually directed toward the underclass of blacks. But whites too, on occasion, were its victims. Without such demonstrations the social and racial order itself, it was thought, would founder or drift toward chaos. Everyone had to subordinate personal autonomy to the collective will. It was the task of leaders to carry out the community's desires, to uphold its sacredness; otherwise they would find that they themselves were the sacrifices offered up to the sanctified ideals.

The weight of the community upon the individual is most dramatically demonstrated in Robin's reaction to the sight of the mob and its prize. Not once does the youth question the social order, only his personal disillusionment, which Hawthorne hints will not last long. Nor, in Christian fashion, does he bind his cousin's wounds or follow the cart to offer the kind of aid that he himself, ironically, had journeyed to obtain. Instead Robin joins the laughter of the ruler, who stands in symbolic disarray. Robin's shout is the catharsis attending any tragedy. First there is the pity and terror of watching someone die, either physically or spiritually, an emotion that Southerners sometimes experienced in much the same way. A boisterous release of tension follows. Someone else has been chosen by Providence, and the creature's misfortune somehow enhances one's own sense of safety. That security, which a system of honor and shame provides, is evinced in Robin's successful initiation into the community. By laughing, Robin acknowledges his oneness with the rest. Hysterical though it is, his response was what the crowd anticipated. In bowing to the onlookers, Robin is morally compromised: he is tainted with their complicity in his own kinsman's downfall. Robin is placed in a double bind. The only way provided for his entry into the community is to join in humiliating his cousin. In a society in which family ties are so intense, family betrayal, even under pressure of community opinion, becomes corrupting. Robin's tormentors appreciate the irony. They enjoy his embarrassment and his submission to their will. He only gains the status of bare toleration, but it is a step up from his earlier isolation.

Even as his kinsman is ushered out of decent society—and out of Robin's family—the youth is welcomed, though scarcely warmly, into the new surroundings. In Robin's reaction there is indeed a hint of oedipal triumph over the major, his sought-for guardian. Robin's shout celebrates the transfer of power from the major to the community. In societies of few opportunities, minimal institutions, and low productivity, the death or removal of any officeholder opens a position that advances by one rung those further down the ladder. That exigency, as much as a son's unconscious resentment of a father's power over him, is a factor in Robin's compulsive laughter.

In a sense, Robin is Everyman on a pilgrimage not toward God but toward place in society, passing youthfully through vales of disorder, vice, and unpredictable evils—the common lot of mankind. One message of the tale is the same as that of *The Scarlet Letter:* "Be true! Be true! Be true! Show freely to the world, if not your worst, yet some trait by which the worst may be inferred." That is a universal maxim, applying not to eighteenth-century New England alone. The closing lines about Robin's prospects in the town may suggest that a new, less vicious approach to life lies in the town's future, one in which some of the virtues of the forest order are brought to the city. But Hawthorne forgoes didacticism. Instead, he deals with human isolation—the great dread of being alone in the midst of many, a theme that runs through much of American literature and life. Robin and his kinsman, the major, are both severed from family ties and from community fellowship. But Robin's future, unlike the major's, is hopeful. The stranger offers him the chance to remain. In effect he says, "If you do as we do, you may be one of us." Also, he implies, "Your success will depend upon your own efforts and rectitude, and not upon the favors of a patron."

Nevertheless Robin, though a good lad, belongs to the world of honor, not of conscience. By no means is he to be seen as a figure transcending the multitude. By similar pressures upon the individual, Southern whites held a race in bondage. To make one's way in Robin's setting or in the antebellum South, one had to adopt the principles held sacred by the community.

At the heart of honor, then, lies the evaluation of the public. It may seem paradoxical but it is not so, as Hawthorne's story reveals. Honor has three basic components, none of which may exist wholly independent of the other. Honor is first the inner conviction of self-worth. Seemingly, that sense of personal completeness would comply with modern notions of individuality: all men are created equal. Robin entered the town certain of himself and of his place in society. But he is not yet modern man, who is fully equipped with independent judgment, ready to experiment, reform, innovate. (So at least we like to imagine modern attributes.) The second aspect of honor is the claim of that self-assessment before the public. Robin calls on others to recognize who he is by announcing his kinship with a powerful local figure. The third element is the assessment of the claim by the public, a judgment based upon the behavior of the claimant. In other words, honor is reputation. Honor resides in the individual as his understanding of who he is and where he belongs in the ordered ranks of society. (When society has pretensions that there are no ranks, honor must necessarily be set aside or drastically redefined to mean something else.) It is, at least in traditional terms, both internal to the claimant, so that it motivates him toward behavior socially approved, and external to him, because only by the response of observers can he ordinarily understand himself. The internal and external aspects of honor are inalienably connected because honor serves as ethical mediator between the individual and the community by which he is assessed and in which he also must locate himself in relation to others.

Honor is therefore self-regarding in character. One's neighbors serve as mirrors that return the image of oneself. This submission to public evaluation prevented outrageous haughtiness and encouraged affability, for if one used the self as mirror as Narcissus did, then self-love would become destructive. It is, for instance, the theme that Jane Austen often explored in her novels: the incompleteness of character divorced from social convention. A point that Hawthorne makes, therefore, is the accepted congruence between personal values and the conventions imposed upon the individual by society. The internal man and the external realities of his existence are united in such a way that he knows no other good or evil except that which the collective group designates. He reflects society as society reflects him. To a large degree, that same morality and psychology applied to the Old South as it once did to the New England that gave Hawthorne his historical and literary inspiration.

The decision to begin with a story by Nathaniel Hawthorne was based upon several considerations. First, the tale seems timeless because the author has universalized its meaning by blurring the specifics of location and time. The action of the story is mythic, partially independent of changes in the social order and disconnected from geographical, religious, political, and economic factors. In truth, the ritual of scapegoating was more typical of the South than the North, at least as we recollect such ceremonies from the past, even the recent past. It is hard to imagine the pagan rite's survival in so sternly Calvinistic a setting as the Boston of 1730, where the vision of a New Jerusalem still lingered from the more idealistic days of the colony's first fathers. In other words, Hawthorne's story reminds the reader, therefore, that the morality of a people—at any time, at any place—may have historic roots and elemental features that civilization and religious doctrine can never wholly efface.

In that light it is possible to say that honor complemented, superseded, and challenged the contemporaneous institutions that men and women carefully nurtured and passed on to descendants over the centuries. Just as ancient social customs persisted despite the hegemony of New England church and state in the story—as it did, on occasion, in history—honor existed before, during, and after slavery in the Southern region. Bondage was an answer to an economic need. The South was not founded to create slavery; slavery was recruited to perpetuate the South. Honor came first. The determination of men to have power, prestige, and self-esteem and to immortalize these acquisitions through their progeny was the key to the South's development. Of course, slavery was wholly compatible with honor in ways that were not so apparent in the godly and commercial settlements of New England and Pennsylvania. In fact, over the course of a parallel and mutually sustaining existence, white man's honor and black man's slavery became in the public mind of the South practically indistinguishable.

Yet the South was not always a biracial or slave society. From the founding at Jamestown to the reign of Charles II it had been as homogeneous as the New England communities continued to be until the Irish invasion of the nineteenth century. With a valuable commodity to sell—tobacco—Virginians first employed apprentices and indentured servants. By such means masters could maintain the honor of unsoiled hands exclusively for themselves. But labor shortages developed in the latter half of the seventeenth century. The supply of poor immigrants declined. There was no choice but to buy Africans in the marketplace. Thereafter whites who did migrate southward, particularly the Scots-Irish in the eighteenth century, settled less often as bonded servants than as free peasants. They either subsisted in the uplands as squatters or smallholders or else ambitiously sought to become slaveowners themselves. They too, no less than Tidewater planters, were imbued with the principles of honor.

At first the legal status of the imported Africans was rather uncertain. In a sense, such confusions did not matter greatly. What was important was that servants—regardless of their standing in law—did the indispensable labor. Probably the introduction of Africans was a reluctant step because of the long-standing distaste of English people for the culture, color, and language of a folk so different from themselves. But what mattered to the whites, as to Hawthorne's Authority, was power, honor, and respect, for which riches and a body of menials were essential no less than in New or Old England of the same era.

Even in the Boston that Hawthorne described, slavery existed without much comment one way or the other. In 1701 Judge Samuel Sewall of Boston offered some pious criticism, but he was at once challenged by an advocate of the acceptability of bondage in the eyes of God. In other communities, even among the Quakers above and below the Potomac, the holding of Africans in perpetual chains aroused little if any initial complaint. But in the eastern provinces, climate, economic tendencies, and, to some degree, a moderate rather than intense commitment to honor hobbled large-scale use of Africans. For the most part, the healthier air of New England and the Middle Colonies drew sufficient numbers of laborers from familiar Old World sources.

These thoughts, induced by a close reading of Hawthorne's text, outline a basic premise of this study: the distinct existence of honor apart from a particular system of labor, a special region of the country, and a specific time in history. Just as Hawthorne universalized the point of his narrative, so we too must see honor as greater, longer, and more tenacious than it has been viewed before, at least in relation to the slaveholding South. It was not merely a Southern phenomenon, though in that part of the continent its tenets were more sacrosanct, more integral to the whole culture than they were elsewhere. After all, in the South today devotion to family and country, restrictive views of women's place and role, attitudes about racial hierarchy, and the subordination of all to community values still remain in the popular mind to an extent not altogether duplicated in the rest of the land. Hawthorne, were he alive to observe this set of Southern patterns, would not be at all surprised. His mythic vision points to the endurance of popular morality against the forces of change.

A second reason for beginning in this fashion is that the present study of Southern honor ends with an incident similar to the one in Hawthorne's story. The pair of stories frames the study and its themes. The latter narrative, a real, not fictional event, concerns a Mississippian who in 1834 killed his wife near Natchez; he paid the same price as that which was inflicted upon Major Molineux in Hawthorne's imagination. The first account leads us into matters of definition and origin. The second brings together the various threads of personal, family, and group life in the Old South, threads that made up the texture by which the Southern ethic was sustained. In history, as in fiction, there is a mythic element, one which the charivari of Natchez exemplified as truly as that presented by Hawthorne.

A third advantage of using Hawthorne's tale grows out of the second. Historians are once again debating the long-disputed question: were the North and South different or the same in most essential features? Was slavery alone the cultural and political dividing line, or was it one major point of departure among others? Like Hawthorne's masterpiece, the topic embraces more than a single, plausible interpretation. From one perspective the answer would have to be a resounding No, they were not at all alike. In regard to the colonial centuries, how could New England, for instance, steeped in religious concerns, organized around tightly knit, orderly villages and well-tended farms, have much resemblance to Southern society? There the church played little role in men's calculations. (Piety and churchgoing were for women and dependents.) Towns were almost nonexistent. The population was scattered thinly throughout the countryside. Rather than raise cereals for local consumption, as was done in New England, planters sought quick profits from cash-cropping. When differing racial mixes in populations and the values emerging from contrary labor systems are added to the equation, one would have to conclude that the issue bears little argument. Besides, as historians are now at last beginning to understand, not only were the initial reasons for the early migrations diverse, according to colonial region, but so too were the populations attracted to these shores. Southern colonists were much more likely to come from the more conservative, rustic, and wilder areas and households of the British Isles. By contrast, the settlers of Massachusetts largely emigrated from the more domesticated areas surrounding London and other relatively sophisticated districts. Likewise it may be said without unnecessary exposition that in antebellum times the quickly industrializing North, with its urban, polyglot populace, had increasingly little in common with the still agrarian, underpopulated, and deeply parochial South.

However, if one were to restate the question of sectional characteristics, adding the dimension of time, the answer might well be quite different. Though the peculiarities that had separated the slaveholding and the free parts of the country from their earliest settlement cannot be forgotten, there once had been a moral perspective that embraced both North and South. That ethical unity, a mixture of traditional Protestantism and folk tradition, made possible a united front against the crown in the American Revolution. A common heritage from Great Britain—devotion to common law and the rights of free men, commitment to familial styles of patriarchy, common language and literary culture—assured a harmony of political interests. Had there been no such ethical consensus, the two sections would have parted company long before they did. Hawthorne's story and its companion at the close of this book illustrate the point. Boston in 1732 and Natchez in 1834, to allude to the pair of ceremonies, resembled one another in terms of popular morality much more than the old colonial Boston resembled its transformed self a hundred years later. Like the latter-day Natchez, the Boston that Hawthorne used as his setting was not the thriving town it was later to become. Young men like Benjamin Franklin found greater opportunities in Philadelphia, New York, or the march westward. Early Boston's institutions were not much stronger than those in the somnolent town of Natchez in 1834. To put the matter as simply as possible: Southern mores did not change, at least not very fast; Northern conventions did.

By the time Hawthorne published his story, his Yankee readers had already begun to repudiate the ethical code that the tale so economically describes. The old means of publicly shaming the deviant had disappeared and been replaced by the relative privacy of the penitentiary system, and an almost exclusive reliance upon the legal apparatus rather than community justice. A "cult of humane sensibility" was so firmly entrenched in the free states by 1832 that Southern habits seemed to many as alien, in some respects, as the

customs of Hindus. As one historian has put it, Anglo-American reactions to slaveholding cruelties—for instance, the buying and selling of human beings as chattel—had "the reflexive force of the taboo
against incest." Northern ideals of equality of all men before the
law, though imperfect in practice as always, undermined the privileges of the wealthy and wellborn. To get ahead required skill at intellectual tasks, not just expertise at manipulating others—or at
least so the ideal became. Honor in the antebellum North became
akin to respectability, a word that included freedom from licit vices
that once were signals of masculinity. The process was not toward
human perfection, as some of Hawthorne's intellectual contempo-
raries dreamed, but at least there was an erosion of earlier forms.
True, as late as the 1790s a sea captain of Marblehead was tarred
and feathered for failing in his duty to rescue victims of a ship-
wreck. The local minister was gratified to report in his diary that
the captain had "experienced . . . just deserts." Nevertheless, mob
actions and this form of lynch law were increasingly condemned, especially by the church. The Rev. Lyman Beecher's assault on dueling after Alexander Hamilton's fatal encounter with Aaron Burr
met a widespread popular response. The custom, which was based
on the ethic of honor, became exceedingly rare thereafter in the
free states. These and other signs of social change in the relatively
short span of one hundred years indicated that honor in Yankee-
dom had become another word for domestic and civic virtue. No
longer did it mediate between a rude, sometimes passionate public
and a belligerent, self-regarding manhood.

The older concepts continued, however, to thrive in the Old
South (albeit with some lessening of their strength by the same hu-
manitarian and rationalizing tendencies that the free states experienced). It was this discrepancy between one section devoted to conscience and to secular economic concerns and the other to honor
and to persistent community sanctions that eventually compelled the
slaveholding states to withdraw. Though they were gradually emerging from the archaisms that Hawthorne describes, pre–Civil War
Southerners had to calculate the value of union when their claims

to respect were met in the North with skepticism, condescension, and finally, contempt.

Another noteworthy aspect of the Yankee author's romance is its demonstration of how a writer can make use of the tension between dying social conventions and those that take their place. Only when traditional honor had expired as a dominant force was Hawthorne able to make such impressive use of it, casting his story back in the time when the ethic was much alive. The New England Renaissance, of which Hawthorne was a leading figure, was an outgrowth of that tension between old and new, a transition largely for the better but with costs that sensitive minds like his understood. Southern writers of the same period were denied that interpenetration of changing social and moral systems, and mourned the departure from old ways without having much vision of what was the matter with the slaveholding status quo. The Southern literary renaissance came much later. William Faulkner wrote of honor with a hard-won, anguished detachment not unlike that of the reclusive New England writer: honor in both its heroic and inglorious aspects was the central theme of so much of his work. There was also the same underlying regret for what had disappeared, the same discontent with a new order that was crass, impersonal, with money, not honor, its chief god. Honor had always required wealth but only as a means to an end. It was not the end itself. In fact, there was even a place for honor apart from wealth—when wealth had been lost or not yet fully reached. Moreover, wealth was always relative, so that in a society of poor folk, the most effective wielder of power laid claims to honor even if his property was not great. But possessions for the mere sake of having and enjoying them was secular accumulation, amoral and self-indulgent, as churchmen as well as men of honor never tired of stressing.

What the North experienced in the 1830s and 1840s of Hawthorne's prime, the South would not reach until one hundred years later—the same span as that which separated Hawthorne from the setting of his story. That persistence of honor as the keystone in the arch of social order prevented Southern writers from achieving much authentic voice in the antebellum days, and even long after. The patterns were too much a part of one's being. They could not be touched dispassionately. To do so would have thrown unwelcome, critical light on the concept itself.

To be sure, exaggerations of honor—excessive touchiness, uncontrolled ambition, shameless servility to a fickle public, self-destructive hospitality, and other manifestations of honor distorted—had always been a major theme of human discourse and representation from classical times to the South of the nineteenth century. These evils were always set in opposition to what was thought to be true honor: the unity of inner virtue with the natural order of reason, the innate desire of man for the good, and the happy congruence of inner virtue with outward, public action.

But as Hawthorne's story subtly explains, honor itself was defective. Its reliance on shame distorted human personality and individualism, forcing even the good man, like Robin, to lose himself in the cacophony of the crowd. The interior contradictions of honor held men in shackles of prejudice, pride, and superficiality. It often existed not in authenticity of the self but in symbols, expletives, ritual speeches, gestures, half-understood impulses, externalities, titles, and physical appearances. All these might conform with rational, innovative thought and action, but often enough they were diametrically opposed. Thus holding men in bondage could not have worried too many Southerners so long as they were committed to the age-old morality. Honor, not conscience, shame, not guilt, were the psychological and social underpinnings of Southern culture.

Finally, Hawthorne's story casts light upon the concept of honor, one too long misunderstood. On a popular level, honor conjures up familiar quotations: Falstaff, "a word . . . a mere scutcheon"; Norfolk in *Richard II*, "Mine honour is my life . . . Take honour from me, and my life is done"; Lovelace, "I could not love thee (Dear) so much, lov'd I not honour more"; Antony, "If I lose mine honour, I lose myself." We think of it more or less as our nineteenth-century ancestors did: knights on prancing steeds, battling futilely as Don Quixote did or nobly in the manner of Walter

Scott's Ivanhoe. Reading Chaucer's prologue to the *Canterbury Tales,* we assume that the knight on pilgrimage rather resembled a stained-glass Victorian representation of a handsome crusader serving God. Chaucer's figure "loved chivalrie, Trouthe and honour, fredom and curteisie." But actually those words have a meaning quite a bit harsher than the attributes of Christian gentility that a modern reader might imagine. Chivalry meant mounted warfare and tourneys, truth was fidelity to a lord, honor and freedom meant reputation and self-sufficiency, and courtesy was deferential manners at court. Clearly honor was not always simply a resistance to cheating on exams, the holding of doors for ladies, or even a quaint prickliness about insults. It was much more complex and also much more pervasive than these images indicate.

This is not to say that Southerners lacked any conception of Christian usages. "Respectability" was as popular a term in the South as anywhere else in America. Influenced by religious advances, transatlantic commercialism, and a secular gospel of humanitarianism, Southerners found themselves—like it or not—being homogenized in the modes of Victorian thought and values. At the same time, the resistance to changes that would otherwise have eroded slaveholding remained a powerful force. The result was admiration for two types of honorable conduct, not just gentlemanliness alone. William J. Grayson, an antebellum South Carolinian thinker, was among the few to put succinctly the two concepts before the public. "What is this quality so Protean in its nature as to be prominent and essential in the christian and the man of the world?" he asked in 1853. "In what does this Janus-faced honour consist? It is not honesty; for nothing is more common, both here and in Europe, than for men of honour to contract debts without intending to pay them. Nor can it be veracity, for the falsehoods of gallantry . . . or diplomacy, are sometimes matters of triumph with honourable men." Swearing, gambling, drinking, wenching, and rejection of the Sabbath custom, Grayson observed, "are not incompatible with the character of a man of honour." Before he closed his essay, however, Grayson meekly accepted the new version of virtuous manhood in which Christian qualities outweighed the older, lustier kind. Southern intellectuals were not much given to challenging customs and forms.

Even in the fast-changing North there continued to be a mingling of older and newer versions of honor. Not all Northerners were pious Victorian gentlemen. Not all were outraged by Southern slavery. Some Yankees even joined the ceaseless flux of plantation expansions west, and most of them were quite at home with Southern popular values. Yet despite the diversity that existed in both sections, the crucial difference between them remained a matter of ethical more than economic priority. As much as the regions shared a common legacy, they yet parted to some degree on perceptions of right and wrong. Differing economic systems may coexist peaceably in the same country. But when moral assumptions diverge, the chances for disunion are much greater. Without grasping the ancient, even pagan origins and continuities of honor, we cannot comprehend the endurance of racism as a sacred, intractable conviction, or the approach of civil war, or the desperate commitment of Southern whites to hold black Americans forever in their power.

2

The Nature of Primal Honor

Like Major Molineux's ordeal, popular concepts of honor grew out of traditions stretching back to far-distant times, to early modern England and even earlier. Southerners were children of the Reformation and humanistic learning no less than other Americans. Like Northerners, they perceived themselves as Protestant in thought, custom, and faith. No other God but the true God ruled their forests and lives. They had a sense of oneness with ancient values—both Old Testament and classical—concepts that still had pertinence in lives of hardship and inequity. "Honor thy Father and Mother," an eye for an eye, the subordination of Eve's daughters to Adam's sons, the shamelessness of Jezebel, the hard vengeance of Jael, the Abrahamic sacrifice of Isaac, the expulsion of Ham, the anointing of David—these and countless other stories, maxims, and rites had a depth of meaning they no longer sustain. Just as some Southerners were religious and others indifferent, so too some whites believed in honor and shame as the biblical stories presented them, whereas others took the ethic lightly. Yet, as evinced in biblical, classical, and popular lore, honor was for all hard law, but inescapable. As the ancient Romans put it, *dura lex, sed lex.* Like the air one breathed, the demands of honor were no more to be doubted than the pursuit of justice, virtue, and godliness, aims with which it was supposed to be compatible.

Among the attitudes brought from the Old World was the ancient system for determining who belonged among the worthy and who did not. The first signs of an archaic honor appeared in the forests—not where Hawthorne's story opens, but in regions beyond the Alps, before Christ, before Rome. The ethic of honor had Indo-European origins. From the wilderness of central Europe and Asia a succession of conquering tribes had come into prehistoric Greece, then, millennia later, into Roman Gaul, Spain, Italy, and Great Britain, and finally, in the last upheaval, by sea from Scandinavia into parts of the once Roman world. These peoples shared a number of ideas about how men and women should behave. They had thoughts in common about the nature of the human body, the mind, the soul, the meaning of life, time, natural order, and death. The linguist Richard Broxton Onians has described these primitive concepts, finding a unity among the Greeks, Romans, "Celtic, Slavonic, Germanic and other 'Indo-European' peoples" and even those dwelling in "early Egypt and Babylonia and among the Jews." Myths, rituals, oaths, grave sites, artifacts, and most especially word roots all indicate a common fund of human perceptions that lasted in popular thought from antique to recent ages.

The overriding principle for these generations of human beings was an ethic almost entirely external in nature. It was easily comprehended and was considered physically demonstrable without resort to abstraction, without ambivalence or ambiguity. Differentiations between what belonged in the public or the private realm were very imprecise. Evaluations depended upon appearances, not upon cold logic. Southern whites retained something of that emphasis. As Walker Percy, the contemporary novelist, once remarked about the South of not long ago, there was an "absence of a truly public zone" completely separate from the interior life of the family, so that the latter "came to coincide with the actual public space which it inhabited." Family values differed not at all from public ones. The attitude helps to explain folk intransigency about race-mixing, for instance: threat to community was danger to home and vice versa. The absence of a public sector, Percy observed, made possible the coexistence of Southern hospitality and "unspeakable violence" in the same cultural matrix, without paradox, without any sense of contradiction.

With these thoughts in mind, the honor derived from the Indo-European system of ethics will be called "primal honor." From the Stoic-Christian system that the English humanists began to cultivate there arose the concept that hereafter will be spoken of as "gentility." The latter notion of honor became the more familiar one, associated with the upper ranks of Southern society from the eighteenth century through the Civil War. The darker, more unpleasant aspects of Southern life betokened the continuation of the archaic forms, kept alive by the exigencies of an inhospitable, dangerous world where masters had to rule in fear. The following elements were crucial in the formulation of Southern evaluations of conduct: (1) honor as immortalizing valor, particularly in the character of revenge against familial and community enemies; (2) opinion of others as an indispensable part of personal identity and gauge of self-worth; (3) physical appearance and ferocity of will as signs of inner merit; and (4) defense of male integrity and mingled fear and love of woman.

In regard to primal honor as personal bravery, Southerners of the nineteenth century boasted that they stood next to no other people. Examples could be cited from almost any public address or ceremony. For instance, J. J. McKilla, at an Independence Day militia banquet in Sumterville, South Carolina, in 1854, offered a typical toast: *"The Palmetto State:* Her sons bold and chivalrous in war, mild and persuasive in peace, their spirits flush with resentment for wrong." Heaping scorn on the "athlete Sumner," the Massachusetts abolitionist, Lucius Quintus Cincinnatus Lamar told Mary Chesnut in 1861 that if the Yankee senator "had stood on his manhood . . . and struck back when Preston Brooks assailed him" on the floor of Congress in 1856, the "blow need not have been the opening skirmish of the war. . . . We are men, not women. . . . Even Homer's heroes after they had stormed and scolded, fought like brave men, long and well." So too would Southern heroes, but if Charles Sumner had only defended his virility, his state would not have had to take up the quarrel, Lamar theorized. For him, as for many, the Civil War was reduced to a simple test of manhood. As Kenneth Lynn ably argues in a study of regional humor, Southerners' touchiness over virility, stemmed from deep anxieties about how others, particularly Northerners and Englishmen, saw them. Yet the braggadocio, the role-playing, the self-deception should not be seen as "gentlemanly masquerade," as Lynn asserts. They meant every word. Look, for example, at Edmund Ruffin, the fiery nationalist who blew out his brains in rage against Confederate surrender. "With what will be my last breath, I here repeat and would willingly proclaim my unmitigated hatred to Yankee rule—to all political, social and business connections with Yankees, and the perfidious, malignant and vile Yankee race": these were the words of his epitaph. Ruffin was no masquerader.

Intimately related to brave conduct and a capacity for hatred was family protectiveness. The impulse was not only a means to assure survival but also a way to avoid criticisms, especially those voiced by one's own family. Thus when the Civil War began, Samuel David Sanders of Georgia mused about Confederate enlistment, "I would be disgraced if I staid at home, and unworthy of my revolutionary ancestors." Moreover, these strictures kept armies in the field. Said a kinswoman of Mary Chesnut in 1865: " 'Are you like Aunt Mary? Would you be happier if all the men in the family were killed?' To our amazement, quiet Miss C took up the cudgels— nobly. 'Yes, if their life disgraced them. There are worse things than death.' " These thoughts differed little from the forms of pagan honor whose descriptions can be found in almost any relevant source.

Insistence upon valor was especially evident in moments of crisis when outside forces threatened Southern integrity. In 1811, as the nation struggled with an ineffective policy toward England's war with Napoleonic France, young John C. Calhoun replied to the Anglophile John Randolph's caution against fighting the British by exclaiming, "Sir, I here enter my solemn protest against this low and 'calculating avarice' entering this hall of legislation." Peace with submission was "only fit for shops and countinghouses. . . . [The nation] is never safe but under the shield of honor." Many years later, William L. Yancey echoed opinions similar to Calhoun's and to those that have inspired loyalists to the ethic of honor ever since Polydamus lost the debate with Hector and the Trojans imprudently followed Hector's impassioned cry for action and left their walls to contest Achilles on the battlefield. The Alabama senator warned the 1860 Democratic convention in Charleston:

> Ours is the property invaded; ours are the institutions which are at stake; ours is the peace that is to be destroyed; ours is the honor at stake—the honor of children, the honor of families, the lives, perhaps, of all—all of which rests upon what your course may ultimately make a great heaving volcano of passion and crime. . . .

The truculence of the Nullifiers had much to do with this concept of morally purifying violence. In 1827, for instance, when South Carolina debated whether or not to challenge federal authority to impose the hated tariff, Robert Turnbull urged constituents, "If you love life better than honor,—prefer ease to perilous glory, awake not! stir not! . . . Live in smiling peace with your insatiable oppressors, and die with the noble consolation that your submissive patience will survive triumphant your beggary and despair." Whether Nullification or, later, secession was wise or fraught with risks mattered little to those zealots determined to retrieve honor, with which slavery was inextricably tied. What concerned them was the necessity for valiant action. Without it, the rest of the world (they asserted) would deem the white populace cowardly and their leaders recreant to duty. The "Submissionists," the opponents of secession, Albert Gallatin Brown of Mississippi claimed in 1860, were the worst enemies the South could have. "If it should cost us the Union, our fortunes, our lives, let them go," he fumed; better that than meekly to "submit to a disgrace so deep and damning."

Southerners were not peculiarly romantic in voicing these sentiments. Equally hyperbolic language came from the lips of Northerners during the American Revolution. Just as impetuous and honor-conscious as a South Carolinian, the Boston leader Josiah Quincy spoke out in tones that a planter would have applauded. "Go, thou dastard! Get thee home!" Quincy exclaimed during the anti-British crisis of 1767. "A rank adulterer [the Tory neighbor] riots in thy incestuous bed, a brutal ravisher deflowers thy only daughter, a barbarous villain now lifts his murtherous hand and stabs thy tender infant to the heart—see the sapphire current trickling from the wound, & the dear Boy, now as he gasps his last, cries out the Ruffian's mercy." Quincy was a Puritan at heart, but he saw no dichotomy between the rhetoric of honor and his religious convictions. For those who urged a more prudent, calculated course, Quincy had a ready retort: "If this, thou blasphemer! is enthusiasm, then will we live and die enthusiasts." It was on such popular notions of valor and bloody conviction that American Revolutionaries relied to unite the colonies to overthrow tyranny. That shared fund of experience and language would eventually be dissipated in recriminations over slavery.

Primal honor also made the opinion of others inseparable from inner worth. For instance, whereas a modern speaker would refer to conscience and guilt, the ancients, to avoid shame, used such expressions as "I wish to be regarded as honest," not "I am honest." It was not that inward virtues were wholly absent. Rather, virtue and valor, apart from social utility, simply were unimportant. Antebellum Southern whites were not, of course, so unsophisticated as the ordinary post-Homeric Greek citizen. Nevertheless, the public character of inner virtue was evident, for example, in a valedictory speech that John Randolph of Roanoke gave in 1828: "I shall retire upon my resources: I will go back to the bosom of my constituents as man never had before . . . and I shall receive from them the only reward I ever looked for, but the highest that man can receive,—the universal expression of their approbation, of their thanks." A man of piety would not have placed human praise so high; God's alone would be sufficient. Likewise, Mississippi politician Albert Gallatin Brown pointed out in the closing days before the Civil War that the "one standard of social merit" in his region was "integrity," by which he meant "unsullied reputation." On that basis, any white man of reasonable status stood "on a social level with all his fellows." Similarly, Charles Casey, an English traveler, noted that Southerners judged one another by outward criteria: "Your temperament, speech, look and act, are all taken by him; and if you can get at the tablet of his mind, you will find . . . your exact worth written there upon."

It followed that those who lacked honor also lacked reputation. Slaves, in both the ancient world and later centuries, were deemed incapable of reliability and therefore impervious to the dictates of community judgment. Similarly, poor whites in the Old South were subjected to the ancient prejudice against menials, swineherds, peddlers, and beggars, who, said William Perkins, an English divine, in 1632, were "as rotten legs and arms that drop from the body." Daniel R. Hundley applied these strictures to the South's hog-driving hill folk in 1860: "Who ever yet knew a Godolphin that was sired by a miserable scrub: or who ever yet saw an athletic, healthy human being, standing six feet in his stockings, who was the offspring of runtish forefathers, or wheezy, asthmatic, and consumptive parents?" As Hundley pointed out, to his own consternation, democratic ideals had modified the older notions of blood purity and asserted the equality of every idler with every hero. By no means was the South, conservative as it was, given to the strict aristocratic principles that had separated peasant from lord since time immemorial. Yet vigorous traces of the archaic stigma against the honorless could be found, particularly in the animadversions against slaves and white "tackeys" or "crackers."

The opinion of others not only determined rank in society but also affected the way men and women thought. The stress upon external, public factors in establishing personal worth conferred particular prominence on the spoken word and physical gesture as opposed to interior thinking or words and ideas conveyed through the medium of the page. At the heart of the matter was the archaic concept that thought itself was a form of speaking. Deep reflection was imagined in very ancient times as a conversation with oneself, rather than a process of ratiocination. After all, this is the very way that children understand the thought process. A psychiatrist once illustrated the notion in the form of a father-daughter exchange:

Father. *What is thinking really?*
Hilda (aged four years, nine months). *Don't know.*
Father. *Well, what do we think with?*
Hilda. *Animals think with their mouths.*
Father. *And people?*
Hilda. *With their tongues.*
Father. *What does a man do then when he thinks?*
Hilda. *He speaks.*

Of course, Southerners were not as unsophisticated as this example suggests. But thought and speech had an intimate relationship that literate cultures no longer sustain. Acquired virtues were therefore most especially recognizable if a man was an eloquent orator, enchanting storyteller, or witty raconteur. These attributes aroused deep admiration. As a writer in *DeBow's Review* pointed out in 1849, like other Southern states "Virginia has a system of oral instruction which compensates for the want of schools, and that is her social intercourse." Family and neighborly visits were not just social events, but training grounds where young and old alike "are taught," the *DeBow's* writer said, "to think and converse," a pairing that demonstrated the assumed congruity between the life of the mind and the life of the community. The writer boasted that this happy sociability gave "intellectual tone" to Virginia society. The oral expressiveness of "an agricultural people" intrigued the writer, though visitors to the South would hardly have characterized the trait as "intellectual." To some degree, then, thought *was* speech; reputation arose in large part from skill in its exercise at gatherings large or small. For the politician in the antebellum South, declared the historian William Garrott Brown in 1902, "There could be no hiding of the personality, no burying of the man in his art or his mission. The powerful man was above all a person; his power was himself." What he was was intimately related to how he used his tongue.

The third organic part of honor requires elaboration: bodily appearance as outward sign of inner merit. Hundley stressed the hardihood of Southern sport as the reason for the white male's prowess, but superior breeding was cited, too. The stereotype was much exaggerated, especially in light of the semitropical diseases and enervating summer climate that afflicted the South's inhabitants.

Poor health, small stature, or any other physical defect carried special opprobrium in the Old South, just as kinlessness did. Yet it could be a spur for achievement. Such was the case with Alexander Stephens, Henry S. Foote, and Robert J. Walker, all of whom suffered unusually from having slight frames and physical disabilities from an early age. Stephens, for instance, always regarded the puniness of his body as a sore trial. A reporter once observed him, late in life, swathed in flannels and an "immense cloak," but his eyes, peering beneath a tall hat, he said, "seemed to burn and blaze," betokening the "invincible soul that dwells in this shrunken and aching frame."

In its most fundamental form, honor was a state of grace linking mind, body, blood, hand, voice, head, eyes, and even genitalia. The blood of a self-regarding nobility transmitted the appropriate qualities. The heart held the intentions that had to be open and honest toward friends and superiors and closed and implacable toward the honorless. The right hand gave the signal of respect in friendship, revenge in enmity. The eyes witnessed honor and looked down in deference or shame. Thus a steady gaze from a slave signaled impudence.

Most important was the head, seat of the social self. Not only was its covering a sign of status—tricorn, periwig, or whatever—but also of sacredness or profanation, by which another's guilt or innocence might be ascertained. In the Waxhaw backwoods of South Carolina, where Scots-Irish Presbyterians had settled, the widow of a clergyman was forced to touch the decayed skull of her murdered husband in 1767; the woman had married a wealthy planter suspiciously soon after her first husband's death. Among the Celts in the community where Andrew Jackson grew up, it was believed that if the woman were guilty her right hand, when placed on the skull, would bleed, identifying her as a violator of nature's law, a murderous woman. For American Indians the scalp lock served as a trophy for the same reason: the magical properties of the head. Whites also used heads as trophies. For instance, the body of an alleged insurrectionary leader of 1835, John A. Murrell, a Tennessee ne'er-do-well and penitentiary inmate, was dug up in 1845. The graverobbers severed the head from the corpse, which had been half-eaten by hogs, pickled it in some way, and displayed their prize at Southern county fairs for ten cents a look.

The genitalia were at once the most sacred and the most vulnerable aspect of the body. Ham had ridiculed his father Noah's nakedness and was banished; he had desecrated the patriarch's most sacred loins, from which descendants sprang. The seventeenth-century French essayist Montaigne described how a young man who had successfully convinced a girl to bed with him was so mortified when he was unable to complete the seduction that he went home, cut off the offending part, and sent it to her out of shame. Quoting from the poet Tibullus, Montaigne concluded, "Not in manly style / Had his limp penis raised its senile head." The French thinker thought the gesture un-Christian but admirable.

There was a most immodest interest in the private parts of the deceased John Randolph, owing to the Virginia senator's bachelor status, odd personality, scanty beard, and high tenor voice. According to William C. Bruce, an authoritative Virginia historian, a physician's autopsy in 1832 revealed that Randolph's "testicles at the time of his death were mere rudiments. These facts simply confirm a popular impression which was universal during the latter part of Randolph's life." The point is not to prove Randolph's defect, but to note the premium placed upon the congruity of outward manliness and its hidden source. It goes almost without saying that the penalty for a slave who dared lust after white women's flesh was castration, first by the law of the slave code, later by community justice alone. The grisliest example of this barbarity occurred as late in Southern history as 1934. A black farmer named Claude Neal, suspected of raping and murdering a white child near Greenwood, Florida, fell into the hands of lynchers. They cut off his penis and testicles, forced them into his mouth, and made him eat and say that he enjoyed it. The next day Neal's body was strung up, nude, in the Jackson County courthouse square.

Not surprisingly, sexual honor was the most curiously ambiguous aspect of the whole concept in the American South, as it had been in prior centuries. The Southern adulation of women needs little elaboration here. But it should be stressed that there was a dual vision of the ideal, one always present in Western popular thought. The Southern woman was supposed to be not only ethereal but also hardworking, politically aware (though never "to mingle in discussion"), and prudent in household management. These were virtues of subservience. "The husband of her bosom," rhapsodized a Southern writer in 1850, "is a man of strength. He has been the partiarch in her abodes. . . . He has kept foes and poverty alike from the door." Her task was to raise sons who would be brave protectors able to meet the intruding world. Thus, he concluded, "day by day, will she train her young spartans to the trial—to the endurance of privation—cold, hunger, toil—no less than the danger and the brunt of the battle." These remarks from a reviewer of a book on women of the American Revolution were not just suited to the subject at hand. They reflected a common, venerable perception: the mother as the moral arbiter of bravery. For instance, during the War of 1812 Sam Houston joined the army. His mother, who had urged him to do so, handed him a musket. Houston recalled her saying, "Never disgrace it; for remember, I had rather all my sons should fill one honorable grave, than that one of them should turn his back to save his life." Then she presented him with a plain gold ring, "with the word 'Honor,' engraved inside it."

Unequal though male and female were supposed to be by the laws of nature, man and woman were expected to make single unions. The heritage of the ages, as Southerners believed, had ordained the rule of monogamy. During the mid-century before the Civil War, pious sentiment softened some aspects of women's traits, stressing their moral purity rather than their weak resistance to temptations. But too much can be made of the Southern notions of woman's irrelevance to the main concerns of life. They were not expected to be mere ornaments, but were to fulfill duties commensurate with male prestige.

Women's sexual powers were formidable. They could damage or destroy male reputation, that of their own men or of others. They could make complaints publicly about men's failings as providers, lovers, and family leaders. Under ancient Anglo-Saxon law such defamers, as these women were viewed, were subject to fierce penalties, and in colonial Virginia and Massachusetts women accused of being common scolds and slanderers suffered duckings. The Virginia legislature in 1662, for instance, pointed out that "many brabling women often slander their neighbours for which their poore husbands are often brought into chargeable and vexatious suites. . . ." Men who were indicted for gossiping also risked punishment, but not of the same severity. For example, in 1642 Robert Wyard of Accomac, Virginia, was required to wear a white garment and hold a "white wann [wand] in his hand" for impugning the character of another's wife. He was given the option of apologizing.

At the same time it was true, without paradox, that nothing could arouse such fury in traditional societies as an insult hurled against a woman of a man's household, most especially his mother. In the Old South, as in the ancient world, "son of a bitch" or any similar epithet was a most damaging blow to male pride. The intensity of feeling arose from the social fact that a male's moral bearing resided not in him alone, but also in his women's standing. To attack his wife, mother, or sister was to assault the man himself. Outsider violence against family dependents, particularly females, was a breach not to be ignored without risk of ignominy. An impotence to deal with such wrongs carried all the weight of shame that archaic society could muster. The symbols of failure were the phallic horns of the cuckold, the jeers of children, the ringing of cowbells and banging of pots, and sometimes ostracism or retribution at the hands of other family heads. At the same time, seduction was the aim of the young man seeking to prove his manhood and challenge the authority of the older generation, a tension that provoked ribald humor, for laughter then, as in Hawthorne's story, was mockery.

Fierce retaliation was therefore mandatory when a daughter, wife, or mother had been dishonored. So it had been in ancient German and Celtic tribes, and so it continued to be in antebellum society. Shakespeare's Leonato mourned his daughter's sexual degradation in a way that many Southern fathers would have recognized:

> Why had I not with charitable hand
> Took up a beggar's issue at my gates
> Who smirched thus and mired infamy,
> I might have said "No part of it is mine;
> This shame derives itself from unknown loins"?

What was at stake in the promiscuity of a dependent woman was her protector's status, without which he could not remain an effective member of society. The unchaste wife or daughter did not betray herself alone. She exposed her male family members to public censure. The inner life of the family was inseparable from its public appearance. Since there was little recognition of a morality apart from community custom, the erring woman had to be condemned along with the husband, father, or brother who was unable or unwilling to control her or to avenge the seducer or rapist.

It might seem paradoxical that men should make demands for sexual restraint on their female relatives, when giving themselves a right to license. But to the traditional mind there was no "double standard" of morality. The sexes differed. They lived separate lives—one in the world, the other in the home, one in exterior circumstances, the other in the inner sanctuary that required vigilant safeguarding. As John C. Calhoun once said, "The moral is like the physical world. Nature has incrusted the exterior of all organic life, for its safety. Let that be broken through, and it is all weakness within."

The male identified that inner part of himself with his women. The woman's responsibility was solely to make sacred that internal space. They should have little cause to defend themselves, a male imperative.[48] This differentiation in moral duty elicited both pride and worry from their sometimes not so self-confident menfolk. In a world without safety, fidelity, privacy, or permanent plenty, the moral order could not be imagined in more benevolent, sexually egalitarian terms.

This presentation has offered some unappealing aspects of honor, at least to modern tastes. It has not tried to show the evolution of honor over time, in order to give precedence to the fundamenals. It most be understood, however, that such transformations did modify the starkest elements. Loyalty to family was transformed into duty to country. Ancient largess became, under Stoic influence, Aristotelian magnanimity, which in turn grew into Christian charity. Virtuous revenge gave way to more abstract concepts of justice. Primitive boasting and haughtiness evolved into condescension toward inferiors, affability toward peers into egalitarianism, courtesy toward superiors into general graciousness. Nevertheless, traces of the old ethic continued, especially in times of crisis such as war or when whites' mastery over blacks was threatened. These trends, admittedly rendered in the sketchiest way here, separated the customs of the South from their most primitive origins, but not by so great a degree that the resemblance between the old and more recent ethical patterns was entirely lost from view. The textures of honor were many, and some of the threads were more colorful and pleasing than others. But the vitality of the whole cannot be questioned for a moment.

As a way to gather these values in a familiar framework, one could propose a second Sermon on the Mount. Jesus had meant to repudiate the ethical standards of the traditional world, but if a man of primal honor had written the homily, it would have taken a form similar to literary historian George Fenwick Jones's rephrasing of Matthew 5 : 2–11:

Blessed are the rich, for they possess the earth and its glory.
Blessed are the strong, for they can conquer kingdoms.

Blessed are they with strong kinsmen, for they shall find help.

Blessed are the warlike, for they shall win wealth and renown.

Blessed are they who keep their faith, for they shall be honored.

Blessed are the open-handed, for they shall have friends and fame.

Blessed are they who wreak vengeance, for they shall be offended no more, and they shall have honor and glory all the days of their life and eternal fame in ages to come.

The primeval code not only affected the way Southern whites thought of themselves and others, but also influenced how they viewed hierarchy, government, and rebelliousness. The concept of honor was designed to give structure to life and meaning to valor, hierarchy, and family protection. But its almost childlike clarity, its seeming innocence, contained inner contradictions. Within the ethic, there was a conflict never wholly mastered, a point at which the resolutions and the alternations of the system broke down. The contradictions became too overwhelming for easy solution. The chief problem was the discrepancy between honor as obedience to superior rank and the contrary duty to achieve place for oneself and family. In the American South before the Civil War, those belonging to the circle of honor were much greater in number than in any other traditional society. Democracy, that is white democracy, made that possible. But even in colonial times, claimants to prestige extended beyond the rigid hierarchy of the gentry class. The result could sometimes be highly violent. The ethic of honor was designed to prevent unjustified violence, unpredictability, and anarchy. Occasionally it led to that very nightmare.

3

Gentility

Honor in the Old South applied to all white classes, though with manifestations appropriate to each ranking. Few could escape it altogether. Gentility, on the other hand, was a more specialized, refined form of honor, in which moral uprightness was coupled with high social position. Such a joining of rank with acquired virtue was vulnerable to all sorts of confusions and self-doubts. As Kenneth S. Lynn has observed, the seventeenth-century Virginia planter was never wholly sure that he was truly a gentleman, at least by the standards of London, the society to which he looked for approval. Often enough the American colonial visiting England met open contempt, and the ridicule rankled. Gentility, most especially its English form, involved mastery of quite subtle marks of status—the proper accent, the right choice of words and conversational topics, the appropriate attire, an acquaintance with various kinds of social proprieties and other rules not easy to follow with aplomb. The mimicking of English customs, styles of architecture, furnishings, and portrait hangings was, for wealthy men like William Byrd II, a way to demonstrate to themselves and others that gentility had been achieved. Byrd was particularly determined. "I rose at 4 o'clock this morning and read a chapter in Hebrew and 400 verses in Homer's

Odyssey," he noted in his diary in a quite typical entry. Such activity had social more than intellectual meaning for him. Nevertheless, the stigma of being a colonial remained. Likewise, in the nineteenth century the Southern gentleman, unless very cosmopolitan, was not always comfortable about his place in the larger context of Anglo-American respectability, however secure he felt at home.

Even as a simple mark of status within the various and distinct parts of the South itself, gentility was sometimes problematical. On the one hand, eighteenth-century Virginia and South Carolina planters established close-knit marital alliances that restricted the circle of gentility to the very wealthiest and wellborn families. There was little difficulty in ascertaining who belonged and who did not in long-settled communities or even districts. But with the territorial expansions of the nineteenth century, the perceptions of gentility underwent corresponding changes. In the newer states of the early nineteenth century, sang their chroniclers, "men of talent and enterprise and women of beauty, intelligence, and virtue" from worthy eastern lineages brought civilization and refinement to the backlands. But it was quickly apparent that the sobriquet "Virginia gentleman," for instance, had become so commonplace as early as the second war with Britain in 1812 that it had lost much of its exclusivity. When the Virginia writer Anne Royall traveled through frontier Alabama in 1818, she identified nearly every fellow countryman as "gentleman," even if he was a tavern-keeper or boatman. Northern visitors were less chauvinistic and more skeptical. In 1858 Corydon Fuller, a book salesman from Ohio, managed to find an occasional "specimen of the best class of Southerners," like Judge Norman of Union County, Arkansas, who was "a Georgian," but "intelligent" nonetheless.

Difficult though it was to tell the genuine article from the fake, three components appeared to be necessary for public recognition of gentility in the Old South: sociability, learning, and piety. Northern gentlemen also assumed these graces, but the order of their priority was quite different, and therefore to them Southern gentility appeared in a curious refraction. Moreover, Southerners themselves did not give the virtues equal weight. Piety was a late addition, a result of the Second Great Awakening early in the nineteenth century. Learning, an expensive commodity throughout the plantation South's history, did not command as much prestige as it did in the New England states. But sociability was the *sine qua non,* from the seventeenth to the late nineteenth centuries, from Charleston to New Orleans, from Richmond to the Ozarks. Despite the different priorities assigned each of the qualities, a favored few seemed to embody them all, thus giving the Old South a reason for pride far beyond what the actual number of such people would have warranted. The culmination of the three graces of gentility was best exemplified in the figure of Robert E. Lee, the man as well as the legend.

The antebellum frame of reference in regard to sociability needs little amplification here. We all know about Southern hospitality—pulling out the wine bottle, opening wide the larder, and plumping up the pillows for any and all strangers. The custom had a darker side that will be treated later. But sociability—"affability," the eighteenth-century gentleman called it—involved more than that. It was a way of identifying the Southerner and distinguishing him from the Yankee. To the Northern observer, the ideal of gregariousness seemed as much a defect of character as a reason for admiration. As early as 1773, for instance, Josiah Quincy, Jr., who was visiting South Carolina to ascertain patriotic sentiments, was appalled—as were many later Yankees—by the prevalence of "men of the turf and gamesters." It worried him that matters of political philosophy and religion were so frivolously set aside for lighter subjects of conversation. At the same time, the New England revolutionary found himself strangely drawn to a Colonel Howe, "a very extraordinary character." Howe was at ease both "in the company of the philosopher and the libertine—a favorite of the man of sense and the female world." If he had faults, who, after all, was spared them? "In short his character seemed an assemblage of a Grandison and Lovelace." Many years later his son, Josiah Quincy, had similar feelings toward the Southern style of gentility. President Andrew Jackson was nothing more than a western savage to Quincy and his conservative Whig friends. Upon meeting the general on his New England tour in 1833, however, Quincy observed that he "was, in essence, a knightly personage—prejudiced, narrow, mistaken on many points, it might be, but vigorously a gentleman in his high sense of honor and in the natural, straight-forward courtesies which are easily to be distinguished from the veneer of policy." The old criticism of Southern graciousness, with its hint of impetuosity, was still there. Yet a strong attraction was felt, too. "Cotton Whigs" like Quincy were not so pious that slaveholding disturbed their equipoise. They comfortably retained some of that worldliness that had always posed a counterpoint to the Puritan and later evangelical style in New England. Aware of these complex reactions in the Yankee soul, Henry James drew a curious portrait of the Southern gentleman in the figure of Basil Ransom, hero of *The Bostonians*. Ransom's touch of violence, like Jackson's, made "courtesy in the hall," as Emerson put it, seem an artifice. So at least it appeared in the eyes of Olive Chancellor, Ransom's obsessively feminist rival for Verena Tarrant's heart. Just as Olive Chancellor rejected her femininity in favor of the suffrage cause, so Ransom needed to proclaim his masculinity in refutation of any and all abstractions. These sectional compulsions were ones that James found fascinating.

By far the most celebrated example of the ambivalence registered between the Northern and the Southern gentleman was Henry Adams's recollections of his Virginia friends at Harvard College in the mid-1850s. A "trio of Virginians as little fitted" for the rigors of intellectuality "as Sioux Indians to a treadmill" enlivened campus life. Especially impressive was "Roony" Lee (William Henry Fitzhugh Lee), "tall, largely built, handsome, genial, with liberal Virginian openness towards all he liked," a figure, in short, who instinctively took command. The youth, said Adams, "had no mind; he had temperament." The Southerners drank, wenched, and got into scrapes over some "imaginary grief," but Roony customarily managed to head off serious confrontations when his cronies stepped out of line. Yet Adams admitted that he found something in common with these unpredictable young men. They were eighteenth-century characters like himself, figures ill-equipped by temperament and class to meet the challenge of the modern world. "No doubt the self-esteem of the Yankee, which tended naturally to self-distrust, was flattered by gaining the slow conviction that the Southerner, with his slave-owning limitations, was as little fit to succeed in the struggle of modern life as though he were still a maker of stone axes, living in caves, and hunting the *bos primigenius,* and that every quality in which he was strong, made him weaker." But Adams had begun to fear that even in this respect one eighteenth-century type might not differ deeply from another. Yankees, he lamented, already preferred "economists over diplomats or soldiers," a shift that left the old gentility irrelevant. Whether or not Adams was wholly accurate either in his assessment of himself or of these specific Southerners, he was keenly aware "how thin an edge of friendship separated them in 1856 from mortal enmity." If matters had been left to the Northern and Southern elite alone, such mixed feelings would scarcely have led to hostilities in 1861. The differences would have simply remained a source of amusement. There was nothing at all fallacious about Adams' stereotype: some Southerners were exactly like Roony Lee—wild but polished, "childlike" but commanding. Yet their ranks were thin, much thinner than legend would have it.

As Adams suggested, the Cavalier was more than a little discomfited when it came to learning. To be sure, Southern ideals of education differed not at all from what early Republican Yankees believed was necessary to equip young men for the world. Study of the classics had always constituted most of what a gentleman, British or American, was supposed to know from books. As President William Brattle of Harvard remarked in 1689, *"Liberali liberaliter instituendi—*Gentlemen must be educated like gentlemen." Over a hundred and fifty years later, William J. Grayson echoed the same sentiment with a South Carolinian accent. "The end of education," he declared, "is to improve the manners, morals, and mind of the Student."[5] Yankee professors would have rearranged the sequence, but it was an acceptable trinity.

Although classical literature endured as the foundation of the

Southern college curriculum much longer than it did in the technically oriented free states, learning itself was not greeted with uniform enthusiasm. Easy reference to Homer, Plato, Horace, and Livy assured Southern gentlemen of one another's trustworthiness, but only so long as the quotations and allusions were familiar. What would the Southern funeral orator have done without a reference to Nestor as a last wreath to fling upon the bier of a "polished statesman"? No encomium to Southern womankind was complete without a reminder of Sparta's brave mothers. To justify nearly any act of self-defense or vengeance, Hannibal's dying words to son Hamilcar or some choice thoughts about Thermopylae always seemed appropriate. It did not take a scholar to report what Cicero had to say about a policy of honor and immortal fame in immediate war as opposed to strategies of peace, wise expediency, and careful military preparation. Far from it. These and other catchwords and maxims from the ancient past were simply part of everyday parlance, along with familiar lines from Shakespeare and Scott's *Lay of the Last Minstrel*. Even gamblers named their horses Bucephelas and hunters called their dogs Scipio.

It was all very well for Southern whites to boast of the high-toned character of their "civilization," but such references signified very little. Nevertheless, year in and year out the *Southern Literary Messenger* and other publications fiercely defended the old curriculum, even if their handfuls of subscribers were already convinced. Willoughby Newton, at the Virginia Military Institute's 1858 commencement exercises, was still extolling the primacy of the classics. Such studies, he told the cadets, prepared them for a military career at least as well as courses in modern mathematics and engineering. Just three years before the war broke out he was urging that what the South needed was a thirst for brave achievement as intense as that which provided "the highest incentives to public virtue" among the ancients.

The purpose of these ritual words was not to sentimentalize the past but to reassure listeners that nothing much need change; the past was yet alive. If it all seemed boring, that too had its uses. New moral thoughts, like new religious inspirations, could be dangerous, but heavy blankets of ancient moral orthodoxies, largely from the Stoic tradition, could stifle uncommon opinion.

Learning, especially of the venerable kind, marked the possessor as a gentleman. Yet in the South at least, too much of it allegedly spoiled the result. There was a strongly anti-intellectual streak in Southern society, one that generations of college students perpetuated so that sociability—and reputation for manliness—would have no rival. Deploring the consequences, Grayson, one of South Carolina's few intellectual squires, blamed the old-fashioned methods of instruction for the problem. Recalling his own days at South Carolina College in the 1820s, Grayson thought an hour or two of recitation with a half-bored professor much too brief and unproductive. Thereafter the student, barely adolescent, was left to his own and others' "boyish devices." Free of adult checks on his behavior, the young man "makes rapid advances in smoking, chewing, playing billiards; concocting sherry cobblers, gin slings and mint juleps; . . . to say nothing of more questionable matters and takes degrees in arts and sciences about which his diploma is altogether silent." Within a year or two, he forgets most' everything. At age thirty, nineteen of twenty graduates can no longer "construe an ode in Horace," Grayson lamented in 1862.

To claim that literary pursuits had no effect at all would seem entirely unfair. At the very least, setting the standard of some degree of learning was bound to exhilarate a few and lead others to grudging admiration for those who did come close to the ideal. Certainly, Thomas Jefferson was totally unselfconscious in advising his nephew Peter Carr (no towering intellect) to study the classics well. His list of authors to be tackled at once was very formidable: Goldsmith's *History of Greece*, Herodotus, Thucydides, "Xenophontis hellenica. Xenophontis Anabasis. Quintus Curtis. Justin." Then on to the Greek and Latin poets, and thence to the moderns—Milton in particular. "In morality read Epectetus Xenophontis memorabilia, Plato's Socratic dialogues, Cicero's philosophies." For a young man of Virginia, the advice was probably more depressing than inspirational.

It is never possible to determine how much literature affects behavior. Yet if the choice of subjects to study ever has a close relationship to felt needs and experiences, it could be argued that the South's concern with classical sources reflected the continued relevance of Stoic traditions of honor and virtue. Thinkers of the ancient world had come to realize that primal honor was an insufficient guide: pursuit of the just, the beautiful, and the true took precedence over popular acclaim for valor. The broader vision was expressed in the Aristotelian ideal of *megalopsychia*. It signified high-mindedness, pride in one's self-worth and achievements, greatness and openness of heart. In the Renaissance, the Stoic concept represented a rejection of self-depising Christian asceticism, the *contemptuus mundi* of the monastery. At the same time, it was a repudiation of ancient Teutonic and Celtic boasting; instead, one's self-assessment should correspond with one's actual, inner worthiness, not with public reputation, as in primal honor. An ability to suffer misfortunes graciously and rejoice in good times moderately was based upon appropriate, modest self-appraisal and becoming restraint. As Montaigne, the French Stoic, put it, "Aristotle thinkes it an office of magnanimitie to hate and love openly, to judge and speak with all libertie."

Southerners often wrote each other as if they were applying copy-book lessons from these expositors of humanistic behavior. While the descriptions may have been quite accurate, often enough the language was stilted and unconvincing. For instance, in 1854 Charles C. Jones, a young Georgian of very high breeding, happened to meet Colonel Charles Suttle, whose fugitive slave, Anthony Burns, was the subject of considerable agitation at the time. Outraged that Yankees could dare think ill of so representative a Southern planter as Suttle, Jones, in a letter home, heaped praises upon him. Suttle, he said, "is a perfect Virginia gentleman, of high standing, well educated, fine commanding, prepossessing appearance," who had to be regarded as "high-minded" as anyone could be. In a word, he was "a gentleman of the *first class*. Perhaps he was. But the description better fit the Aristotelian ideal than any unpretentious Virginia squire. Hyperbole, though, should not be thought simply a sign of Southern romanticism; rather it was a part of the ritual speech that invoked ancient humanism for current application. Lord Bolingbroke, Edmund Burke, and other advocates of gentility who preceded the romantic era would have understood and approved Jones's choice of compliments. At the same time, such uses of language and models no longer held their appeal in the North. By confusing humbler aspects of honor with lofty gentility, Jones seemed morally insensitive. Even sympathetic Yankee conservatives were beginning to weary of such stalwart defenses of slaveholders on the grounds of a spurious "high-mindedness."

In reviewing the more admirable characters of the American past, however, Southern and Northern gentlemen could come to quick agreement about the appropriateness of the Stoic model. George Washington, John Marshall, and other exemplars of the role aroused orators to flights of erudition, regardless of their sectional origins. For instance Edward Everett, the New England attorney, dwelt upon George Washington's Ciceronian qualities. "The ancient philosophers," he said, "placed the true conception of perfect manhood in the possession of those powers and qualities which are required for the honorable and successful discharge of the duties of life, each in the golden mean, equally removed from excess in either direction, and all in due proportion." Washington, he continued, fulfilled these traits better than "any other chieftain or ruler of ancient or modern times." Such inner strength did not, Everett said, find popular support. "Thoughtful valor" in a chieftain gains only modest approval; whereas "gallant rashness" takes the laurels. In magistracy, "discreet" measures for the public good win meager assent, but "selfish management" is easily condoned. In council, the "well-urged" argument for reasonableness obtains faint applause, while the emotional appeal "delights the ear, and sometimes maddens while it charms." The gentleman, he summarized, was one who "disarms Fortune" with the power of prudence, regardless of its unpopularity. The Northern version of gentility stressed dignity, reason, sobriety, and caution; the Southern ideal made more concession to warm-heartedness, generosity, and expressiveness. But in either case high-mindedness, a summation of all these traits, was the social ideal, one that combined grace with honor as the Stoic tradition had fashioned it.

The difficulty was, however, that in the antebellum South gentility and learning became increasingly incompatible as white democracy eroded the old deferences to hierarchy. Even after new schools and colleges were established, the leaders were defensive. When the University of the South was founded, for example, the early recruiters catered to the raw planter mentality. They arranged the school year so that in the winter months the student could "engage in the sports which make him a true Southern man, hunting, shooting, riding; when he can mingle freely with the slaves who are in the future to be placed under his management." School studies would occupy the summer and fall, when the young man was of little use to anyone on the plantation.

If many planters were skeptical of learning, so too was the yeomanry. The University of the South's founders could not repel an intruding world. Hundreds of Episcopalians gathered on the Sewanee mountaintop in 1860 to lay the first cornerstone for the "heavenly city." But mountain folk trooped to the windy site as well, attracted by the chance to gape at militia uniforms, well-dressed matrons, and processions of bishops in billowing vestments. They soon wearied of prayers and long speeches. "I saw fighting, horse-trading, gambling, all conducted openly and vociferously and without the least regard for the ceremonies that were being conducted around the cornerstone," one participant later recalled. No one dared silence the "country-people" or tried to stop the drinking and gaming. The juxtaposition of the fancy and plain, the decorous and the vulgar accentuated the code of gentility—setting its adherents apart from lesser folk—but also served to remind them of the social fragility that so limited Southern genteel learning.

The chief problem facing the gentleman who wished to be known for his learnedness and erudition was not solely the presence of slavery in the society. Matters scarcely improved when that institution was gone. Rather it was the stress upon sociability and manliness as the highest significations of honor that obstructed a free pursuit of the life of the mind.

As a result, even the defense of the South's most cherished institution—slavery—earned the intellectual few tangible rewards. As Professor Drew G. Faust has observed, those who undertook the task of demonstrating the legitimacy of slaveholding did so in order to prove their loyalty to the South, a fidelity rendered suspect by their concerns for high culture. Surrounded by a "brainless" squirearchy and mired in the routines of country living, such thinkers as William Gilmore Simms, William J. Grayson, and Beverley Tucker commiserated endlessly with each other in long, self-pitying letters. They disliked the vulgarity and ignorance that they discerned in the Southern masses, even in the planter class itself. The Southern thinker was always a man apart, covering his vulnerability as an intellectual by glorifying the "home institution." Aloof by necessity, he could not share the boisterous pleasures of the neighboring squires and yeomen. "Shy when they are frank; sad and thoughtful when they are uproarious; solitary when they crowd together," a Southern intellectual like Simms, even as a boy among playmates, recognized his differentness. As a youth, Simms recalled, it had made him feel resentful and morbidly despondent, attitudes of mind lasting a lifetime. Still more provoking to Simms and his friends was the intellectual's impotence in politics and even in regional letters. Quarterlies drew few subscribers. "There is something wanting among us," lamented Simms's fellow sufferer William J. Grayson. The "quarterly review," said Grayson, "is a head without a body, a portico without a temple. It is not Hamlet without the ghost; but the ghost without Hamlet. We have little to review."[14]

Westerners dwelling in plantation societies in the West Indies, Ceylon, and other far-off places have generally lacked the self-confidence, sophistication, and intellectual stimulation necessary to match the creativity of metropolitan centers. The South was no exception, though the Revolutionary Fathers briefly provided a remarkable deviation. But in the more democratic milieu of the antebellum South, when Southern life was under fierce criticism abroad, that Revolutionary heritage died out. Paralyzed by recognition of his own irrelevance to planter society, the gentleman-intellectual claimed to have no ambition for "the admiration and subserviency which great wealth secures its professor," as William J. Grayson loftily declared. But another device for reconciling oneself to ineffectuality was to mask learning in personal eccentricity, an approach that John Randolph, Edmund Ruffin, and Beverley Tucker adopted. Such methods ensured that planting neighbors, easily affronted by erudition that they could not understand, would not be resentful.

By the late antebellum period evangelical Christianity had severely altered the characteristics that defined the ideal Southern gentleman. "High-mindedness," magnanimity, and a sense of self-worth continued to be adjuncts of manly gentility, however imperfect their realization in practice. But much more easily discernible and therefore more readily acquired was piety. That virtue, however, was also the subject of some ambivalence in the public forum. A long anticlerical tradition among the upper classes of Virginia and the Carolinas was bound to affect the way men perceived religious attributes.

During the eighteenth century, under the influence of the rationalism of the Enlightenment, the Southern model of honorable conscience conformed with the classical heritage. For instance, Jefferson advised his nephew Peter Carr in these secular terms: "Give up money, give up fame, give up science, give up earth itself and all it contains, rather than do an immoral act. And never suppose that in any possible situation or under any circumstances that is best for you to do a thing tho' it can never be known but to yourself, ask yourself how you would act were all the world looking at you, and act accordingly." The inner motivation rested upon Stoic, not Christian precept. One was to imagine public scrutiny, not expect alienation from God or even one's own sensibilities. While Yankee schoolmasters, fathers, and clergymen would not have any objection to such propositions for right living, they were much more likely to include Scripture and works of the church fathers in their lists of suggested reading, particularly Richard Baxter, Philip Doddridge, and other Protestant advisers to the soul. The supremacy of honor as the criterion for excellence of character was much more intense in the Southern gentry code than in the puritan moral scheme. "Health, learning and virtue will ensure your happiness," Jefferson later urged his nephew; "they will give you a quiet conscience, private esteem and public honour." Not surprisingly, the skeptical squire of Monticello said nothing about either divine blessing or the curse of alienation from God in the event of failure.

The difference between conscience as part of honorable bearing and conscience as an inner voice of God might seem slight as far as the actual way gentlemen behaved. One could forgo the committing of wrong as easily by one injunction as the other. Nevertheless, the Christian approach quite clearly had a more telling effect in encouraging moderation, sexual continence, repression of anger, and postponement of desires, because guilt is a more internal and self-dependent mechanism than shame.

In contrast to the eighteenth-century deistical notion of conscience, the diary of Michael Wigglesworth, written in mid-seventeenth-century Massachusetts, exemplified what Henry Adams, two centuries later, called the cultivation of "self-mistrust," an essential ingredient in Christian guilt. *"The last night a filthy dream and so pollution escaped me in my sleep for which I desire to hang down my head with shame and beseech the Lord not to make me possess the sin of my youth and give me into the hands of my abomination,"* wrote the Boston merchant. "I despair of ever pleasing God by my endeavours in the world. . . ."

Whether Wigglesworth's remarks were heartfelt, or merely ritualistic, one seldom found similar expressions among churchgoing aristocrats of Virginia in the seventeenth or the eighteenth centuries. Though devout in his own way, Landon Carter took a much more sanguine view of his relations to God. "Dispair," he said, almost in conscious reaction to the New England mode, "is the worst disorder that a human Creature can fall into; but in a planter it is a disease unto death; therefore God keep me clear of that." The difference was not just a matter of personality. Carter was concerned with thanking God for blessings received and pondering the meaning of human mortality. His soul took care of itself, in a way Wigglesworth would have found most capricious and self-centered.

By the 1830s, however, religious precept, somewhat democratic in character, transformed Southern gentility. As Professor T. R. Dew of William and Mary College put it in 1836, "He who obtrudes upon the social circle his infidel notions, manifests the arrogance of a literary coxcomb, or that want of refinement which distinguishes the polished gentleman." Aside from a few genuine intellectuals like Jefferson, most eighteenth-century gentlemen were deistical only out of convenience. With revival enthusiasms at work among Baptists, Methodists, and Presbyterians, the ranks of the gentry gradually came to accept Dew's position, which was only slightly premature.

Southern colleges, seminaries, and academies all sought to inculcate the new evangelical prescriptions. For instance, in 1839 Francis Lieber, a German refugee and professor of philosophy at South Carolina College, tried to combine the Stoic and Christian traditions for the edification of young college men. His advice was a prediction of the cosmopolitan style that clergy and laity alike would admire in the coming Victorian age. The gentleman, he said, was self-disciplined, uncomplaining, modest, but firm in rectitude. He was dedicated to progress, and he rejected the "splendors of plume, lace and cut" of his forbears in favor of democratically "plain attire." Influenced by another professor of moral philosophy, Robert Henry, a young student at South Carolina College named James Henry Hammond, reflected the new democratic and Christian orientation. In his class notes from 1828 he wrote, "Honor is that principle of nature which teaches us to respect ourselves, in order that we may gain the respect of others. No man desires the respect of one class of Society exclusively and therefore the law of honor will influence our conduct towards persons of every quality." Lieber would have agreed. Even a slave, Lieber said, could manifest the nobility of gentle conduct despite his lowliness, gaining esteem from those below and above himself no less than a master could. As William J. Grayson later observed, the Southern gentry would appreciate

Lieber's effort because "a religious spirit has interfered" with the old understanding of gentility and "modified the temper of society."

Bookstores in the South found a ready market for sermons suited to pious tastes, at least in the well-settled Eastern communities. Men who would spurn the emotion of camp meetings would place a devotional book by their bedsides. In 1830 Hugh Grigsby of Norfolk, for instance, confided in his diary his intention to find more of "Allison's sermons. They suit my taste wonderfully. They breathe a spirit of moral excellence and manly piety," being the work of "an elegant scholar and accomplished gentleman." Grigsby was one of many who combined gentility with evangelicalism in the South. Such men as he and General John H. Cocke of Fluvanna County, Virginia, had their counterparts in other Southern states. They gave to benevolent societies, subscribed to religious journals, and welcomed missionaries to their parlors.

Looking backward, Southerners of refinement marveled at the change that had come over their region during the prior fifty years. In 1862 William J. Grayson recalled the evils that once had detracted from the cultivation and Christian aspirations of Carolina gentlefolk. As a young man, he remembered, he had stayed at the house of a Major Hazzard, an elderly veteran of the Revolutionary War, and Grayson's first cousin once removed. One night the major had secretly left the house to join other irate planters in pursuit of supposed black insurrectionists. Seized, tortured, and condemned in a perfunctory freeholders' trial, the slaves were hanged. Then "their heads were cut off, stuck on poles and set up along the highway." To their credit, Grayson boasted, the young gentlemen there were so disgusted by the sight that they took down "the hideous butcher's work" and buried the remains.

In addition, the "churches were filled. Sunday was kept sacred," Grayson noted; also the Yankee invention of the Temperance Society had become a fixture in some quarters of the gentility. Whereas in Revolutionary times men were "more jovial and talked louder as they drank deeper," one seldom heard any more a "smutty allusion" in decent company. These remarkable changes, attributable to growing associational life, he thought, made mockery of the laments sometimes heard about the loss of old-fashioned virtue in the Carolina low country. Grayson's pontifications, however, were considerably overdrawn. Even he was not altogether convinced that progress and Christian evangelism were unmitigated blessings. Like others of intellectual bent, he mourned the fact that lesser men adopted these imports from the Northern cities to gain the social power to replace older families like his own. Nevertheless, he welcomed the changes and pronounced them advantageous for the genuine attainment of "a noble purity, strength, and elevation of character."

Nearly every Southern community could boast a representative of Christian gentility. Such individuals went far beyond the usual customs of a grudging charity. Instead, they were kindly toward lesser folk, strangers, and even neighbors whom others despised. Their self-regard was very much involved in the doing of good works, in both formal and informal ways. They gave substance to the meaning of gentility. Such figures as John Belton O'Neall, General John Hartwell Cocke, Chief Justice John Marshall, and Charles Cotesworth Pinckney exemplified the role with the naturalness of manner that only a few gentlemen genuinely possessed. Moreover, they supported noble, often national causes—for black colonization, Bible societies, temperance organizations, and the other paraphernalia that the rich in both sections thought necessary for God's glory and patriotic advance. Their efforts were not always appreciated, but they had the social rank and necessary self-possession to stare down complaints. Likewise, clergymen like Charles Colcock Jones of Georgia and Bishops Barnwell, Otey, Elliott, Pettigrew, and Wilmer—all well placed and well intentioned—provided a satisfying retort to those who perceived the South as godless, licentious, and indifferent to nineteenth-century progress. The presence of such men must be noted, but it would be travesty to claim them as the sole representatives of Southern honor. There were other kinds considerably less pious, benevolent, and self-sacrificing.

As a means of contrasting the ideal model of gentility with the ordinary styles to which most Southerners were loyal, the familiar example of Robert E. Lee seems the most efficient. We shall not meet in these pages many others of his stature or moral bearing. Yet it is important to remember that such figures, as even the Ohio book agent in Arkansas recognized, set a standard that affected Southern life far out of proportion to their number. Though Lee assumed legendary proportions in the hands of Southern—especially Virginian—historians after the Civil War, the myth was based upon genuine attributes. Jefferson Davis summed them up in 1880 when he called Lee "a gentleman, scholar, gallant soldier, great general, and true Christian." Lee's scholarship left much to be desired, but on the other points he was a figure of considerable interest, however hackneyed the portrait has become in the redrawing.

Lee's father, "Light Horse Harry" Lee, might be said to have typified the eighteenth-century squire as accurately as his son set a model for the next generation. Born of distinguished Virginia lineage, Richard Henry Lee had left his Princeton studies to serve in Washington's army at the outbreak of the Revolution. With customary bravado, he refused Washington's offer to make him his aide-de-camp, declaring, "I am wedded to my sword and my secondary object . . . is military reputation" with hope of deserving "your Excellency's patronage" as "a stimulus to glory, second to none in power of the many that operate upon my soul." His fulfillment of that pledge need not concern us here. Hero and three times governor of Virginia in the 1790s though he was, Light Horse Harry had no gift for business. Ann Carter, his second wife and the mother of Robert E. Lee, watched helplessly as he despoiled his own and her ample estate in unrealistic speculations. Still worse than the constant, humiliating dunning by irate creditors was the serious maiming suffered in a Baltimore anti-Federalist riot over entry into the war with England. Unwisely he had taken the unpopular side in the dispute; one man stabbed him twice in the face and another tried to remove his nose with a knife. The humiliation broke Lee's spirit. He went into self-imposed exile to the West Indies and died in 1818 in Georgia not having rejoined his Virginia family.

Perhaps the fact that he was little acquainted with his own father was one reason for Robert E. Lee's devotion to children, something he had not experienced firsthand. Once early in the Civil

War, when he was stationed in western Virginia, Lee came upon two dozen little girls in "white frocks and pantlets," running and giggling about the yard at a large party. "It was the prettiest sight I have seen in the West, and perhaps in my life," he remarked. Such a sensibility was rare among Army men. In any event, Lee was endowed with an unusually affectionate nature. Reared as much as a member of the Carter family as of the Lees, young Robert showed early all those graces that a proper Christian gentleman should manifest—with children, slaves, women, and fellow men.

In contrast to the diffidence of his father, Robert E. Lee was particularly attentive toward his progeny. Military duties, however, kept him away from the home he loved. When his son and namesake was three years old, Lee returned to the Arlington plantation from the Mexican War. The boy, dressed in the customary frock and with hair "freshly curled in long golden ringlets," waited impatiently for the father whom he had not seen for two years and did not remember. Amidst the greetings, Lee exclaimed, "Where is my little boy?" He then seized the child of a visiting relative and kissed him. "I was shocked and humiliated," Lee's son recalled, but quickly added, "I have no doubt that he was at once informed of his mistake and made ample amends to me." Judging from his further recollections and the affectionate letters that the younger Lee received, his surmise was certainly accurate. In the accepted style of the day the father showered advice upon his children. "Honor and fame are all that men should aspire to," Lee asserted. With steady application and valor, "they will at last be won. . . . Hold yourself above every mean action. Be strictly honorable in every act, and be not ashamed to *do right*," he wrote his son Custis in 1851. Absence from home made such suggestions poignant reminders of an involuntarily neglected role. But even at a distance, Lee was determined that his youngsters should grow in grace. When present to supervise them, he did not, as his own father had done, act indifferently. He was especially keen that the boys should learn sports. Robert, Jr., for instance, reminisced that his father "gave me my first sled, and sometimes used to come out where we boys were coasting to look on." Moreover, he allowed them an intimacy not altogether common in that day of austere patriarchy. He even let the little ones "climb into bed in the morning and lie close to him, listening while he talked to us in his bright, entertaining way."

Though not the scholar that Davis claimed, Lee was indeed the Christian. He read devotional volumes, from the Bible to the Book of Common Prayer, from Thomas a Kempis to pamphlet sermons. His faith was largely emotional, not cerebral or rationalistic. As pious as any Northern evangelical, Lee constantly resorted to prayer, for friends and kinfolk, for his state and country, for the men he led and those he fought. There was a "primitive" quality to Lee's piety, according to one scholar, but resignation to God's will, faith in the literal word of scripture, and a sense that the "fratricidal" war was a divine visitation upon the land for the sins of all Americans were common opinions among the religious folk of the time. One could not really be a Southern gentleman without such views, according to many in the upper ranks of late antebellum Southern society.

Lee's attitude toward slavery and its relation to Divine Providence was typically Anglican, a mixture of condescension and twinges of guilt of an indefinite sort. "In this enlightened age, there are few I believe, but what will acknowledge, that slavery as an institution, is a moral & political evil in any Country." But his sympathies, he admitted, lay chiefly with the owners, for, after all, the slaves were better off in America than in Africa. He relied, he said in 1856, upon "the mild & melting influence of Christianity" to effect any progress toward emancipation. Christians, he wrote his wife, should press for "the final abolition of human Slavery" but look always to the God "who Chooses to work by slow influences; & with whom two thousand years are but as a Single day." Lee was unexceptional in maintaining such views: they were the standard opinions of a class that exploited black laborers, but wished them well, that bowed to fast-gathering metropolitan opinion but did nothing to hasten the hour.

We need not dwell on Lee's other much-praised attributes. Douglas S. Freeman explained them well. "If blood means anything," wrote the great Virginia historian, "he was entitled to be what he fundamentally was, a gentleman." Nevertheless, his connection with the ancient ethic deserves comment. Without that tie, his decision to join the Confederacy would be inexplicable. Lee's partial doubts about slavery scarcely relieved him from the weighty obligation that the tradition of honor imposed. "I wish to live under no other government," he wrote in the last days before secession, "& there is no sacrifice I am not ready to make for the preservation of the Union save that of honor." The stipulation was irremovable. He was no Southern nationalist. Few Southerners were. Lee always viewed the struggle as a "civil war," not a "war between the states," or for "Southern rights."

Though a much more complicated figure than his image as the "marble man" suggests, Lee was utterly simple in choosing his destiny. He had no faith in the cause he served. None was needed. Two interconnected factors, and those two factors alone, explained his decision to resign his commission, return to Virginia, and accept appointment under the new government. He wrote Anne Marshall, his sister, about one of them: "I have not been able to make up my mind to raise my hand against my relatives, my children, my home." From the earliest times in Western history, the cardinal principle of honor was family defense. To war against one's own family was a violation of law—a law that, unwritten and often unspoken, superseded all other claims. To Lee, as to nearly all Confederates, that commandment, whatever its source of inspiration, pagan or Old Testament, could not be violated. It helped to drive the upper South out of the Union. Who did not have kinsmen further South? In time a sense of abstract nationality, transcending family and *deme,* might have been constructed upon the secession effort, but certainly not in 1861, when archaic honor and a sense of insult superseded notions of a truly separate nation.

The second reason was equally a matter of conscience—one arising from the primal code as much as from Christian heritage. As Mrs. Lee wrote a friend, "My husband has wept tears of blood over this terrible war, but as a man of honor and a Virginian, he must follow the destiny of his State." The Old Dominion was not an abstraction in Lee's mind. Inextricably it was bound up with the life and heritage of the Lees, Carters, and other clans with which he was associated, the living and the dead. Lee had no choice in the matter. Culturally, morally, spiritually, he was compelled to forsake the Union. On this count he is sometimes accused of a narrowness of vision, but the complaint itself is parochial. Lee could not escape either fighting for or against his kin. The option simply to exile himself would not have occurred to him. By any standard that was the coward's way out, a rejection of what Lee's God had set before him as moral choice.

This brief description of General Lee has not been included in order to throw a sentimental light upon the Southern code or to prove that such old Southern apologists as Freeman, Ulrich B. Phillips, and Philip A. Bruce were wholly justified in highlighting the magnanimity, kindliness, and childlike innocence of the plantation order as a whole. Rather it is designed to show the range of the Southern system. Honor was always more than the sum of its parts, and it could bring out the best in men as well as the worst. Many Southern gentlemen would have agreed with Lee, however, when he said in a wartime reflection, "A true man of honor feels humbled himself when he cannot help humbling others." For him "the forbearing use of power does not only form a touchstone, but the manner in which an individual enjoys certain advantages over others is a test of a true gentleman." Such men resided throughout the South, even in its roughest, most unformed regions, a point that the modern cynic might deny. But unhappily the number of such men was small, their influence sometimes circumscribed more than legend would concede.

Nevertheless, for all their imperfections, gentility and honor together were not only functional aspects of Southern life but, at times, creative ones as well. Without the conflicts arising from the two intertwined ethical patterns, without the intimate context they provided for natural reactions and passions, without the sense of family and communal continuity they afforded, a major source of American nationalism would be missing. One of the most serious problems that faced the ancient Greeks was the difficulty ordinary citizens had in recognizing duties and fidelities higher than those to immediate kin and locale. To some degree the same kind of virulent particularism that had made union of city-states against common enemies so hard to achieve also afflicted the Confederacy. Dissidence and even rebelliousness behind Rebel lines were not invariably signs of an emergent, modern style of individualism and diversity, but rather of an ancient localism, one that had plagued all sections of the country during the American Revolution. But the Southern states that experienced war and then Reconstruction, as W. J. Cash had observed, developed in the Redeemer period and after a greater sense of regional identity than that which had led to secession. However fractious Southern whites had been during the fighting, the war experience provided memories and myths upon which a sense of sacred collectivity was based. As initial bitterness faded and celebrations of old glories became ever more stylized, that impulse for valor and immortal honor—what the Greeks had called *arete*—was transformed into a sense of national loyalty, without loss of its regional origins. The Southern concept of patriotism was constructed upon faithfulness to a particular place and people and their past, not upon some abstract idea such as "democracy" or "freedom," principles generating few sparks in ordinary men's minds unless they were conceived as synonyms for personal and familial security and self-regard. It is no accident or irony that the region most renowned for its particularity, its separateness, its experience with both glory and defeat should also be the most nationalistic, not only in the last century but in the present one as well. It was never the abstraction of "liberty" that animated Southern patriotism, but rather the concrete determination to uphold personal and community independence from overt or insidious attempts to destroy it.

Before we proceed to the familial and community aspects of Southern ethics, one final observation is mandatory. The ancient philosophers and their humanistic interpreters, in early modern England and in the South as well, often spoke of the "laws of honor" as if they were as readily apparent as the Ten Commandments. They were not. Honor was accorded on the basis of community decision.

The method of reaching that conclusion involved many contingencies. Any action, *ex post facto,* then seemed logical if it was regarded as conforming to those "laws." In like manner, writers of history, like those in other social sciences, must impose a coherence, regularity, and rationality upon the subject at hand. In both cases, however, the process of necessary ordering distorts, because, as Faulkner intimates, much of human existence is really inchoate even if it lives on in memory. We speak of rules of behavior in the past. They were not rules, not immutable or even logical. At best they were acceptable options. The strategies and the priorities were more like trails across a field. In the South the "rule" was, in fact, simply the unplanned, customary path that in most instances enabled the antebellum sojourner to avoid rough terrain and dangerous cliffs in the course of moving over the social landscape. If for some reason the road was blocked, less desirable detours could be taken. To stray too far from the familiar way, however, was to confuse the order of nature. These paths were not always well marked. Misjudgments were frequent, and community evaluations were sometimes ambiguous, perhaps wrongheaded. One had to improvise. Yet the main objective of fidelity to custom could not be cavalierly repudiated. In any event, why people behaved as they did cannot be entirely encompassed in so broad a category as "strategies." One must allow for irrationality—including collective irrationality, as in Hawthorne's story.

Yet honor, for all its variations—from primal valor to Christian graciousness, from bloody deed to "right reason"—provided a means to restrict human choices, to point a way out of chaos. Thus it helped Southern whites to make life somewhat more predictable than it would have been otherwise. It established signposts of appropriate conduct. It staved off the danger of self-love and vainglory and in the circles of the genteel, it elevated moderation and learnedness to virtues of self-disciplined community service. Since honor gave meaning to lives, it existed not as a myth but as a vital code.

4

Family

At the heart of the Southern family lay a problem not always satisfactorily resolved. At what points and to what degree should a father exercise his authority? When should he transfer his property and his power to the upcoming generation so that the sons, most especially, could learn how to command with dispatch and confidence? The problems inherent in the cycle of growth—the transition of child to man, and thence to father—were not peculiar to the South. The origins of familial tensions lay in two aspects of social life. First, there was the veneration of forefathers and their traditions, a genetic foundation that provided sons with inspiration but also the formidable challenge of living up to almost mythological heroes from the family past. Second, and more importantly, childrearing practices in the antebellum South subjected the young to flawed prescriptions of shame and humiliation and the ideals of hierarchy and honor, a mode in sharp contrast to the conscience-building techniques of pious Yankees. Even Southerners realized that the manner of inculcating youth to conform with familial and public customs and values was not always efficacious, but though they recognized deficiencies they resigned themselves to the evils, regarding them as being as incurable as human nature itself.

The weight of tradition within a family was the first yoke upon the rising generation. "Blood" was not an abstract concept but a determination that could so type a child that a sense of unworthiness could well develop. Like horses, human beings were supposed to exhibit traits of lineage. "I know him very well," wrote James Simmons to Governor John Manning in reference to a young aspirant for political appointment. "He comes of first rate Carolina stock and his breed is good. You can rely on him." On the other hand, "bad blood" was also supposedly a fair predictor of future prospects. Typical were the derogatory comments of Samuel A. Townes of Alabama to his brother George in regard to their sister's children. She had married a General John Blassingame, whom both brothers despised. Unfortunately, gossiped the rising young planter, "Blassingame blood circulates" in the youngsters' veins, and two of "Elizas children have already developed some of the villanous [sic] blood. Maria & John take after our family in our warm, open & honest intercourse with the world, but Elizabeth in some degrees & Aurelia *particularly* has all of the low cunning slandering & mean propensities of her detestible [sic] father and poor Eliza does not attempt to eradicate them."

The parades of patriarchs stretching back sometimes to ancestors in Scotland, Ireland, Ulster, Wales, or England provided standards of accomplishment, status, and character to be matched—or, as in Samuel Townes's estimation, to be overcome as best one could. Family declensions, attributable to some deficiency of genetic inheritance or personal waywardness, could be located on every hand. They provided signposts of danger to be avoided. Meanwhile, newcomers to higher rank seemed to arrive from nowhere and assume vacated positions, defying the supposed laws of inherited characteristics. As James H. Hammond wrote his son Harry, "Genius and imbecility, Chivalry and poltroonery and meanness were always strangely mixed up among the Salt water people. . . . There were old families undecayed—decaying and decayed and new families founded by successful overseers and factors, and then an unusual amount of loafing fishermen, hunters etc." The historian Chalmers Davidson has observed that of the four hundred large slaveholding

families in South Carolina in 1860, only fifty had roots traceable to
great wealth in colonial days. Their gains, however, were someone
else's losses, and the danger of slippage was never far from the
thoughts of wary elders in the upper classes. Like Hammond, who
had warned that idleness slackened "every nerve moral and physical," John Randolph of Virginia urged a young nephew to beware
those who idled their lives away in expensive habits. They would
"become in form, as well as in fact, poor folks." Anxiety to preserve and ambition to recover family fortunes were constant refrains
in advice to the young. Somehow the "good blood" had to pre-
dominate over the bad.

A most telling sign of the special intensity of family lineage was
the pattern of naming newborns. Ofttimes distinguished surnames
replaced the ordinary Christian name—Peyton Randolph, Langdon
Cheves, Preston Brooks, Whitemarsh Seabrook, Otway Byrd, Beverley Tucker, Landon Carter—a custom not so readily found in polite
Northern circles. By these talismans, perhaps, the threat of family
dissolution could be prevented, as if there were some special magic
in the christening itself. The surname taken from the maternal side
and used as first name did not necessarily represent veneration of the
mother, but rather honored her father. Women contributed to the
honor of the family name chiefly through these means, since their
own accomplishments were so strictly confined to the traditional
duties.

More than in the free states, the mystique of names carried considerable meaning in the family and the community. If the bearer
of the name came a cropper, the original figure so honored felt
sorely abused. For instance, a distinguished judge in a western
North Carolina county, where Scots-Irish family loyalties were especially strong, had been pleased to let his name be used by common folk as a hopeful prediction of a newborn's character and
future renown. But one day Judge Saunders addressed the courtroom before passing sentence on a man convicted of larceny: "Hear
all you people present; when you go home, tell your wives and
neighbors to name no more children after me. Consider the situation in which I am placed; compelled in discharge of my duty, to

pass sentence on this poor wretch to receive thirty-nine lashes on his bare back, and he is a man bearing my full name, Romulus Mitchell Saunders."

More commonly, sons received family names, not those of prominent individuals, local or national, and upon them the fathers' immortality rested. In a letter to Theodore Dudley, John Randolph, for instance, advised the young man to make a name for himself not solely for the good of mankind but for the glory of his family, too. Randolph presented a list of all their important relatives, as inspiration and also as practical notification about whom to reach for cousinly assistance as occasion might arise. First, Randolph called attention to their mutual connection with Dr. Bolling Hall, "a valuable counsellor." Bolling's "great grandfather, on the mother's side" was one Robert Bolling, Randolph continued, "brother to Drury Bolling, my maternal great grandfather . . . which Drury and Robert were sons of Robert B[olling] . . . by his second wife, Miss Slith [*sic*, Stith?]; (his first being the grand-daughter of Pocahontas, by whom he had one son, John, from whom, by his first wife Mary Kennon, my paternal grandmother sprang.)" The ritual incantation of "begots" might appear to be a casual recital, yet whether it came from a querulous maiden aunt or from a wealthy bachelor uncle, the implications could not be lost on the dullest lad. Randolph then pointed to the various branches stemming from that impressive trunk: "Bollings of Chesterfield and Buckingham, in the male line" and "Curles Randolphs, Flemings, Gays, Eldridges, and Murrays in the female." Throughout the stress was upon the males of the tribe, whether on the maternal or paternal side.

This tendency was still observable as late as the 1930s. In a letter to "Cousin Eloise" a North Carolina clergyman recalled how, a few years before, a Mrs. Jacobs of Wilmington had written to say that "she was a grand-daughter of Col. Axalla Hoole who was killed at Chickamauga. I never had heard of her before," the minister said, but she declared that "I was her only relative in North Carolina" and should baptize her little daughter. Thus, last Sunday "I Baptized the great-grand-daughter of Col. Axalla Hoole who died at

Chickamauga. Mrs. Jacobs is the daughter of Cousin Ada Lawrence, who is the daughter of Col. Hoole. Col. Axalla Hoole was my grandfather's half-brother, and also your grandmother's brother, wasn't he?" The repetition of Hoole's name, rank, and manner of death revealed the talismanic nature of family pride. Such incidents were fondly recalled because the rituals of family remembrance assured continuity and the preeminence of fathers past in the lives of their progeny. Scarcely a Southerner today could not repeat some similar anecdote.

By emphasizing male ancestors on both sides of the family tree, several aims were accomplished. First, it helped to cement solidarity between grandchildren and grandparents, whose attitudes toward their offspring's mates were often crucial to family harmony. Second, it gave mothers and wives reason for pride as bearers of their fathers' names. And finally, it served as guide for the sons. Abiel Abbott, a Yankee clergyman in Charleston, remarked how the children of David Ramsay, historian and planter, conducted themselves in the knowledge that they were "the offspring of illustrious ancestors & parents whose names are embalmed in the national history. . . ." The relation of the dutiful child to ancestors and to community was thus made clear; one could not easily escape to pursue one's own hopes under such circumstances. Duty to fathers came first. The future, even the present, rested on the past.

In contrast, Northern naming practices were swiftly changing during the early years of the nineteenth century, part of an evolution that had begun much earlier. According to historian Daniel Scott Smith, the shift demonstrated the waning power of the father and the growing sense of freedom from the past. Each individual looked toward a future in the pursuit of personal, not strictly familial interests. In Hingham, Massachusetts, a fairly representative New England community, the increase in nonfamily Christian names was dramatic, particularly after the American Revolution. The ratio changed from 10 percent for males and 30 percent for females at the turn of the century to 30 percent and 40 percent respectively in the Civil War era. The transformation suggested a desire to promote an instrumental kind of individuality.

Just as rich folk enjoined their children to match the high achievements of the family ancestors, so too did the poor refer to some kinsman as representing the best ideals of their clan. The ownership of slaves, it is often asserted, was the aspiration of such people, a factor helping to mitigate envy and resentment of the planter ranks. But actually the prospect of respectability identified with a particular ancestor or kinsman, who may or may not have owned slaves, urged the poor boy to match that record. The example might not be very grand: a summer service in the Revolutionary War as private, or superior hunting skill. Sometimes a reputation for leadership in an obscure backwater or even a claim to have been reared in a prestigious part of Virginia before a westward relocation stirred pride. Glorious or objectively petty, the claims were revered all the same. "My mother was a Gholson," boasted Riley Wyatt, a Mississippi doctor of humble Alabama stock. A maternal first cousin, Samuel J. Gholson, who had served Mississippi in Congress, provided him with a sense of family prominence that could yet be retrieved, despite his father's obscurity and widowed mother's abject poverty. Likewise John Hewitt of Tennessee recalled a kinsman named Reaves who was two generations away from "ancestors of high birth and education." Both Reaves and his wife, "three generations" from literacy, subsisted in the hills on a "hog and hominy diet" until Reaves defied his less ambitious mate and set off alone to become a typesetter in an obscure village scores of miles away. Later he called for her and the children to join him, after he had mastered the craft. His inspiration came from a crankish great-grandfather, a recluse who had had considerable education. Thus the aspiration to change and get ahead was not necessarily a purely bourgeois objective, as a modern perspective might lead one to assume. It could be an outgrowth of family pride—simply the ancient desire to be *somebody,* to create a lineage.

Just as some rich families sought merely to retain status that was inherited, so too did poorer folk find well-being in just holding on. Family honor of this kind did not require soaring objectives. Belonging to an old and large clan was sufficient. Such was certainly the case in the Scots-Irish settlements that dotted the Southern hinterlands. In Mecklenburg County, North Carolina, for instance, John McKnitt Alexander and William Baine Alexander populated the region so thoroughly that they and their neighbors no longer even used the surname, so common had it become. Legal documents sometimes identified Alexanders by their middle, not their last names. Likewise, in Cumberland County, a recent study points out, a Scottish name was almost an assurance of election to local office during the early nineteenth century. After all, who could vote against a fellow clansman?

As late as 1940 this kind of adherence to family names and their evocations still endured. In Kentucky, a rural sociologist discovered that only 5 percent of all males had names not affiliated with traditional family first and middle names. Over 70 percent of the men were named for their fathers. Like their ancestors before them, Kentucky hill people used the word "generation" to mean common lineage from a single patriarch, not a certain age group (for example, the "older" or "younger" generation). A great-grandfather and great-grandson belonged to the same "generation," with "sets" grouped by different family heads distinguishing one line from another: the "Old Dick set" of Browns, for instance, "Old Dick" being the common progenitor. The same pattern had existed in Mecklenburg, with the "Clerk Isaac" set and "Long Creek Isaac" set of Alexanders. These customs suggest the persistence of very elemental means of preserving patriarchy. They helped to make everyone feel loyal not to an immediate father alone, but to a whole weighty series of fathers.

For the most part naming patterns reflected the strength of the patriarchal order across the gradings of wealth and rank. No doubt when elaborate studies are conducted—none currently exist for the antebellum era—class and geographical variations will be found. But the key pattern, naming sons for paternal forebears, will no doubt show little change over time, except in districts where unusual urban growth and a new order of things was underway. Moreover, the naming patterns will probably be found to have little relationship to the ownership of slaves or the lack of that form of property. For the poor, the weighty responsibility to live up to ancestral standards of performance did not impinge upon the upcoming generation as much as it did in old families of power. Nevertheless, in the South the compulsion to advance was particularly tied to familial considerations. This attitude spanned the social classes and helped to give the South its sense of regional wholeness. At the same time, it encompassed a basic social ambiguity: one could only be truly individualistic by conforming to ancestral prescriptions.

If there were some ambiguities in the emphasis on ancestral success and personal autonomy, there were even more contradictions in the manner of childrearing. Contrary to southern opinion, child discipline was not rigid and stern, at least not as assumed. The patterns were very similar to the habits of western Europeans and British folk stretching back to the precolonial era. In essence the approach, like the society itself, relied chiefly upon principles of shame rather than conscience, with three clearly identifiable components: (1) the early and continuing ambivalence of mothers toward their offspring, leading to a combination of near-smothering love and emotional withdrawal; (2) the abrupt assertion of fatherly authority at the "clothing" stage, approximately four years of age; and (3) socialization into a community in which sexual differentiations were demanded, with honor and shame the chief principles upon which social and moral hierarchies, including those of race, were insistently enforced.

Southern white mothers, rich or poor, had reason for dissatisfaction with their fate. Although some writers have maintained otherwise, these matrons had little conscious awareness of what should take the place of their rounds of drudgery and their subservience first to father, then to husband. Their little stage for life's dramas was confined to the family circle. There was no escape. Yet it would hardly be fair to claim that Southern mothers were incapable of unqualified love for their children. On the contrary, mothers lavished caresses upon their little "Cherry Cheeks," as one plantation matron called her youngest. Whether rich or poor, there was no lack of fussing over small ones, especially when they were peevish. In fact, babies were almost public property, so fondled were they by neighbors, kin, slaves, and visiting strangers. White plantation children were even more indulged than yeomen's infants. After all, there were the ubiquitous mammies to give succor and nourishment. For instance, William Faulkner, like generations of Southern men before him, declared his loyalty to the memory of his "Mammie," Callie Barr, who "gave to my family a fidelity without stint or calculation or recompense and to my childhood an immeasurable devotion and love." In his opinion, Callie Barr was "brave, courageous, generous, gentle, and honest . . . much more brave and honest and generous than me." The sentiment was heartfelt but not unusual.

On the male side, too, there were also "significant others," as if fathers alone could not fill the role assigned them. The attention given to infants and toddlers by "uncles," both kin and black, as well as grandfathers, cousins, and tutors to the older children, had a more reserved character than that offered by the women, but there was nothing at all lacking in the way of genuine attachment. J. G. Clinkscales, for instance, attributed his own understanding of manhood less to his neurasthenic father than to "Unc' Essick," whom he called "one of the best and truest and noblest men I ever knew—white or black." As the child grew older, these male figures became increasingly important in the formation of the child's character and social demeanor. By such means the child learned early his role as a member of a community of men, not just of a parental and sibling group. He also learned that houseservants were considered members of the household; they were the master's "black family," just as the master's offspring belonged to the "white family."

In order to understand the Southern mode, it is necessary to explain its Northern antebellum counterpart. Roughly speaking, in the Jacksonian era a pious, mother-centered form of childrearing was gradually replacing the older traditions of coercive, father-centered practice. To be sure, there was no categorical uniformity in the homes of Yankees any more than in the South. Some Northern families were as conscious of lineage, honor, and patriarchal authority as Southern families were. Nevertheless, one may safely refer to the Northern evangelical scheme, with its origins in Quaker, Congregational, and Presbyterian theology and ethics. Whereas the Southern child was to learn the rubrics of honor and shame, the religious mode set the criterion of conscience and the imposition of guilt. Devout parents did not rely so much upon whippings, slaps, and furious verbal abuse, but upon internal, self-regulative prescriptions. Sermons, tracts, and exchanges of advice among pious mothers in a community all stressed the centrality of conscience-building, based upon the individual's relationship to God rather than an identification with community values of honor and reputation. The inculcation of conscience was a time-consuming, onerous task. It required patience and skill, whereas the Southern style was much less calculating and reflected more concern for the convenience of the adult than for the instruction of the child. Only mothers had the time, or, frequently, the interest to perform the duties demanded of the pious approach. In the South, fathers still held the reins of power, even over child discipline, but their concern was all too often intermittent. As a result, there was some uncertainty in Southern mothers' minds about how strict or lenient they should be in the absence of paternal advice or direction.

To raise up God-fearing, hard-working, and well-motivated children, the evangelical Yankee mother sought to channel the young person toward wholly effective self-mastery. Mrs. Taylor, a Boston adviser, for instance, recommended in the fashion typical of her times that early schooling could do much to restrain "the violent and obvious acting of *self-will*," but the process had to begin much sooner—as soon as the baby left the crib and began to move about. "A mild system," in which fathers were prepared to "strew a few flowers" and not always play the part of "master," was "always to be preferred, if possible: yet . . . [discipline] must be firm," she argued. "System," not inconsistent reaction to childish behavior, was all-important, with each child treated with impartiality, regardless of sex or age. Mrs. Taylor warned that parents who had come into new wealth were likely to be uncertain about how to raise their children to the standards appropriate to their new station. Yet religion, rational planning, and acceptance of good advice on parental practices could overcome the deficiency, she said in her 1825 book.

A major means of achieving these lofty ends was to withhold affection from the wayward child, rather than to react with a boxing of the ears in the heat of the moment. In 1832, by which time the style was thoroughly developed, the parents of a deceased four-year-old New England boy published a memoir of his upbringing. The regimen for John Mooney Mead included "withholding from him whatever he cried for, and when he was fretful, they did not pacify him by caresses, or by bestowing what he desired, but by directing his attention to something else." Only once in his brief life did the child feel the sting of the switch, at fourteen months of age. The punishment, however, was accompanied by appropriate words of admonition, not just a grumpy "don't do that." His father, a Congregational minister, and his mother constantly assured him that he had erred but could be restored to favor by making amends to his loving parents, who were ready to embrace him at the first sign of contrition.

As the child of evangelical parents grew more independent, the imperative to reflect upon consequences became more insistent. Gradually the young person discovered that the checks on conduct grew from within and were no longer related to fear of provoking adult anger. Theodore Parker, the abolitionist and fiery preacher of Boston, remembered how at age five he had nearly killed a turtle. But he had surprised himself when he had refrained. Racing home, he breathlessly asked his mother Hannah why he had not struck the turtle that had frightened him. She exclaimed, "Some men call it conscience, but I prefer to call it the voice of God in the soul of man. If you listen and obey it, then it will speak clearer and clearer . . . but if you turn a deaf ear or disobey, then it will fade out . . . and leave you all in the dark without a guide." In many respects the story could have been told by a planter's son, for in the antebellum years more and more plantation families fell under the evangelical sway, with conscience the objective sought. Yet not many Southerners would have considered the incident a turning point in their moral and religious development, as Parker did. Although there were anxieties aplenty in such inculcations, Parker and many like him felt their wills reinforced by encounters with temptations overcome. From such experiences they learned that parents cared very much about them and their future prospects, even if there was little outward show of affection in the form of kisses and hugs.

In contrast, white Southerners reared children to value honor as much as, if not more than, godly conscience. Like the Puritan conscience, honor could be internalized, and when it was violated, guilt was likewise the response. It did require self-restraint, but based upon pride, not divine commandment. Honor reconciled both habits—to make all due allowances for another's provocations with self-denial and restraint and, when required, to react impulsively for the sake of self-esteem and public reputation. Although there might seem to be a dichotomy between adult violence—the Southern record of personal altercations and duels—and the parental demands for children to forswear aggression, there was none. The North Carolinian William Pettigrew advised his younger brother that "as far as it can be done, we should live peaceably with our associates; but, as we cannot always do so, it is necessary occasionally to resist. And when our honor demands resistance, it should be done with courage." Nor was it impossible to promote both Christian conscience and the conscience of honor in nearly indistinguishable ways, as Lee's advice to his sons evinced.

In regard to deference for the older generation, conscience and honor arrived at the same point from somewhat different perspectives. Conscience-building evoked respect for old age as a general abstraction. One should be kind to the poor elderly, not just to the wealthy aged. Honor, however, was much more discriminatory. "Honor thy father and mother," but it was considerably less important that one be deferential to the "uncle" in the cabin, the stranger at the gate. Nevertheless, among gentlefolk of the South, whether the source was Christian or simply traditional, the well-bred child was expected to manifest courtesy. Familial pride demanded it. But it was also simply the right thing to do, and by all and sundry it was thought to be both Christian and honorable, as if the two ethical patterns were always one and the same. The strategies for judging and exemplifying personality in relation to status were part of a young Southerner's training from the earliest age, but it was also a matter of plain moral duty.

The raising of children to a code of this variety by no means implied that parents rejoiced when youngsters were brutal toward the helpless and alien. Nor should it be inferred that the Southern gentility lacked conscience, as some critics of slaveholding, then and more recently, have maintained. Yet the early introduction of the modes of honor did serve to blunt sentimentality about the unfairness of hierarchy. Thus honor was more than a manifestion of Southern high-spiritedness and community prejudices about race, sex, and family pride. It entered the very texture of upbringing.

Insofar as honor was woven into the lives of very small children, it was a source of familial and personal strengthening. Among the natural benefits—and they were substantial—was the full expression of love between parents and children. There was a natural outpouring of spontaneous feelings, for, as was mentioned earlier, to speak was to think, to feel was to express emotions openly. Whereas fathers in Northern and evangelical households tended toward distance and reserve, and mothers worried lest they allow maternal indulgence to jeopardize God's favor upon the small one, Southern parents were almost too devoted to their children. In particular, the eldest child, as one would expect in a patriarchy, enjoyed special interest. As Freud once said, "A man who has been the indisputable favorite of his mother keeps for life the feeling of a conqueror." That was indeed the hope of the Southern parent. But one could be equally favored by an adoring father, too. "If only I could get a squeeze at that little fellow, turning up his sweet mouth to 'keese baba!' " wrote Robert E. Lee to his wife when far from the home that he loved. At its best, a lofty appreciation of personal worth and status could grow out of that sense of familial belonging. "A certain high-mindedness"—Stoic and humanistic *megalopsychia*—one Southern writer has said, "went with Corinthian columns and self-immolating black mammies."

In terms of social ideals, one could do much worse than to set before the child those principles of gentility already described. In homes where piety as well as patriarchy reigned, the Christian ethos and the concept of genteel honor could seem almost perfectly in harmony. Such a style contrasted with the stiff demeanor and sometimes destructive inhibitions that a rigorous and overly introspective "self-mistrust," as Henry Adams said, engendered in Yankee souls. For the children of the Rev. Charles Colcock Jones, Presbyterian and slaveholder of Georgia, or of the North Carolina Pettigrew family, or of many other planter families, conscience and honor could be and were wisely combined. Patriarchy did not necessarily involve a complete submission to parental will. Southern fathers expected a degree of liveliness, even independence from the young. But among those who belonged to the high gentility especially, the child was to honor the father's position as much as the father himself. Much was often said in correspondence and diaries about letting the children find their own way in the world—on the plantation and at school as youngsters, in the larger sphere when young adults. Indeed, fathers were even willing to gamble on their sons' success by presenting them with patrimonies to manage at a surprisingly early age. Nevertheless, an egalitarian or even brotherly relation between father and child was not the aim (even were it possible in any society). No less than in Northern, evangelical households, the Southern parent of high gentility perceived the child as a moral figure to be molded as if made of clay, not as an independent personality with talents, interests, and temperaments to be developed for individualistic rather than family needs.

Some fathers assured themselves of filial respect by withholding intimacy. This was also meant to be instructive, insofar as it encouraged the child to seek self-protective reserve in relations with others. Advice reinforced this parental example. In 1850 a planter wrote to his son, "Be kind and civil to every one but intimate with none." A Mississippi plantation mother in 1864 told her daughter, "It is best not to be Intimate with any body nor confide to[o] much in anyone" because "our best friends are our greatest enemies."

Other parents took a less formidable line. But in either case, there was always much intrusiveness and constantly repeated advice about conduct. Many if not most parents presumed that whatever the manner of their own behavior, it was worth emulation. Cultural relativism had not yet arisen: there was, most believed, only one way, one road to achieve success. The consequence was, on the whole, fairly salutary. Children are amazingly adaptable, Southern whites no less than any others. But for some, the burdens that moral parents laid upon the child were too absolute. They could be torn between love and shame, respect and rebellion, especially when parents discovered that ideals had not been met and personal whims and desires had been allowed to run free. At such times, in families where honor was the chief goal, the admonitions took this form: "Avoid as much as possible low company," advised a Natchez plantation mistress in 1859; "[A]ssociate with the refined for your manners soon tell what company you keep—Recollect dear Son you have a name to preserve." Characteristically, there was no mention of a jealous God to serve, an immortal soul to save.

The reins of guilt and shame, internalized from an early age, could be extremely dangerous, especially if the "significant other"— fathers, mothers, widows, guardians—placed severe moral demands upon themselves and expected offspring to do likewise. "Overindulgence" was often thought to be the reason for so many sons having become prodigal in the upper social ranks. But they also appeared in highly upstanding families, to the grief of distinguished fathers and grandfathers. Thomas Jefferson, for instance, was often didactic in his solicitude for his daughters and their children as well as for the offspring of his sisters and brother. Yet he was generous-hearted and informal in personal relations with the young. How it grieved him, though, when, as so often happened in planter families, the young did not grow in maturity and self-discipline. Charles Lewis Bankhead, his grandson-in-law, Lilburne and Isham Lewis, his nephews, and other relatives were involved in spectacular scrapes, usually a consequence of alcoholism. Such ne'er-do-wells were a special curse in the rural South, though Northern families of similar repute had their share as well.

In households where fathers were not so distinguished, not so committed to public service, high aims were perhaps less determinedly set before the growing youngster. Some fathers offered ex-

amples of manliness so physical and primal that the young son had
little difficulty duplicating in his small world what he observed in
his father's behavior. "Minister as he was," recollected Reuben
Davis, a Mississippi lawyer from middling stock, "my father never
doubted that it was part of his Christian duty to knock down any
rascal who happened to deserve such discipline." His code did not
resemble that of Thomas Jefferson, nor that of a Boston Brahmin.
For the former, a Roman disdain for insult and a certainty of inner
integrity forbade such unseemliness. For the latter, time itself was
too valuable to be wasted in minor disputes. Sense of self was such
that the slights of others were not to be taken seriously, in the fashion of a gamecock. But for the late-eighteenth- and early-nineteenth-
century Southern planter class on the frontier, the rules to impart
to the young were simple, clear, and, in context, healthy. Andrew
Jackson recalled the advice of his widowed mother before her death,
when he was still very young: "If ever you have to vindicate your
feelings or your honor, do it calmly," she had warned. "Avoid quarrels as long as you can, but sustain your manhood always." Equally
uncomplicated was Reuben Davis's credo: "A man ought to fear
God and mind his business. He should be respectful and courteous
to all women; he should love his friends and hate his enemies . . .
eat when . . . hungry, drink when . . . thirsty, dance when . . .
merry . . . and knock down any man who questioned his right to
these privileges." For an oral, rather fluid slave society, these were
all virtues that made good sense, unrefined though they were. Perhaps there was the danger of a childish naiveté implicit in so transparent a scheme. Still, it had a vitality, and as long as men and
women so raised were in touch with their feelings, it could produce
admirable results.

As in the North, Southern mothers played the dominant role in the
care of infants. But in the South, among both rich and poor, fathers
were not invariably diffident about their offspring. Demonstrative
themselves, they expected to see early signs of manliness in sons and
vivacity in girls. "Give little Molly a thousand kisses for me," wrote
George Braxton, a Virginia planter, to his wife in 1755. "Remember

me to the children and tell em I will be mad if they are naughty,"
declared Levin Joynes affectionately in 1788. The pattern rather resembled modern-day rural father-child relations. According to a recent anthropological study, black fathers in northern Florida treat
their progeny similarly. The father "holds the baby, kisses him and
talks to him," but when the baby becomes "hungry, tired, or needs
to be changed he is returned to the mother." Nevertheless, the father "demonstrates pride in him, relates to him in an affectionate
way, and provides emotional . . . support for him."

Although proud of their youngsters as extensions of themselves,
Southern antebellum fathers devoted little routine time to them.
The same was equally true of upper-class Northern fathers during
the period. Busy with financial and commercial enterprise, the
Amorys, Appletons, and Lawrences and similarly well-placed fathers
had no time for superintendence of their young. Besides, it would
have been indecorous to show too much affection, which was best
left to nurses and mothers to provide. In the South, fathers were
busy with less profitable but equally gratifying and socially functional duties—muster rolls, courthouse visits, hunting parties, and
other activities that conferred status but not always reward in coin.
Whatever the utility of their excursions abroad might be, Southern
fathers were not as tied to plantation and hearth as modern historians have pictured them by way of contrast to the work-home
dichotomy of the antebellum Northern and modern style. By whim
more than by design, fathers lavished affection on their young one
moment and were utterly preoccupied with other matters the next.
The haphazardness in Southern father-child relations was in stark
contrast to the Northeastern upper- and middle-class, evangelical
norms of behavior. Travelers frequently remarked upon the irregu-
larity that characterized so much of white Southern life, including
childrearing. For instance, children of merchant bankers in Boston
were very early introduced to the notion of keeping strict accounts,
accepting the parental idea that they should note *"every cent* you
receive, and *every cent you expend."* Rare was the Southern planter
who required such monetary exactness. An early introduction to the
stables was more appropriate.

In times of crisis fathers often demonstrated the utmost concern, as if, perhaps, to make up for prior inattention. When William Beverley of Virginia buried an infant boy in the mid-eighteenth century, he wrote a close friend, "I vainly thought he would be an exceeding great comfort to me in my old age . . . but now he is gone the way of all flesh, I shall endeavour not to be fond of any thing in this world." Two months later he still was inconsolable and mourned that he had not himself "died in his room," instead of the boy. Antebellum fathers, no less than their colonial forebears, were distraught in crises of illness and death.[28] Yet fathers spent little time hovering over the cradle; it was not quite respectable or manly to be too domestic. At the same time, the child was frequently seen as an extension of themselves.

Beyond the efforts to keep a child alive, a chief objective in child-rearing was to encourage the very young to be aggressive, even ferocious. Otherwise, reasoned the traditionally minded parent, the male child would be so severely checked and overprotected that effeminacy might ensue. Thomas Jones, a Chesapeake planter, rejoiced in the eighteenth century that his two-year-old "runs about the house, hollows and makes a noise all day long, and as often as he can, gets out of Doors." Very young children learned that they were supposed to grab for things, fight on the carpet to entertain parents, clatter their toys about, defy parental commands, and even set upon likely visitors in friendly roughhouse. Girls acted with the same freedom from restraint as boys. Their introduction to the proprieties of ladyhood came much later.

When a boy developed speech and was presented with his first pair of breeches, an early sign of manhood for four-year-olds, his parents' impatience to see him a self-reliant, competent, and virile soul grew apace. Moreover, it seemed only proper to entrust young children to the care of older siblings and young slaves. Busy with household and farm duties, mothers thrust children into sometimes irresponsible hands. Resentments could arise but also affections. Brantley York of early nineteenth-century North Carolina, for instance, had a healthy and straightforward love for his older sister. He remembered how at age four he had to accompany her to the

Old Field School in frontier Randolph County; she was "minding" him for mother. He did not object to the tedium of school, an activity in which he could not then share. He noted that she had always been "my nurse." There was a "rough sympathy and helpfulness," a Yankee visitor thought, in the way poor white children acted toward their younger siblings. The same was true for the vast majority of gentry families in the nineteenth-century South.

It is always risky to generalize about such matters as childrearing. Every family, ancient or modern, has its own peculiarities. Moreover, different styles were coming into fashion in the mid-nineteenth-century South, ones largely connected with the advance of evangelical religion. It would be an error to insist that honor alone was the principle guiding Southern white childcare. Particularly in the upper South, but elsewhere too, Southern matrons and fathers sometimes recognized the failings of the traditional approach. "How bad it is," said one Virginia mother in 1804, "for children to be so giddy & extravagant." But for an extended example, we return to the case of Robert E. Lee, because he so well epitomized the way Southern gentlemen were becoming accustomed to react toward the young. Lee's solicitude about how problems of discipline ought to be handled in a very young child's life was evident in a letter of 1837, posted to "Dear Markie," his artistocratic wife Mary Custis. "Our dear little boy," wrote the pious young father, "seems to have among his friends [i.e., his elders] the reputation of being hard to manage,—a distinction not at all desirable, as it indicates self-will and obstinacy." Lee readily admitted that the world saw in such behavior of a three- or four-year-old healthy signs of aggression. Nevertheless, the army regular continued, "it is our duty, if possible, to counteract" such feelings and impulses so that they could be quickly brought "under his control." Lee explained that he tried to reason with the youngster and to warn him against letting "his little faculties" become "warped by passion."

Most Northern as well as Southern evangelical parents thought early checking of that vice was an absolute necessity. Parents with more traditional views also agreed, but they often lacked the psychological strategies to instill it. Also, the parents' daily example was likely to undercut their words. Turning his attention to the topic on a much later occasion, Lee wrote "Markie," "You must not let" the youngest boy "run wild in my absence, and will have to exercise firm authority over all of them. This will not require severity or even strictness, but constant attention and an unwavering course. Mildness and forbearance will strengthen their affection for you, while it will maintain your control over them." These sentiments indicated that in the South, among the small number of evangelicals in the upper class, inner integrity, self-discipline, and personal achievement were all goals to which parents and children were to aspire. In this they differed not at all from the Northern evangelical pattern. Similar regularity could be found, too, among some of the families in the Southern yeomanry.

One should not assume, though, that Lee's style of fatherhood was the rule to which all other forms of childcare were exceptions. In making that assumption, as we in this age may be inclined to do, we should recognize two factors. First, Southern scholars today are likely to have been raised in rather similar ways, ones that encourage educational, possibly high religious objectives. To universalize those attitudes and to transpose them back in time would be all too natural. Second, Southern archives are full of family papers in which these same principles are set forth in letter after letter. After all, the kind of people who would leave voluminous testimony to their achievements and thoughts, for later family—and eventually public—edification, were already predisposed to strive for great, often godly ideals. But what of the thousands who did not squirrel away family treasures in ribboned bundles? There is no way of knowing how representative the paper-keeping evangelical whites were in the Old South. One must suspect, however, that there were more traditional parents—ones who were not careful about keeping home records—than there were those who did so.

Typical of the better sort of old-fashioned father (one who did write down his thoughts for posterity) was John Horry Dent. An Alabama slaveholder originally from low-country South Carolina, Dent established an uncommonly efficient plantation in Barbour

County, near Eufaula. Sober, industrious, civic-minded, and well read, he was probably more typical a Southern parent than Robert E. Lee.

In childrearing, as in life, the rugged aristocrat from South Carolina believed that neither church nor womankind should interfere too much in checking manhood in the very young. For him, worship services were accommodations to the needs of matrons, old people, and other dependents. Personal uprightness, he maintained, had almost no connection with Sabbath observances. Unless one had to be present for a marriage, christening, or funeral—all of them family more than spiritual events—he believed the wise planter should stay clear of church, where hypocrisy and sanctimoniousness flourished. In that respect he carried on the traditional anticlericalism of the eighteenth-century squires of the Carolinas and Virginia. Dent would have been horrified, however, had anyone suggested that he was repudiating conscience or denying its importance in the moral development of the young. Nonetheless, he rhymed his deepest convictions in 1858:

> Honor and shame from all conditions rise;
> Act well your part and their [sic] the honor lies.

In keeping with these views, Dent's affection for his young was ordinarily casual. He made an exception, however, of his eldest son Horry. Upon him he lavished his hopes, until Horry died in Confederate service. According to Dent's recent biographer, his papers made few references to the others. The unhappy results of parental insensitivity were evident as the other two boys grew up. The youngest son showed no promise at all; he clerked in a small store. The second eldest, Herbert, was a constant trial, misbehaving from an early age. When a teenager, he killed a horse, lost another, and shot a slave in the leg—all accidents, perhaps. No doubt such scrapes were intended to catch the father's attention, by these if no other means, but Dent scarcely blinked an eye. After the Civil War Herbert, unable to hold a steady job, was still dependent upon the old man. In 1880 Dent lamented that he had "spoiled" Herbert. He consoled himself that most other planters of his generation had also overindulged their sons. Like other former slaveholders, he mused that slavery had been a curse after all: it had sapped the will of the young to learn self-reliance. Actually, the fault lay elsewhere.

5

Sexual Honor, Expectation, and Shame

The encounter of antebellum Southern male and female was intense, competitive, and almost antagonistic. Intense, because all exchanges were, in a society that placed so much value upon personal contact and close relationships. Competitive, since independence was a social goal that women, despite the contrary requirement of subordination, shared with men. The struggle, however, had to be subterranean and devious, for men alone were given the privilege of expressing their feelings openly. Antagonisms grew out of the conflict, but also out of the misogyny that arose from male fear of female power.

It should not be supposed that these attitudes were peculiar to the Old South alone. They had always existed. Nevertheless, antebellum Yankee women, at least those in the upper and middle classes, had begun to question, with increasing insistence, their age-old subjection. In response, Southern spokesmen reacted to the threat of unfamiliar notions of feminine rights by articulating long-held assumptions. Southern men were not, as one authority recently claimed, "would-be patriarchs." They were the genuine article, and intended to remain so eternally. One writer, for instance, declared in 1845 that "the husband acquires from the union increased capacity and power," but that the wife simply brought a "feebleness that solicits protection—a singleness that requires support." These prescriptions were not the product of Victorian sentiment. Rather they expressed ancient convictions in contemporaneous terms.

Southern male honor required that women be burdened with a multitude of negatives, a not very subtle way to preserve male initiative in the never-ending battle of the sexes. Female honor had always been the exercise of restraint and abstinence. "She cannot [that is, ought never to] give utterance to her passions like a man," commanded T. R. Dew of William and Mary College. She must "suppress the most violent feelings," yet show a "contentment and ease which may impose upon an inquisitive and scrutinizing world." The advice that planter Bolling Hall of Alabama gave his daughter in 1813 was typical of the social ideas of womanhood that had been handed down for generations. "If you learn to restrain every thought, action and word by virtue and religion, you will become an ornament," he promised. To be sure, Yankee parents had made the same sort of prediction in prior years; many still did so, although the winds of change were abroad during antebellum times.

Of course, everyone knew forceful women, stern in rectitude, commanding in personality, but by no means were such formidable matrons recognized as part of a formal matriarchy. They held power by virtue of willfulness, not prescriptive right. Aunt Rosa Mallard in Faulkner's *The Unvanquished* exemplified the type. She did what she deemed necessary to preserve family fortune, but always in the name of the owner, Colonel John Sartoris, who was away at war. The same type appeared often in real life. "Grandmother" James, recalled Emily Semple of Alabama, "was looked upon as a severe old lady whom everybody feared, even her sons and grandsons." Yet even she could not get her "jovial" husband to attend Methodist camp meeting, although later she did successfully use her powers of purse, as his widow, to ensure the occasional appearance of her sons at services. Among the lower classes, too, some women possessed the necessary grit. " 'Granny,' " said Vance Randolph in reference to an old farm woman, "was regarded as a chimney-oracle, and her grown sons and grandsons consulted her about many matters which they did not mention to their wives. Illiterate and superstitious she was, and filthy and disgusting in her personal habits, but [with] magnificence about her, a sort of couraged pessimism. . . ."

Reversals of role—the hen-pecked husband, the scolding wife—offered a deviance that supported the prevailing view by negative example. How such individuals were handled by gossip and sometimes public humiliation will become evident in the course of these pages. Enforcement of gender and family conventions was community business, at least among the common folk of the Old South. All ranks of men agreed that women, like other dependents upon male leadership and livelihood, should be subordinate, docile. As Dr. James Norcom of North Carolina put it, "God in his inscrutable wisdom, has appointed a place & a duty for females, *out of which* they can neither accomplish their destiny nor secure their happiness!!"

The difficulty was that if one did not marry, there were no appropriate alternatives. Women's money-making occupations were chiefly confined to doing the work of other women in the home—sewing, managing a house as landlady or paid housekeeper, supervising children as governess or teacher. It was acceptable for widows to manage the business in which their husbands had been engaged, but spinsters, unless milliners or dressmakers, seldom started a firm on their own. Unlike their Northern sisters of comparable education, Southern women could not even teach school without feelings of guilt and self-consciousness. Leaving Alabama for Georgia, Margaret Gillis, for instance, thought that her employment as a plantation music teacher would provide new fulfillment as well as a way to survive the Civil War. "Well I have braved all opposition, and the displeasure of those who love me, and come here to teach," she wrote in her diary. "I thought I never could be contented without teaching," but "how my heart aches," she discovered, as homesickness and a sense of social declension overwhelmed her. Her worries were justified. Dr. James Norcom of North Carolina, gossiping about a physician's widow named Mrs. Sawyer who had to take up music teaching to earn her living, admitted that her occupation was respectable, but barely so. Few ladies wanted to know the musical arts, he claimed, and those few were all that stood between Mrs. Sawyer and "starvation."

Feminine dependency was woman's fate, no matter how much she secretly wished that it were otherwise. When brides were much younger than their husbands, the latter held the initiative, even in regard to planning the household. Fifteen when her father literally gave her to Thomas Merrick, Caroline had nominal charge of nursery and kitchen, but her husband interfered whenever it suited him. For instance, he abruptly moved the family to New Orleans when she was twenty and already burdened with three babies. Without any consultation, he purchased a house that she had never seen. Suppressing her disappointment, she only admitted later that "the home chosen was not such as I should have selected," being miles from the busy city life. Yet she lived there for fifty years, long after her husband had died. James H. Hammond's wife Catherine also had to hide her resentment when he went to New York from South Carolina to buy all the china, glass, tableware, curtains, sofas, and bedsteads for a new mansion in Columbia. Catherine had only the pleasure of reading his letter about the trials of shopping. "It takes so long to look all around," he complained in hopes of sympathy, "and even after one finds the right place it requires several visits to get what you want." Henry Burgwyn's wife was so young and eager a bride (Yankee though she was) that she delighted in her furnishings and possessions, which, she rejoiced, were "all Henry's taste." Soon she found, however, that there was little left to do. She undertook excursions by foot, accompanied by roving hogs, until the neighboring ladies in New Bern made fun of her Yankee energy. Walking, especially alone, was thought indelicate.

Marital squabbles were inevitable. Yet the wise woman tried to loyally suppress her misgivings as she had been commanded by parents, teachers, ministers, and friends. Chafing under some criticism from her husband, Mary Louisa Williamson of Alabama's Black Belt confessed that his arbitrariness had added to "the cares that devolve upon a wife." But "in the evening" she once more "*vowed to love, honor, and obey my husband.*" The local preacher stressed the obligation that Mary Williamson felt in surmounting her anger. "Listening to the Minister," she wrote, who assured her "that 'those were *ties,* that neither angels nor men could render void,' I felt perfect confidence in the strength and vitality of my *love*"—although "once or twice since the fervor and steadfastness of my faith has wavered." Like the slaves who often heard in the white people's church about the necessity to obey, women were commanded to defer to male authority. The spiritual message had its effect. Out of necessity women adjusted to the pattern and took situations as they came. The process made them sometimes a trifle hard.

Toughness beneath the soft exterior had its origins in childhood. Girls, it will be recalled, were raised without much sexual differentiation from their male peers from birth to the boys' "clothing" stage. During that first period of childhood they too were indulged, fretted over, and given every opportunity to make demands, and even allowed the sort of wild outdoor activity that led to easily preventable accidents. In frontier Alabama, Colonel Semple's aristocratic daughter Emily Virginia Semple remembered that she was accustomed to bruising herself by running in the yard, age four, with a sunbonnet drooping over her eyes. Finally her father ordered the inconvenient article removed, to prevent her from "butting my brains out." Her mother, fearful of the ill effects of sunlight on a girl's white complexion, refused, and won the dispute. At an earlier time in Southern history mothers were not so solicitous about ladylike appearance and behavior. In 1769, for instance, Agan Blair of Maryland reported that for several days past "Betsy and her Cousin Jenny had been fighting," to the vexation of all, and after repeated threats of whippings had failed to restore order she had finally intervened, although neither child was her own. Southern colonial women were averse to strict regulation of young girls. An Englishwoman visited the Blair plantation on the eastern shore and brought along a "little girl," who was much "to be pitied," declared Agan Blair. "This poor thing is stuck up in a chair all day long with a Coller on, nor dare she even to taste Tea fruit Cake or any little Triffle offer'd her by ye company. . . ." Fathers like William Byrd II often preferred their girls over sons, not because of some loosening of patriarchal requirements, but because, at least in part, daughters were often less aggressive and more easily handled than boys.

Although stricter controls became more fashionable in the antebellum era, a degree of indulgence often continued for girls into the next period of their moral and physical development after the age of four. J. G. Clinkscales remembered that in his pre–Civil War childhood, "many of the young ladies could ride as well as their brothers, and not a few of them could handle firearms with great accuracy and skill." Fathers took their girls fishing. Sometimes they went on hunting trips, too. In Mississippi, John J. Pettus's sisters accompanied the boys on their sporting forays in the forests. Thomas Page of Virginia recalled that girls ran about the plantation yard "wishing they were boys, and getting half scoldings from mammy for being tomboys and tearing their aprons and dresses." Half-scoldings were also half-approvals. Just as boys showed courage in hunting, schoolyard fighting, and other vigorous business, so too did girls sometimes prove very brave souls. J. G. Clinkscales's sister Barbara, for instance, went after an old sow, a dangerous beast, that had been devouring baby chicks. She took her father's muzzle-loading shotgun and "emptied a load of bird-shot into the anatomy of the notorious chicken-eater." Needless to say, however, mothers insisted that the girls learn womanly chores, feeding the farm animals, sewing, and mending. Like the boys, they also learned the lessons of tyrannizing slaves, sometimes in very unladylike fashion.

Early and late, Southern critics complained that girls were taught to be just as aggressive and difficult to manage as boys. Colonel Landon Carter hardly ever had a good word to say about the manner in which his son and daughter-in-law raised his grandson and granddaughter. From his point of view both children were excessively indulged. Little Lucy imitated the gross manners of her mother, to the old colonel's distress. Carter, however, believed (correctly or not) that "the first she has entirely ruined by storming at me whenever I would have corrected him a child; and the other has already got to be as sawsy a Minx as ever sat at my table." In 1831 Moses Curtis, the North Carolina schoolmaster, had trouble with a girl of thirteen who refused to answer a question, for which offense he thrashed her with thirty blows over a three-hour morning session. Obstinately, she did not submit with proper deference until mid-afternoon. Family and personal pride could be as powerful a force in girls as in boys. Teachers, parents felt, had little right to punish girls severely, if at all. Even James Norcom, a stern believer in parental corrections, thought that schoolmen should not be allowed to use physical force upon either girls or boys, for it degraded their sense of personal integrity and honor, particularly so after the age of twelve or thirteen.

Family pride and sense of honor were important attributes for girls to share with their brothers, for two main reasons. First, they encouraged resistance to matches based largely on sexual attraction. Although tomboy behavior was acceptable at an early stage, as soon as they reached menarche girls abruptly had to recognize their vulnerability to male aggression. Sexual experiment had to be forbidden, not for reasons of morality alone but also to prevent unwanted young men from violating girls' chastity. Illicit pregnancy forced marriage on the one hand or social ostracism on the other. It was hard for Southerners, like the Irish folk from whom so many of them sprang, to imagine that illicit sex was merely a search for pleasure; the ulterior motive had to be greed for lands and social advance. Or else it was simple gallantry—a licentious expression of masculinity that motivated the rogue. Hence, young girls were warned to remember their parentage as well as their self-respect. Second, the development of family honor in the young virgin served the purpose of reinforcing courage.

The familiar stereotyping of Southern ladyhood—the glorification of motherhood, the sanctity of virginity, and the noble self-sacrifice of the matron—had a very important social purpose. Such concepts ensured at least outward submission to male will. They incorporated the ideals of inner constraint and hardihood within the framework of the softer feminine values of modesty, reserve toward outsiders, and warmth of affection toward the men who were significant in women's lives. Moreover, the hymns of praise to virtuous womanhood made the ascriptive disadvantages of the gender more bearable. They elevated the negative features into admirable qualities.

Some scholars have argued, however, that these idealizations were mischievously self-deluding. The myths failed in their purpose, leaving misery in their path. Mythology pretended that every woman could think herself a belle, and at the same time offered no inkling of the distresses of motherhood that awaited most belles. So the legend of ladyhood might seem from our perspective today. But all societies have their conventional illusions, which are designed to make the unbearable somewhat less frightening. Besides, no one knew of any alternatives. Companionate marriage would have to await changes in women's property rights, prospects of decent employment for wives and mothers, and a culture devoted to egalitarian principles generally. Until then, the feminine ethic had to encourage submission to reality.

It is sometimes argued that Southern young women suffered needlessly in silence, that worries were voiced only in private, not in public as they should have been. Yet the reason for reticence was not anxiety lest the myth of the ladyhood be shattered. Instead, the injunction to hold the tongue was a demand for stalwartness against adversity. That mattered much more than delicacy. The latter was a luxury thrown aside when women had to meet difficult times—agrarian disasters; sudden changes in fortune, whether from bad luck or male inadequacy; epidemics; or, most especially, military catastrophes and losses during the Civil War. Women were expected to nurture a capacity to bear burdens with grace, courage, and silence. That social ideal far outweighed any girlish dreaming about being a belle, a fancy to be indulged only in the brief sojourn from paternal control to husbandly dominion. Thus to appear poised, forbearing, and hopeful, especially when things went wrong, was to please friends and relations. In fact, it signified inner stamina.

The ideal of feminine courage and honor almost replicated that of men under such circumstances, and certainly it found expression in legends of female heroism in Civil War recollections and novels. But these values were still traditional ones; they did not at all point toward a modern feminism. Rather, they reflected the ancient view that mothers of brave men had to be brave themselves. By and large, many of them were. The aspiration and actuality were conjoined, particularly under the bitter duress of war.

In happier, more settled circumstances women were supposed to be uncomplaining and docile. When Mrs. Gildersleeve, a Georgia physician's wife, found herself pregnant once again, she took herself promptly to bed, "so great," friends gossiped, was her "disappointment." It was a quietly emphatic way to respond to bad news, but somewhat too transparent and self-indulgent to win her much sympathy from the other matrons.

Mrs. Gildersleeve's unhappiness about facing the ordeal of childbirth was no sign of a present-minded spirit at work in the womanly conscience. Childbearing was an ancient and sacred calling of the gender. Few in the Old South disputed so self-evident a proposition as that. For instance, Mrs. Chesnut stood by a wife, a newcomer in the community, who was thought to be barren. She told her circle of friends that the woman had actually had three babies but lost them all. "Women have such contempt for a childless wife," Mrs. Chesnut commented. "Now they will be all sympathy and kindness. I took away her 'reproach among women.'" Mrs. Chesnut knew whereof she spoke: she was exceedingly conscious of her own unfruitfulness.

Barrenness in women, like kinlessness, which was also much dreaded, had always been a point of shame, and sufferers were contemptible or at best pitiable in the eyes of others. To be sure, Southerners were not so primitive and brutal about the matter as archaic peoples had once been. Nevertheless, family continuity was highly prized and childlessness was a sore grievance. The married woman who disappointed her husband and relations in this respect could scarcely help having feelings of incompleteness. Moreover, it cut her off from a source of personal power—the duties of nurture—and from sense of fulfillment as a woman. C. Vann Woodward and Elisabeth Muhlenfeld, students of Mary Chesnut's literary diary and of her sad, dramatic life, speculate that one of her many trips north away from the dull plantation routine in the 1840s was prompted by a nervous depression, the cause of which was related to her in-fertility. Indeed, her antislavery convictions might well have been connected with the problem. Mrs. Chesnut, reared to slaveholding wealth and enjoying all its privileges and responsibilities, had fewer political than domestically moral objections to the institution. A major component of her assault upon the system was the thought that "we live surrounded by prostitutes" whose offspring populated the quarters. "Thank God for my countrywomen—alas for the men! No worse than men everywhere, but the lower their mistresses, the more degraded they must be."

What drove home the point was her attitude toward her lusty father-in-law, James Chesnut, Sr. and his attitude toward her. How bitter it was for her to record that "these people take the old Hebrew pride in the number of children they have. . . . Old Mr. C. said today, 'Wife, you must feel that you have not been useless in your day and generation. You have now twenty-seven great-grandchildren . . . «Me a childless wretch. . . . Colonel Chesnut, a man who rarely wounds me . . . And what of me! God help me—no good have I done myself or anyone else, with this I boast so of, the power to make myself loved. Where am I now, where are my friends? I am allowed to have none. (*He did not count his children!!*)»'" An autocrat—like the Russian czar or the emperor of Austria, as Mary Chesnut described him—the old planter earned her deep respect and even admiration and affection. But he was father, she suspected, of a mulatto line. Practical, jealous of his property, and completely unsentimental, Chesnut, Sr., she mused on more than one occasion, "was born when it was not the fashion for a gentleman to be a saint." The wonder was, she thought, that he had not been "a greater ty-rant." The sins of slaveholding which her husband's father so regret-tably exemplified in her mind were not unconnected with her own sense of blameworthiness for not providing him with grandchildren, a task that the blackest "wench" in a slave harem could do.

In maintaining what appears to us as a "double standard" of sex-ual behavior, Southerners were not very self-conscious, most espe-cially in the early years of the Republic. Differences in the very phy-siques of the genders properly signified inequalities in "points of honor," declared Thomas R. Dew of Virginia, basing his arguments upon such eighteenth-century English authors as Addison and Burke. Thus, he continued, men could retrieve "a lost character" by a simple "reformation" of former promiscuity (though their wives should not provoke them with tears but entice them back with winning ways). On the other hand, a woman ought not be touched "even by the breath of suspicion," and could never fully recover her good name once it was blemished. Honor and interest combined to repress feminine lustfulness, but basically the sanction was external: fear of social ostracism. As proprietors and protectors of female virtue, fathers, brothers, and husbands were brought to public shame by the tarnished woman. Needless to say, Southern churchmen sought to impose a higher ideal of chasteness upon men, but they, like Dew, could not repudiate the ethic that condemned womanly sin and excused male vice. As a result, hard custom, undergirded by common-law jurisprudence, held the South to the traditional "double standard." In contrast, middle-class Northerners were gradually forsaking that view, and instead deeming women by nature morally superior and more self-controlled than men.

Three broad categories in the realm of sexual ill-conduct reflected the general structure of Southern ethics: simple male fornication, which, under some conditions, was not even disapproved but almost sanctified; second, adultery, particularly female adultery, for which the remedies of the aggrieved husband were sometimes violent; and finally, certain (but not all) varieties of miscegenation. In each of these situations public response depended upon broad, customary expectations, but in practice these were modified by perceptions of how the principals conducted themselves.

Simple male fornication hardly requires much elaborate analysis. Yet it is worth mentioning that middle-class evangelical and Yankee ideals on this score were different from the mainstream of Southern mores. Although most Northern males doubtless had sexual experience before marriage, physicians and clergymen urged the duty and the healthiness of male continence. Ralph Waldo Emerson shocked his English friends Thomas Carlyle and Charles

Dickens by observing that in his homeland "young men of good standing and good education . . . go virgins to their nuptial bed, as truly as their brides." After witnessing scenes of vice in Paris in 1848, he resisted carnal temptations by recalling "the dear and comely forms of honour and genius and piety in my distant home," who "touch me with chaste palms moist and cold, and say to me, You are ours." It was all very well to exhibit manliness in self-denial, as Victorian advisers like Emerson declaimed, but cold, chaste palms were not much in favor in the South. Neither the economy, the system of race control, the concepts of family life, nor even the understanding of gentlemanliness and social status stimulated the kind of repressive psychology that male continence involved.

Attitudes toward male fornication were permissive. Male lust was simply a recognized fact of life. To repress natural impulse was to defy nature itself, leading to prissiness and effeminacy. Outright libertinism also suggested unmanly self-indulgence and inner weaknesses. But a healthy sex life without regard to marriage was quite in order. Fathers and mothers tacitly expected their boys to be adequately prepared for marriage. After all, the virgin male could too easily make the first wedding night a veritable disaster, hardly an auspicious beginning for a lifetime union. Young men made sexual experience a point of honor and boasting among themselves. Older men found that a masculine odor of mild indiscretion enhanced their respectability—if certain rules were followed. In his diary, Hammond defended his own inclinations, noting that "Casar [sic] spared no woman—that in all ages & countries down to the present day & nation the very greatest men . . . have been addicted to loose indulgences with women. . . . Webster & Clay are notorious for it & President Harrison got his wife's niece by child." Hammond gave more credence to these stories than they probably deserved; he had committed similar blunders, and his misery at having been caught led him to find solace in the misadventures of others. Yet Hammond's remarks were fairly representative of the male perspective. In 1852, James L. Petigru gave an account of a dashing Carolinian and the young wife of an aged physician at a Virginia vacation hotel. On a midnight call, the doctor discovered the half-clothed couple leaving a neighboring room and chased them about the corridors, waving a shotgun. To the amusement of the other Southern guests, the lover managed to slip away undetected on the morning train. Such matters were delicious fare for the Carolinians.

In the American South, as in England and France, sleeping with a woman was an informal rite of virilization. The obvious way was to pursue a black partner. If the initial effort were clumsy or brutal no one would object, in view of the woman's race and status. Moreover, black girls were infinitely more accessible and experienced than the white daughters of vigilant, wealthy families. On a visit to Charleston in 1809, Alexander Wilson of Philadelphia observed the contrast between the "frigid insipidity" of "melancholy" upper-class "females" and the "negro wenches" who were "all sprightliness and gayety." A young white virgin male had only to down a few jiggers, light a "segar" to steady his nerves, and ask a passing black to "find him a girl."

Chancellor Harper of South Carolina scoffed at abolitionist objections to such carnal pairings. He said that after the "warm passions of youth" had cooled, the ordinary planter's son realized that he was "connecting himself with one of an inferior and servile caste." He then invariably turned to court "the female of his own race," who offered "greater allurements." The essay by Harper in which these remarks appeared implied that a class of enslaved black women performed a useful service: their availability made possible the sexual license of men without jeopardizing the purity of white women. Prostitutes performed that convenient service in free societies; fallen women, it was thought, kept the rest of the world in good moral order. Slave companions did the same in the Old South.

Unrestrained promiscuity by men was by no means uniformly condoned, but discretion was the mark of a gentleman. One should not flagrantly presume upon another man's territory, in home or quarters. If the "Lothario" lacked repute, woe betide him. For instance, if a poor boy or man "stole" another's slave girl, the penalties were stiff, even though the intention was strictly temporary cohabitation. Though a rich but wayward youth might beat the charge with a good lawyer or an appeal to the outraged master, men of low standing faced serious problems. In South Carolina, when John L. Brown, already known for "dissolute habits," ran off with another man's slave, he was caught, tried, and sentenced to hang for "negro-stealing." Judge John Belton O'Neall recommended commutation and Governor James H. Hammond complied. Brown received thirty-nine lashes on the back instead. Obviously the master and the community sought to set a stern public example, a warning to those without slaves to keep their hands off the valuable possessions of the better element.

Overseers who took liberties in the quarters were a constant cause of complaint. Their activities disrupted life among the slaves and led to demoralized work habits. But at least they did not "steal" their prizes away. When a yeoman boy—eighteen-year-old Levin Johnson of Mississippi, for instance—ran off with a "handsome mulatto" girl, lawyers pleaded the client's immaturity, nonfelonious intent, and remorse. He and the girl had spent the night on a wharf-side steamboat, and for this Johnson was almost sent to the gallows. His sentence was commuted to life in prison. Masters did not invariably go to law for redress, however. J. J. Lyons of up-country South Carolina discovered that the female slave clerk of his store had been sleeping with one of the Perry clan. Since Perry belonged to a leading family, legal action would probably have failed before a jury. At their next meeting Lyons horsewhipped the young blade unmercifully. Many such examples could be given. The main lesson was not "thou shalt not fornicate with black women," but rather "thou shalt take care to do so at no other man's expense."

A second and much more serious issue of sexual misbehavior, the infidelity of a married woman, could no more be separated from questions of status than could male improprieties of the kind just mentioned. By and large women of planter rank were too strictly supervised to have much experience with infidelity, though the "flirt" was a constant source of scandal and fascination among the ladies. Certainly the kind of feminine license that prevailed in the upper classes of seventeenth- and eighteenth-century England and France had no Southern parallel even in the aristocracy of the colonial and early national South. But if grand jury presentments, foreign travelers, and itinerant clergymen are to be given any credence at all, the lower classes of the hinterland South were fairly casual about marital arrangements in general and adultery in particular. Conditions of moral informality gradually diminished under the auspices of revival enthusiasms and church discipline. In fact, a major and unstudied reason for the rise of evangelical churchmanship throughout the South after 1800 was that it provided an effective means for more orderly, sober folk to demarcate and insulate themselves from an element with roistering traditions stretching back to British origins. So little work has been done to describe the ethical and cultural structure of the yeomanry outside the churchgoing crowd that historians are caught between the romantic and bourgeois presentation of Frank Owsley on the one hand and the familiar stereotypes of poor-white depravity on the other. Nevertheless, the backwoods Southern yeomanry, particularly in the early antebellum years, was no more morally refined than the pre-Wesleyan working classes of England. Therefore, most examples of feminine adultery—and of responses to it—involved the middle and lower orders of the white South, not the wealthy, churchgoing matrons of Charleston and Richmond.

The attitude toward feminine adultery was scarcely casual, but it was not a matter of criminal violation. Although grand juries and remonstrating citizens urgently requested that antebellum state legislatures punish adulterers (particularly female ones), lawmakers steadfastly refused. In South Carolina, for instance, bills to provide penalties for adultery were introduced in 1844, 1856, and 1860. None passed. By common law, sexual offenses of this kind had been under ecclesiastical jurisdiction, but when the church was disestablished in Revolutionary times, sexual policing duties were not transferred to other tribunals. In New England, by contrast, adultery had initially been a statutory felony, punishable by death and later by less sanguinary but quite humiliating penalties. Southerners did not believe that the machinery of the state should intervene in matters of local morality. After all, common law provided a husband with the necessary legal right to seize his wife from a seducer by force and to apply to her whatever physical chastisement he felt suitable—within limits. Citizens could band themselves against a local malefactor, with appropriate results, but state intervention on a comprehensive scale, it was thought, would have overtaxed the limited resources of central power.

Nevertheless, for the individual husband two alternatives for handling an adulterous wife did exist within the law itself. Neither was socially approved, and both therefore were seldom used. The first was criminal conversation, a tort action. Only men could sue under this ancient theory of trespass. The common-law rationale was that men, having proprietary claims upon a wife's property, should not be obliged to support children by another man and have their own offspring's legitimacy questioned. Samuel Johnson claimed that "confusion of progeny" was the central problem in a woman's unfaithfulness and accounted for the universal disapprobation of it, but the real problem was, of course, protection of male ego, honor, *and* purity of bloodline. James Hammond thought the absence of criminal-conversation actions from the routine judicial calendar was a mark of Southern moral superiority. It was not. The action was rare simply because it was not well known, and that circumstance was a function of its embarrassing connotations. Criminal conversation was a suit for damages against an adulterer for the loss of a wife's labor, affections, and good name. Who wanted to admit that he was a cuckold? An example of the ambivalent feelings involved arose in a South Carolina case before Justice Elihu Bay in 1820. The husband sought $5,000 in damages from his wife's seducer, but the husband then had to admit that his wife was utterly promiscuous before she had run off with her lover. Bay thoroughly denounced the wife's seducer as "the villain *spider of society*" who had heaped "dishonour" upon the husband. Five thousand dollars was not an excessive compensation, he declared. Nevertheless Bay ruled that condonation (the husband's toleration of his wife's earlier concupiscence) had to be presented to a jury before the court could assess the extent of punitive damages to be awarded.

Thus filing a criminal-conversation action ran counter to notions of how a man should act under trying circumstances. "Mortification of mind" and "depression of a husband's happiness," as Justice Daniel Huger of South Carolina declared, constituted the basis of such suits, not the medieval notion of a poor man with no other recourse available to him seeking redress against a lecherous overlord. In America each man was to defend his own honor as a freeholding citizen. Money damages were unsuitable.

Divorce, though always a more familiar way to gain freedom from an unfaithful wife, presented similar difficulties. In South Carolina neither husband nor wife had access to that remedy. In other parts of the South, divorce was rare, either by state legislatures or by equity or chancery courts. Hoping to reduce, not increase, the number of applications, some Southern state legislatures began in the 1820s to relinquish the power to grant private bills of divorce and confer the jurisdiction upon the bench, where stern common-law jurists were supposed to stand impervious to political, democratic demands. But under pressure of changing notions the lawmakers did liberalize the grounds, reflecting a curious conflict of motives that deserves further investigation. Nevertheless, the number of requests was always slight relative to population size. In 1821 fifty-five divorce petitions reached the Tennessee legislature. Ten years later the number of pleas had risen to sixty-six, hardly an impressive increase. In Alabama the number hovered around 63 per year from 1849 to 1854, then leapt to 105 in 1855, a rate sustained until the Civil War. In Georgia, 291 legislative divorces were submitted between 1798 and 1835, but the acceleration was really confined to the last two years. How many were actually granted remains unascertained, but the number was not high. In North Carolina, according to one estimate, only one in twenty pleas was honored in 1810, four in twenty-two in 1813. No doubt the ratio gradually improved over the next forty years. Yet careful work with county and state records still remains to be done to discover the patterns of the average state assembly and trial judge.

Since divorce pleas early in the century ordinarily arose from members of the poorer classes, gentry legislators had little difficulty in withholding the privilege, as common-law tradition enjoined. An example was the 1813 case of John O'Quin of Wayne County, North Carolina. He and his friends, among whom was a magistrate, caroused at a village house of prostitution one evening. When he woke up the next morning he found himself bedded with "a *Huge Mass of Creation,* purporting to be of the Female Sex, who called herself MARY JACKSON." She announced that the drunken magistrate had married them the night before. Shortly thereafter Mary Jackson joined the troops going to the Canadian front in the war with Great Britain. O'Quin pled for release. The lower chamber rejected the bill, no doubt with much guffawing about how young men should not mix pleasure with the serious business of matrimony. Yet, as always, there was a rationale behind seemingly arbitrary decision making. A fool and his honor, it might have been said, were soon parted. O'Quin's misfortune, in a sense, made more valuable a wiser man's respectability. One's moral reputation was supposed to conform with one's social position, which, as we know, was a very ancient concept. Rich men were imputed to be wise, poor to be foolish. Therefore, examples of folly should be presented to the public in the form of clownish folk like O'Quin. Judge Eugenius A. Nisbet of Georgia admitted that in the handling of divorce cases, legislators were most often influenced by such factors as who the parties were, rather than the circumstances of the case. "The wealth and standing of the parties," he said in 1835, "their political and social relations, or perhaps, the personal beauty and address of the female litigant, controlled in many cases the action of the legislature." Negative decisions, then, meant the very opposite: a disapproval of petitions from the stupid, ugly, and poor, regardless of the inherent merits of the plea. With clear consciences, the politicians thus reaffirmed the sacred character of marriage and male honor by rejecting socially unimportant litigants, the class that overwhelmingly dominated registries of divorce actions.

No less significant than the class status of the plaintiff was evidence of his manliness in the handling of his travails. Without it, chances of winning a divorce from an adulterous wife were slim. In

1833, for instance, John R. Sexton, an illiterate yeoman of Blount County, Tennessee, sought freedom from a most incorrigible wife. Not only was Elizabeth Sexton unfaithful, but, said one deponent, she used her husband's bed to entertain two men at a time. By another deposition, she had sex "three times in broad day light with one David Hammontree," whom she called "much of a man." Finding her rutting under a bush with a stranger to the neighborhood, the local deacon reproached her. Elizabeth retorted, "My ass is my own and I will do as I please with it." The divorce committee was unimpressed and rejected Sexton's plea as "unreasonable." He had observed these goings-on without taking appropriately manly action. Even when a wife deserted a yeoman husband to turn up as a prostitute somewhere else, the husband's chances of winning a suit depended less on the wife's shamelessness than on the manner in which the husband managed the situation. In the minds of legislators—men of the world—the hidden requirement was a confrontation with the lover(s) and, one may safely guess, administration of some firm corrective to the erring wife. If the husband could not control her, he was not to be awarded community approval in the form of divorce. In North Carolina in 1813, Peter Riley argued that he had had to leave his sluttish wife "to protect his reputation." But from depositions there was no sign of his chastising his rivals or his wife. The petition was denied. In the same year, before the same committee, Frederick Ward of Lincoln County, North Carolina, was not freed from marriage, even though his wife had repeatedly cuckolded him, left the state for "New Spain" (Louisiana), and there remarried. He, too, had not fulfilled the unwritten demand.

If, however, a poor man could demonstrate that his wife had been moved by the enticements of a rich seducer, then he stood a decent chance of winning his case. After all, the reasoning went, any man might be deceived by a daughter of Eve who proved too easily swayed by pretty promises and fine clothes of a gentleman. In divorce cases, as in criminal-conversation actions in English settings, the higher the standing of the adulterer the greater the sympathy for the husband upon whom he supposedly preyed. Thus Thomas

Taylor, husbandman of Bedford County, Tennessee, gained a total divorce from Nancy Nuzum in 1821. She had threatened to pile up fifty-dollar debts upon the yeoman, ridiculed his poverty, and boasted that the child she bore belonged to "a gentleman and she wold take it to him that he wold Dress it." Just how accurate the accusations were could scarcely come to light now, but they apparently impressed the committee. Indications of a clandestine unfaithfulness, cleverly hidden even from neighbors, also gave the unsuspecting husband a winning hand. James Trotter, for instance, had witnesses to testify that his wife had deceived everyone for years. Her misdeeds came to notice only after she had abruptly admitted her promiscuity and departed for Petersburg to become a streetwalker. He, too, gained freedom at the hands of a legislature that was generally niggardly about handing out divorces to poor folk, or indeed anyone at all.

On the surface, these decisions appeared whimsical. Yet they were judgments based upon the principles of a traditional ethic. The courts and lawmakers never put honor into statutory or judicial form because it was commonly understood that there should be a division between the workings of the law and the stalwart defense of a man's sense of self. As Joel P. Bishop, a nineteenth-century legal specialist, explained, "The government does not take cognizance of all the laws of human association existing in a community." Breaches in "the law of honor," he said, belonged in that category. The young or foolish fellow who bound himself to a notoriously brazen woman such as Mary Jackson, or one under suspicion of wantonness, such as Betsey Sexton, had to pay the price of his folly or ineffectuality.

Unpleasant though violence was, the most socially approved course for a husband with a wayward mate was to take the law into his own hands. Even judicial experts all but suggested that physical retort was the proper means of retrieving lost honor. On matters of sexual honor the law took account of community opinion. Tapping Reeve, in reference to common-law precedent about adultery, conceded that "where a man finds another in the act of adultery with his wife, which is the greatest possible injury, yet the husband is not justified . . . to avenge his own wrongs." Nevertheless, he continued, the husband was only guilty of manslaughter, to the lowest degree, and liable to suffer "burning in the hand to be inflicted gently," probably with a cold iron. Texas law on this issue was much more straightforward than even common law. According to Article 1220, still on the books, a killing under circumstances in *flagrante delicto* is justifiable homicide. Other states were less bloodthirsty, but juries were loath to convict on even the mildest charges of manslaughter under provocation.

Miscegenation between a white male and black female posed almost no ethical problems for the antebellum Southern community, so long as the rules, which were fairly easy to follow, were discreetly observed. First, the relationship, even if long-standing, had to seem to be a casual one in which the disparity of rank and race between the partners was quite clear to any observer. Second, the concubine had to be sexually attractive in white men's eyes. The lighter the skin, the more comely the shape, the more satisfactory the arrangement appeared to be. Third, the pairing could not be part of a general pattern of dissoluteness. If the wayward white was alcoholic, unsociable, and derelict about civic duty or work, then his keeping a mistress became a subject of general complaint. But gentlemen of discretion and local standing were able to master these simple conventions and suffer very little public disapproval.

Moreover, a man should by all means never acknowledge in mixed company his illicit liaison with a woman, black *or* white. Whispers among members of the same sex did not constitute public exposure. In a conversation among the ladies, Mary Chesnut referred to a genteel old reprobate and how his family reacted to his midnight doings in the quarters. "His wife and daughters in the might of their purity and innocence are supposed never to dream of what is as plain before their eyes as the sunlight," she observed. "They prefer to adore their father as model of all earthly goodness." If someone had violated good taste and brought up the matter in their hearing, however, then all family members, the "sinner" included, would have been disgraced. Transcendent silence was the proper policy.

Needless to say, rules of silence were not always scrupulously observed in Aristotelian fashion. Deathbed contrition occasionally led to breaches of the taboo against personal, public confession. Lieutenant-Governor Winston of Mississippi, for instance, freed his slave mistress and their son by will in 1834. As he had no wife or heirs to bear the disgrace, however, there was no public outcry in that frontier state. David Dickson of Georgia bequeathed an estate of half-a-million dollars to his lovely mulatto daughter in 1885. A North Carolina planter required that a mulatto should share equally in an estate with the legitimate line. A Virginia planter freed his lifetime mistress, then over sixty years old. In all such cases, public reaction—as well as the outrage of heirs—was intense. Usually, however, the law upheld the validity of wills. What was most galling to survivors about these incidents was not just the loss of estate that they entailed but also the exposure to public criticism.

For obvious reasons, a mulatto girl posed less danger to a family's well-being than a mulatto male, unless, as Southerners sometimes fancied, an unsuspecting white male tried to marry her in the mistaken belief that she was white. Ella Thomas, a plantation matron, read a novel in which a bewitching girl who turns out to be the daughter of a mulatto slave and a "Col. Bell" becomes engaged to a young slaveholding gentleman. "I must say I was sufficiently *Southern*," the Carolinian diarist declared, "to think him justifiable in breaking off the engagement after a great deal of suffering." After all, there were the future generations to think of. Richard Mentor Johnson had little trouble over his concubinage with Julia Chinn, a well-brought-up mulatto. A Jacksonian congressman and senator, he kept her in safe seclusion on his Kentucky plantation until her death in 1834. But Johnson tried to introduce their two attractive daughters to Washington society, and the effort made his love life a matter of notoriety. When he ran on Van Buren's ticket, he became the only vice-president in American history to gain the office by narrow Senate election, having failed, by reason of his domestic unorthodoxy, in the electoral college. Had he left his daughters on the Kentucky estate the issue might never have become a scandal, although by the mid-1830s marital regularity had become an evangelical prescription for public office.

The real difficulty was the mulatto male who was the offspring of a planter's union with a mulatto slave. The "bleaching" process, as Southerners perceived it, enhanced his attractiveness to white women and also provided him with a pride in blood hardly suited to the black race and its place in society. Bennet H. Barrow, for instance, became highly incensed when some young mulatto sons of a neighboring planter came riding through his slave quarters in their fine clothes, accompanied by mulatto girls imported from New Orleans. "As I rode up to them," Barrow gloated, "I never saw any thing humble as quick as they did, forgot all their *high breeding* and self greatness." He scared them off with hard talk and whip-cracking. When he complained that "people submit to Amalgamation in its worse Form in this Parish," he was not so much referring to the sin of biracial intercourse as to the impropriety of raising mulatto males to levels that encouraged "impudence."

There was always the chance of a drastic mistake. Since white girls were often quite intimate with their brothers, it followed that their fathers' mulatto offspring would hold a special attraction for them. In the catalog of Southern nightmares, none loomed more ominously than the notion of a pairing of sister with black male. "Would you have your sister marry one?" was not just a cliché. It exposed a taboo that the possibility of incest further strengthened.

The probability of incestuous amalgamation was exceedingly low, but once in a while incidents did occur. For instance, in South Carolina's Union District one Colonel William Farr, a bachelor, took as his "bright mulatto' mistress the daughter of his half-brother. Fan, as she was called, bore him a son named Henry. Farr did not openly admit to being either the father or the uncle of the boy, and his wealth and reclusive habits helped to prevent a community outcry. As he said, he did not "wish to make a blowing horn of everything he did." Moreover, he cultivated a friendship with Judge John Belton O'Neall. Nevertheless, Farr and his mistress were an un-

happy pair, sometimes seriously hurting each other in furious alcoholic battles. As his health and disposition deteriorated, Farr prepared for the future by sending his son, named Henry, to boarding
school. The boy was expelled as soon as his origins were known,
however, and he had to finish his education in Indiana. To assure
mother and son a competence, Farr bequeathed them half of his
$60,000 estate, the other portion being assigned to Judge O'Neall as
a precaution against a challenge. Shortly before dying, however,
Farr replaced O'Neall as beneficiary with Dr. William Thompson,
his physician. Presumably the judge had lectured him on debauch-
ery once too often. Upon his death in 1837, the colonel's white kinsmen by his half-brother disputed their mulatto relatives' rights to
the inheritance. As Farr had anticipated, however, Thompson
stoutly defended the original settlement through various trials and
appeals. The plaintiffs claimed that Fan's African magic was the
only possible explanation for Farr's perversity: he must have been
somehow poisoned or mesmerized into mental incompetence, the
lawyers argued. With Judge O'Neall abstaining, the final court ruling upheld the will by a verdict of two to two (a majority would
have been necessary to overturn it). However distasteful the circumstances were, the jurists really had no choice. South Carolina pro-
bate law, bowing to common social practice, decreed the proportion
that a concubine should receive, a singular fact that Hammond and
others were loath to mention when defending slaveholders' virtue
from abolitionist attack. Farr's will met the stipulations, and his
mental competence was never in doubt.

What was genuinely significant about the case was not the decision of the bench. Rather, community toleration of Farr's living
arrangements was noteworthy. That toleration was based on the
fact that Farr had not advertised his deviation. He did not take his
concubine to public places or impose her presence upon relatives.
She acted as his servant. Moreover, his kinsmen had a vested interest in checking any public outcry, so long as Farr kept them unin-
formed about the contents of the will. Under conditions so bizarre,
it was best not to make a fuss. And it must be remembered that the
mulattoes involved were so light-skinned that driving them out

by charivari or some other coercive community action would have been morally confusing.

Nearly all examples of female intercourse with black men from the antebellum period involved women with defective notions of their social position—hardly surprising in view of the deep horror the violation of this taboo inspired in the community. Sexual attraction, fascination with the exotic, and most of all a sense of gratification in submitting to the dark lover were all involved. One may also be sure that the blacks in question were unusually gifted— and bold—lovers, whom a white man might well envy. No doubt black vengeance through white jealousy was much of the attraction that the black lovers found in these poor-white girls. Some of the slave lovers were conjure-men whose tricks promised the adolescent girls their hearts' desire. Elizabeth Pettus of Fluvanna, Virginia, for instance, was intrigued with a conjure-man named Bob, who seduced her with the threat that he would use magic to break off her match with Dabney Pettus "if she did not conform to his humours." She gave in. Likewise, Lydia Bright of Norfolk in 1803 went to bed with slave Robin because he had promised "that he would conger for to get Benjamin Butt, Jr. to be her husband." In Anson County, North Carolina, Mary Dunn, a serving girl, watched with fascination as a slave named Warwick used a ball of twine and a pan handle to fashion some sort of zodiac in the farmyard dirt. She whispered to a neighbor that what his magic had revealed to her was "so ugly she would not tell." The secret was not hard to guess: he came to her that night.

Placed in close proximity to slaves and themselves enjoying very little standing in the community, girls like Mary Dunn, Elizabeth Pettus, and Lydia Bright heard much about black sexual prowess, but also about their own duty never to touch the forbidden fruit. Even for these adolescents, poor as they were, there was much self-respect to lose. Yet the temptation was great to see for themselves what it was like to bed with a virile slave. No doubt there was much truth in Edward Long's comment that lower-class women in England were "remarkably fond of the blacks, for reasons too brutal to mention. . . ." Likewise, in the colonial and early Republic eras some American women of wayward disposition made no color distinctions. Needless to say, husbands of such prostitutes or "debauched" girls, as one witness called Mary Dunn, easily won divorces. If their spouses had only white bedmates, however, husbands did not automatically gain freedom.

Judging from women's responses to accusations of unnatural amalgamation, one might safely argue that they were often mentally retarded or else had a very poor self-image. An exception, however, was Betsey Mosley, mother of a black baby. In reply to her outraged husband, she said "that she had not been the first nor would she be the last guilty of such an act and that she saw no more harm in a white woman's having a black child than in a white man's having one, though the latter was more frequent." Usually the woman either felt deep remorse over her indiscretion or brazenly prostituted herself in defiance of husband and family.

One avenue of escape did exist: a claim of having been raped, a claim that Southern whites have continued to prefer to believe even into the recent past. (The Scottsboro case of 1931 and incidents arising during the same period in rural Alabama are among the more famous illustrations.) Thus Governor Hutchins Burton of North Carolina was called upon to review a Davidson County case in 1826, one in which a girl's poor-white family sought to salvage some respectability by insisting that she had been coerced by a wealthy planter's handsome slave Jim. Like Mary Dunn, Polly Lane was a serving girl—bored, lonely, overworked, and fascinated by her lover. Fantasizing about fleeing to Cherokee country in Georgia where they could escape notice, the pair stole money from Jim Palmer, the overseer. Palmer caught slave Jim, however, and threatened to have him hanged. Jim fled to the woods where Polly, whose complicity had not yet been discovered, brought him food and comfort. Weeks later another slave overheard her wailing in the woods about her upcoming pregnancy. To escape humiliation, Polly had to claim that she had been brutally assaulted that very morning. She denied pregnancy, and the jury, true to racial custom, ignored the evidence of her swollen belly. Jim was sentenced to hang. Jim's owner, however, hired a young lawyer named J. J. Daniel, who beseeched the governor to delay execution until the color of the child could be ascertained. It was a fact backed by "the highest *authority* of Medical Jurisprudence," declared Governor Burton's Raleigh medical consultants on the case, that rape victims could not become pregnant. Conception depended upon "excitation" or "enjoyment of pleasure in the venereal act." Since Polly was clearly pregnant, Jim's defense was probably true, they reasoned. The governor granted the respite, and the Davidson County community undoubtedly spent the winter wagering about the complexion of Polly Lane's forthcoming baby.

Jonathan M. Smith, a semiliterate member of the clan to which Polly Lane belonged, fumed that "trifling white people all ways" had "purtected" Jim from the punishments he deserved. In every way possible, he sought to hurry Jim to his appointment on the gallows. But to Smith's chagrin the child arrived thirty-nine days too early to conform with the date of the supposed rape, and only the most prejudiced observers in the Lane faction could deny that the child was mulatto. In this instance, the community concluded that Polly Lane was so depraved and her family's status so problematical that Jim should be granted his life. Petitions to that effect, organized by the planter elite and signed by the presiding judge, sheriff, county militia general, clerk of court, and half the jurors, provided Governor Burton with ample grounds to proclaim a reprieve, with transportation out of state. The latter was a sad necessity, since the Lane faction would not have permitted Jim to survive otherwise. To Jonathan Smith's mortification, Polly was charged with bastardy, but it is doubtful that the infant lived very long. It was so easy to allow an unwanted child to die of neglect.

Miscegenation of this kind suggested a weakness in the moral and social sense of the white female by the standards of a primitive culture. Likewise, white men who showed a disregard for consequences displayed similar problems of self-identity. A considerable number of men involved in such situations clearly exhibited signs of immaturity before their break with sexual and race conventions. Keith Thomas has discussed the similar phenomenon of seventeenth- and eighteenth-century Englishmen who had liaisons with socially inferior mates. Their motives, he says, may have had Freudian roots. Such men, as Freud interpreted them, could not direct both their sexual drive and their affections toward the same woman. Instead, they divided their women into the double image of ancient tradition—the madonna and the harlot. This dichotomy, Thomas explains in Freudian terms, arose because the philanderer feared his own feelings of jealousy of his father's role in the marriage bed. The son idolizes his mother, but finds these feelings no less overwhelming and dangerous than his attitudes toward his father. In repressing his fantasies, he splits the sexual and the affectional impulses in his relations with women. Sex becomes associated with an inferior, an expendable woman whom, outside of wedlock, he both enjoys and socially despises. But the wife whom he should love and protect, Thomas suggests, becomes a source of resentment. He blames her for his confusion and accuses her of coldness. Driven to indecision and self-hatred, the adulterous husband cannot have a complete relationship with either his mistress or his wife.

Whether the problem was psychological, cultural, or both, these factors of filial rebellion and moral dissolution played true to form in the marriage of Thomas Foster, Jr., and Susannah Carson, a young couple living in Adams County, Mississippi, in the 1820s. Foster, the son of the twentieth wealthiest planter in the richest county in late Jeffersonian America, was a representative "dissolute." His father had carved out a $100,000 estate near Natchez, and at Foster Fields, center of his many plantations, he and his wife Sarah raised a large brood of children. New to wealth and unsupported by religious faith or intellectual aspirations, Thomas Foster, Sr., thought material benefits would suffice to sustain the next generation. Son Thomas, upon his marriage, received two plantations and the requisite number of slaves. He was simply to carry on his father's career. A college education would have been superfluous, Thomas, Sr., and his wife Sarah believed.

Thomas's sixteen-year-old wife, whom his parents had selected, was the daughter of James Carson, an Irish refugee from the 1798 Rebellion, land speculator and part-time Methodist preacher. She was supposed to bring to a close the young Thomas's already worrisome profligacy. But two years of married life and the prospect of a second child led to his rebellion against domesticity and parental surveillance. The late months of pregnancy were commonly referred to as the "gander months," because during that period husbands traditionally found outlets other than their wives for their sexual interests. Thomas was no exception; like the barnyard creature, he had gone prowling. Shortly after his wife Susannah returned from her confinement at her parents' house in Natchez, bringing with her a newborn son, she discovered her spouse lying naked in a slave cabin with Susy, the couple's cook, a handsome slave who had been a gift from his father.

Faced with Susannah's tears and anger, Thomas Foster, Jr., was dutifully remorseful for a day or so. Two years of chaos, tears, and threats of blows followed. Finally Susannah went to her husband's parents to explain why she had to have a divorce. By then Susy had displaced her in the master bedroom and was wearing her mistress's bonnets. The pattern that Susannah Foster recounted in her petition for divorce scarcely deviated from the scenario that most Southern women so humiliated described in their marital histories: threats against the children's lives, verbal abuse of the wife, declared preferences for the mistress as companion and bedmate, occasional vows to reform, self-pity followed by defiance once more, increasing alcoholism, and rejection of respectable company and association with low tavern friends.

In 1826 Thomas fell ill. With thoughts of impending death on his mind, he even agreed that his father could shackle Susy and prepare to have her sold. General William Barnard, a son-in-law, assisted Thomas Foster, Sr., in arranging Susy's sale. Before the transaction was completed, however, Thomas recovered. Secretly he met Susy at the tollbridge tavern outside Natchez where he and his racetrack friends had often gathered. Crossing the ravine at the western edge of town, the pair fled to his second plantation. There they lived until, in 1830, Thomas sold Susy and other slaves to his eldest brother Levi for half their worth. Depressed and half dazed from alcohol, Thomas was convinced by Levi and another brother, James Foster, Jr., that this was the only solution to his habitual indebtedness. In the following year Thomas Foster, Jr., died, before Chancellor John A. Quitman had rendered a decision on the divorce petition Susannah Foster had initiated some four years earlier.

What happened to Susy, the rejected paramour, after her sale to Levi, then a plantation owner in Franklin, Louisiana, is not known. She had been a daughter of Abd al-Rahman Ibrahima, a "prince" in the House of Timbo (located in present-day Nigeria). Misfortunes in war had led to Ibrahima's sale to black traders, and in the 1780s Thomas Foster, Sr., then a struggling planter in Spanish Mississippi, had purchased him and appointed him his chief driver. The daughter shared her father's aristocratic bearing, and no doubt Thomas found her an exotic partner. In his old age Ibrahima wished to see his homeland once more, and Thomas, Sr., perhaps embarrassed about his son's misbehavior, at last agreed. The two old men, master and driver, had a mutual grief to bear in their final days. At least, however, Ibrahima never learned that Thomas had forsaken his daughter. New York philanthropists made possible his return to Africa; he died within sixty miles of Timbo in 1829, the same year and month that Thomas Foster, Sr., passed away. Susy's sale did not occur until the following year. The denouement would have pleased the senior Foster, who had placed such hopes upon his son's eventual repentance. It would have been another blow to Susy's father, however, a Muslim whose sense of honor and dignity far outdistanced that of his master and his master's sons.

Despite such problems as those of the Fosters, it is only fair to add that even in the rough world of the Southwest, sexual misconduct probably declined during the antebellum decades. In the wilderness regions where white women had been in short supply in earlier days, ratios of men and women started to even out. Men could find marriageable partners and resorted less to irregular arrangements. Churches and church discipline encouraged domestic honesty. Education and prosperity helped to reduce the disorders, sexual and otherwise, that accompanied depressing struggles against disaster. It would carry matters too far to call Thomas Foster, Jr., a member of an endangered species. "Black sheep" were a ubiquitous curse.

But new, rather Victorian social attitudes were reaching the gentry class and, through revivals and clapboard churches, the yeomanry as well. Nevertheless, in the persistent war between "civilization" and primal ethics the principles of honor, shame, and pride still had enormous strength. Certainly the guns that blasted the walls of Fort Sumter did not destroy the ancient code as well. Instead they expressed the determination to keep it holy.

Part Two

•

Public Ethics

6

Hospitality, Gambling, and Personal Combat

Welcoming strangers, taking risks at cards or sport, and defending personal honor were all characteristics that Southerners eagerly seized on to identify themselves. Although Southerners boasted loudly enough about these inclinations before the Civil War, afterward they became articles of sacred memory. In the 1880s, for instance, to illustrate the hospitable and gentlemanly ways of fellow Virginians in the old days, George W. Bagby, a Richmond journalist, described how "Colonel Tidewater had come half the length of the State to try a little more of Judge Piedmont's Madeira, to know what on earth induced Piedmont to influence the governor in making that appointment, and to inquire if it were possible that Piedmont intended to bring out Jimson—of all human beings—Jimson!—for Congress?" Leisure, graciousness, and quaint concerns, Bagby and others of his kind fancied, had been more or less the rule until the Civil War.

Indeed, it is not at all hard to be seduced by the image. Although some recent historians would claim that Colonel Tidewater was really Mr. Moneycrop, an avaricious profit maker rather than a gentle soul, countless diaries and letters suggest that Bagby's portrayal, despite its wistful romanticism, caught something of the ambience of Southern life. Take for instance the hunting expedition of Dr. Thomas Ravenel and T. W. Peyre, his neighbor in Pineville, South Carolina. Peyre arrived early to get a fine start, but Ravenel first had to visit a distant field for a word with a driver and overseer there. After the delay, Ravenel and company returned home so that he could change horses. This gave Ravenel the opportunity to while away another half-hour in the outhouse. The party mustered once more and headed for the woods. By the time the hunters reached the scent, the dogs, tired and thirsty, could not be roused from a convenient pool. The lunch hour approached, and all went home. On the second day, the hunt finally took place, and ended in triumph, though Peyre had had to prevent several side excursions beforehand. Peyre had enjoyed the human spectacle, Ravenel the chance to make a common business into an elaborate two-day ritual. What else was there to do in the July heat in the country anyhow, except to fashion something out of the materials at hand—the doings of wildcats, hounds, and people?

Yet behind the agreeably slow pace of Southern gentry life, the friendships joyfully affirmed by hunting, the barbecues, the wild nights at cards and drink, and even the fights, there often lay cheerless anxieties and unmanageable furies. Minor doings, pointless trips, and complaints about the "wuthless" hands merely punctuated the boredom that greeted nearly every rising sun. As Thomas Chaplin of St. Helena Island noted in his diary, "Christmas Day— DULL, DULL, DULL." In the summer, moist, unrelieved heat sank the most sanguine spirits. "Bitten by fleas, buzzed by mosquitoes, poisoned by wild flowers, tired of drinking warm water . . . and so sleepy as to be almost in a state of id[i]ocy, I 'take my pen in hand' to write you about our exciting Sunday," sighed one Virginia resident to another. Duels also served to enliven routine. "Our city," wrote a planter of Franklin, Louisiana, "is becoming as usual at this season exceedingly dull" and "our good citizens are diverting themselves in performing feats of arms, there have been four or five duels within the last week. . . ."

Gregariousness and conviviality were a way to give drama to life. No one can stand too much reality, particularly if one day is very much like yesterday and tomorrow. The comings and goings of relatives and friends, the thin excuses to go up to the courthouse, the interminable "friendly" games, and the personal contests of arms and fists attested not only to Southerners' desperate need to conquer *ennui* but also their compulsion to find social place in the midst of gatherings. That was the great charm of the South, the willingness to create good times with others, but behind that trait was fear of being left alone, bored, and depressed.

Thomas Carlyle, the reactionary Scottish-reared author whom the Southern literati so much admired, put into words a feeling that bedeviled the Southern white: "Isolation is the sum-total of wretchedness to man. To be cut off, to be left solitary: to have a world alien, not your world, all a hostile camp for you; not a home at all, of hearts and faces who are yours, whose you are! . . . To have neither superior, nor inferior, nor equal, united manlike to you. Without father, without child, without brother. Man knows no sadder destiny." Harriet Martineau, one of the most sensitive students of nineteenth-century American character, recognized the importance of honor as originating from fear of solitariness. "Where honour is to be derived from the present human opinion," rather than from loftier notions of "truth and justice," she said, "there must be fear, ever present, and perpetually exciting to or withholding from action. In such a case, as painful a bondage is incurred as in the pursuit of wealth." Especially was this so, she believed, in the South. The more "American" or Yankeefied the white Southerner was, the more he feared losses as a moneymaker. The more Southern he was, the more honor icily gripped his thoughts. The two preoccupations, to greater or lesser degree, functioned together, mocking Southern claims to leisure, individualism, and stability superior to other cultures. "Fear of imputation is here the panic, under which men relinquish their freedom of action and speech," Martineau observed.

Under these circumstances, the most pressing Southern fear was not death so much as dying alone. That was a veritable nightmare. Corydon Fuller, a Yankee itinerant in Arkansas, walked into a tavern and found a group of drinkers poking fun at an old alcoholic's dying twitches on the barroom floor. Contempt masked their own worries; laughter covered fright. Dread of aloneness helps to explain why sometimes even refined folk, as well as less educated ones, feared so much the night, graveyards, ghosts of dead kinspeople, and nameless "ha'nts," hidden emblems of one's own uncomfortable memories of wrongs and omissions. "Do you remember the conversation we had with your Aunt Wales?" asked Henry Cumming of his wife in 1825. The old lady had been startled by a "bird that flew in at the window and again out towards the Church yard." Not two weeks had passed before Aunt Wales's husband died, he reminded her. "Her unreasonable apprehensions have certainly been realized in a most remarkable manner. . . ." The bird signified, however, her forlornness, not her husband's doom. Indeed, some years later, Maria Bryan, another relative, remarked that Aunt Wales was "one of the most unhappy persons I know, lonesome & disconsolate, & [thinks?] herself forsaken by the world & her friends."

The lack of privacy, the hostility toward those who wished to be alone to read or think, the overabundance of alcohol to nurse self-pitying male egos, the scarcity of lending libraries, books, and literary societies, the low state of education, the distances between people of similar intellectual interests, the temptations of hunting, fishing, and just aimless wandering in search of company—all these characteristics of Southern social life gave special meaning to special gatherings. People came together not just to celebrate a holiday, mourn the dead, pay respect to the sick and dying, join the wedding party, go to camp meeting, muster the militia, attend the election poll, or entertain the visiting relative. They came to escape solitude as well. In an oral society, where words and gestures counted so much, the opportunity to exchange ritual words or hear them eloquently pronounced was deeply cherished. "The man who wished to lead or to teach," the late-nineteenth-century Georgia historian William Garrott Brown recalled, "must be able to speak . . . [and] charm . . . with voice and gesture." Those like William L. Yancey of Alabama earned special authority with their amazing oratorical gifts. "How such a great man mounted the rostrum, with what demeanor he endured an interruption, with what gesture he silenced a murmur,—such things were remembered and talked about when his reasoning was perhaps forgotten," Brown wrote. What mattered was the sense of community and reconfirmed loyalties that such occasions aroused.

Three kinds of events in which the personal strategy of the principals gave meaning to life and strength to reputation seemed particularly suited to the Southern ethos. The first was the host-guest relation, a frequent transaction despite (or else because of) the great distances separating one farmhouse or plantation from another. The second was strictly a male encounter (with clergymen uninvited): gambling and horse racing (with women present in the more sophisticated settings). The third was supposedly a rather private affair, the duel. But here no less than in the barroom brawl or fistfight, the whole male community was involved. Each ritual encounter in this sequence was more antagonistic than the previous one, but all three helped Southerners determine community standing and reaffirm their membership in the immediate circle to which they belonged. In all of them honor and pursuit of place muted the threat of being alone and provided the chance to enjoy power in fellowship.

The first of these strategies has been the least well understood. Scholars have treated hospitality largely in terms of the Southern economy: was there much or little conspicuous consumption? Undoubtedly the purchase of grand estates, exquisite furnishings, coaches, and thoroughbreds was confined to a much smaller proportion of the planter class than legend and popular tour excursions today might suggest. The building of Melrose, Gunston Hall, and similar lordly sites served to substantiate the claims of their planter-owners to rule. Some Marxist historians like Eugene Genovese and Raimondo Luraghi have emphasized that obvious function, and they have taken to celebrating the "prebourgeois" spending habits of the slaveholding elite. Others have blamed Southern backwardness partly on such misuse of capital. Gaudy display, they reason, solidified planter control over awestruck yeomen, but drained off funds that might have been spent to improve general economic conditions. But it is really doubtful that fancy improvidences really had an adverse effect upon the Southern economy as a whole. More serious inhibiting factors were ubiquitous habits of familial defensiveness and whites' suspicion of collective and governmental enterprises. The slave system certainly encouraged white labor inefficiency, for reasons too well explained elsewhere to need amplification here. These were more important causes of economic backwardness than the occasional appearance of a columned palace in the wilderness. Besides, the Old South's exhibitions of enormous household wealth could have been easily matched by the homes of Boston merchants and Philadelphia bankers, individuals seldom accused of frivolous investment. In any case, as Jane Pease wisely says, "it would be hazardous," at this point of historical study, "to rest any significant part of an argument about Southern failure to develop economically on assumptions about the impact of Southern planters' consumption patterns." The argument is a dead end.

To understand the social meaning of hospitality—the relationship of an individual and family to outsiders on home turf—it must be treated in its constituent parts. The individuals involved, the circumstances of the moment, the relative standing of host and guest made all the difference. It should be no surprise that outward appearance, ascriptive signals, and prior relationships gave context and meaning to the encounter between host and guest.

First and foremost, hospitality in its broadest definition was family-centered. The planter of means was obliged to share good fortune with less well-fixed kinfolk or be severely criticized for Yankeefied tightfistedness. When no other agency existed to care for the weak, the family was the first and often sole resort. Northerners likewise felt obliged to extend the helping hand, and did so with no less and no more willingness than Southerners. However, there was, one may speculate, a sense of deeper obligation in the South, if only because the slaveholding states were slow to find public means to house the dependent and indigent—asylums, hospitals, poorhouses, or rooming houses. Moreover, it was much more dignified for a widowed distant cousin, like Edmund Ruffin's relative Mrs. Lorraine, to accept an invitation for a visit that lasted over a year than to request a handout. One never knew when misfortune might descend. Helping kinsfolk was both more personal and more consoling than other means.

Yet even within the family circle, hospitality was often exploited by one or the other party as a means of exercising personal power. Although keeping a fine house or throwing barbecues for the neighbors did have many social purposes in a community, in some instances the prime reason for lavishness of expenditure was strictly familial. J. Motte Alston, for instance, recalled that his wealthy grandfather, nicknamed "King William," used sumptuous dinners to keep his Charleston family under surveillance. Every Saturday night the table was set with the best china, silver, and linens. All sons and daughters, their spouses and children had to attend. "Only a valid excuse was received for not so doing." Guests, too, could make use of the seeming friendliness of the custom. "Grandmother" James of Livingston, Alabama, had lent a cousin a thousand dollars, which he postponed repaying. She packed her trunk and arrived by coach for an unannounced visit. After the typical effusions of welcome, she stated her business and her intention to stay indefinitely until the bill was met. An order on the planter's Mobile factor was in her hands the next morning, and "the old lady returned home in great good humor."

The dependency of relatives upon the good will, good humor, and generosity of those better off was a mortification only exceeded by being thrust onto the public charge. We have already seen the contempt in which traditional societies held individuals who lost the ability to manage for themselves or never had it in the first place, particularly orphans, spinsters, and poor widows. No writer has caught the desperation and pathos of such circumstances better than Tennessee Williams, whose plays, especially *The Glass Menagerie, A Streetcar Named Desire,* and *The Eccentricities of a Nightingale,* explore the theme of unavoidable dependency in once proud families. In *The Glass Menagerie* Amanda Wingfield, an East Tennessean and former Mississippi "belle," dreams of entertaining a "gentleman caller" for her daughter Laura, who is crippled both physically and emotionally, as if the chance to do domestic honors for a marriageable man would itself transform their sad existence. Laura's ineffectuality and passive refusal to imitate her mother's coquetry of earlier days drives Amanda to say, "What is there left but dependency all our lives?" She had seen the fate of women unfit "to occupy a position." They were "barely tolerated spinsters living upon the grudging patronage of sister's husband or brother's wife!—stuck away in some little mousetrap of a room— encouraged by one in-law to visit another—little birdlike women without any nest—eating the crust of humility all their life!" To be sure, some families surmounted the strains, making dependents feel needed and loved. But the role of kinfolk host, though it offered the chance to give succor disguised as hospitality, was scarcely any more enviable than that of recipient. Both parties to the transaction felt coerced by custom and duty, and at the least the danger of mis-apprehension and resentment was ever-present. More fundamentally, permanent dependency contradicted tacit expectations that help in time of family need would later be returned under similar exigency.

With strangers, however, the rules of hospitality were consider-ably more discretionary than with relatives, who could not be cast aside without loss of family repute and guilt-laden recriminations. Not many planters lived grandly enough to live up to the regional self-acclaim about lavish entertainment. First of all, the living quar-ters were often exceedingly uncomfortable for permanent residents, let alone for visitors. Heat, dust, and ever-worrisome insects some-times undermined household resolve to make even spacious dwell-ings presentable. Neither slave nor mistress took pride in keeping good order. Cultural ideals that stressed male good times over do-mesticity, special occasion over routine habit made for a haphazard struggle against dirt and disrepair. An anonymous Virginia diarist reported that at one small farmer's house in Louisiana, he and his companions literally had to strip off their clothes, but still found themselves "a la cooty," so full of fleas was the house. Mrs. Sarah Hicks Williams, a Northern woman, blamed the disorder of her North Carolina neighbors' houses upon "the want of system." The cause, however, lay more in the depression of will that semitropical climate and unspecialized work habits engendered. Not willful laziness, as outsiders imagined, but a sense of paralysis gripped even the well-bred planter's matron. There was too much to do and little to show for the effort once things were done. Instead it was easier to immunize oneself with the distractions of talk and drink for the men, seeing friends for the women. Cornelia Spencer, from the long-settled town of Chapel Hill, North Carolina, where order was a source of community pride, found conditions all but intolerable among kinsfolk in frontier Alabama. They had "solid silver castors" and delicate china, but had not bothered to plaster the walls. As a result of inattention, there were "holes in the walls—holes under the doors[,] holes in the windows—." The cousins nervously fretted about her obvious discomfort, but she did nothing to relieve their embarrassment. If, at times, inquisitive strangers were greeted with less cordiality than they anticipated, the reasons should not be hard to imagine.

As far as one can tell, the wayfarer who stopped for the night was treated with considerable suspicion, particularly if the request for lodgings came unexpectedly, without the accompaniment of a special claim to hospitality—a letter of introduction, or a blood rela-tionship quickly ascertained between the visitor and host. If such conditions were met, the visit could become a celebration, a wel-coming into the family circle. If the newcomer could produce proper introductions, he or she was ordinarily recognized. When John Bernard, Harriet Martineau, Frederika Bremer, John F. D. Smyth, James K. Paulding, and many other writers of travel accounts ap-peared on the doorstep, their presence could be a great source of gratification, about which the host could brag for months thereafter. A Mrs. Matilda Houston rhapsodized that through Virginia and the Carolinas, she and her party spent not a "sixpence," so welcome was her presence, at least so she claimed. Others who bitterly com-plained that Southern hospitality was more legend than reality often reflected the indifference that their standing elicited. "Of such hospitality the traveller will find nothing," declared Francis Hall, "except indeed, his rank or character would be such, as to give eclat to his entertainers." Charles Latrobe said that the guest who came unrecommended was made to feel himself "the party obliged, and that obligation could never be repaid." A poor appearance certainly was construed as beggary, a powerlessness and dependence that incited contempt, not sympathy. Elkanah Watson, for instance, discovered that he could not obtain lodgings at the same isolated North Carolina household where some years earlier he had been handsomely treated. The sole difference was the state of his clothing after a harrowing ride through dust and storm. John Cornish, a young Northern clergyman in low-country South Carolina, feasted royally one evening at Squire Wistal's plantation, where his letters of introduction commanded the host's respect. The next night, however, a less well-to-do planter turned him away on a stormy December night because he was without horse, money, and decent, dry attire. A slave put him up in the master's corn crib in exchange for half a "segar." Even if he was admitted to the inner premises and greeted warmly, the weary traveler was more than likely to sleep "in a room with others, in a bed which stank, supplied with but one sheet, if with any," Frederick Olmsted reported, and offered no "fruit, no tea, no cream, no sugar, no bread" (except corn pone), because these and most other amenities were not to be had. Yet by local standards these houses and their residents were supposed to be above the ordinary level of hospitality and refinement.

Strangers to the South were often surprised to discover that money was at times accepted, to defray the costs of the host and even to make him a profit. Such travelers' anticipations of largess led to immediate disenchantment. Yet their hosts did not thereby violate the concept of hospitality, at least not in every instance. The charges were a means to make a distinction between family-centered obligation and the treatment of an alien. The cash transaction signified the termination of obligation, and was sometimes even used when fellow Southerners arrived on the scene without invitation. For instance, Mrs. Elizabeth McCall Perry found herself and her party far from their destination, Laurens, South Carolina, as a heavy storm and sundown were approaching. They took shelter at the home of a Mr. Barksdale, brother, it turned out, of her husband's chief antagonist in an upcoming law dispute and election.

Aware of the delicacy of the situation, Barksdale was welcoming but formal. Only at loss of his own reputation could he have refused her altogether. Sensitive to his feelings, Mrs. Perry volunteered to pay for the horse feed, meals, and inconvenience. With perfect understanding, he suggested she pay $2.00. The sum was far less than a hotel would have charged, but if he had graciously refused any payment he would have put the Perrys under an obligation inappropriate to the circumstances. Two dollars was exactly the right sum to charge.

As this example reflects, hospitality could not be divorced from honor, nor honor separated from the coercions of public opinion. To refuse an offer of magnanimity—even if only a drink in a grog shop—was to insult the donor, by throwing doubt on his claim to worthiness as a companion. At all levels of society, even the lowest, hospitality could often signify a test of status, a means of discovering who a stranger thought himself to be and what he thought of those urging him to join their pleasures. Corydon Fuller, who had observed the dying drunkard in Arkansas, might have been intimidated to accept a glass from the merrymakers dancing about the corpse. But just as guests had to meet the situation demanded by their entertainers, so too was the host under firm obligation. Drink-treating at election times, for instance, was by no means simple bribery but rather the demand of male constitutents that the office-seeker thereby prove his manhood, indifference to heavy financial loss, and claim to the respect of those accepting his bounty. The title of office for the one, the grog for the others seemed a fair exchange. On a somewhat grander plane, Thomas Jefferson "felt bound in honor" to entertain any and all worthies who passed Monticello during and after his presidency. Wellborn folk swarmed there in the summer months on their way to spas, and each gentleman was certain that his support of president and party entitled him to the personal gratitude of the host. Meeting that expectation was a major factor in Jefferson's financial troubles in his declining years.

In all the coercions and obligations that surrounded the custom of hospitality there ran an undercurrent of deep mistrust, anxiety, and personal competition. Thus, for instance, James Hammond gloomed that his career had been destroyed by the jealousy of rivals: "Manning could not conceal it. He built his fine home in Clarendon to beat me"; nevertheless, "I beat them in their own line—furniture, balls, & dinner parties." When men gathered at each other's houses, the appointments were as much on display for their benefit as for the comfort of the inhabitants. Although the dwelling might impress the yeomanry, it mattered much more if the house and furnishings awed the neighboring planters. The necessity of pleasing equals aroused some grumbling: it was expensive and often unappreciated. Thomas Chaplin "found dinner" for his fellow huntsmen on the Sea Islands, providing "five times as much as the men could eat" because the example of others had made him "afraid there would not be enough." Apparently Chaplin's associates thought that the competition had grown too keen and that everyone was spending too much. Therefore they voted to fine those offering more than "six dishes of meat for dinner" in order "to prevent competition." The fifty-cent penalty, however, was not likely to have the sobering effect Chaplin anticipated. Edmund Ruffin objected less to the competitive aspects than to the wastefulness of encouraging "loungers and spongers" in the name of " 'the hospitality of old Virginia.' " Ironically, he hoped that Yankee ways of thrift would find a Southern home the better to whip the North in the struggle for sectional preeminence. But for better or worse, hospitality, like slavery, was an intrinsic part of the antebellum scheme of things.

The strain of hostility that these illustrations evince, if seen in the context of the Revolutionary and post-Revolutionary eras, might appear to be the result of the infant country's political uncertainties about democracy, slavery, and republicanism, the dislocating effects of economic and territorial expansion, and the growth of centralized institutions and industries. These abrupt transformations, early republican historians are accustomed to say, invoked deep-seated frustrations, worries about present and future, and nostalgia for a simpler past. No doubt the equivocal response to a stranger at the gate was in part a function of these anxieties, particularly as the Civil War approached and Northern and foreign strangers came under general suspicion. Nevertheless, host-guest antagonisms long preceded the era of dynamic growth and continued long afterward, when the South, sunk in defeat and poverty, experienced too little change, unless for the worse.

Ambivalence had in fact always been the underlying factor in traditional hospitality. Guest and host were supposed to show respect for each other, and failure to do so sundered the transaction of honor in which they were engaged. For the moment they were to set aside their struggles for supremacy, but the reciprocity could not obscure the distinction between the roles. The stranger in a tavern, for instance, was invited to be the first to drink or at least be the first to receive the gift of a glass from the rest. But he was under obligation to play host to the next round—thereby making equal all parties present, each in turn serving as guest and host. The coercion implicit in that situation should be evident, but so should the brittleness of the feelings under the restraint of the hospitable code. As the tongues grew looser, the jokes broader, the sly remarks more cutting, the same conventions that compelled outward friendliness then turned to anger, and the fists and oaths flew thick. Hospitality was meant to be a ritualized truce in the rivalries of men, but instead it was sometimes prelude to violence, particularly among the less gentle planters and the yeomanry. Certainly the top echelons of society seldom indulged themselves in this fashion, but as Dickson Bruce points out, violent behavior was part of the general culture of the region. Whether men competed gracefully under the formal rules of hospitality or furiously in the violence that sometimes resulted, the drama of these strategies was their appeal, and status their prize.

Gaming, the second kind of ritual occasion for the muting of rivalries, was related to hospitality and often appeared, along with alcohol, in male society. Southerners, like their Scots-Irish and English forebears, loved sports, hunting, games of chance and skill—in fact, any event that promised the excitement of deciding the inequalities of prowess among men, or among men and beasts. Whatever the uncertainties and daily risks of life might be, for a moment or two at least, games dramatized vicarious triumph and misfortune within a structure of set rules. As in the case of hospitality, money could and did change hands. But unlike its role in the host-guest relation, money in the context of the game or sport served as a means to ratify obligation and deference, not to terminate them, no matter how cheerily the winnings jangled in the pockets of the bettor. The point of play was the distribution of honor and status. Although men invariably expressed an indifference to the outcome, the depth of their involvement belied the outward show. Once the play was joined, it engaged all participants in a special, enclosed world. All-night sessions over cards were a proverbial custom early and late in Southern history. John B. Nevitt, a Natchez planter, reported in his diary in 1828 that he entertained forty guests and "sat up all night" over "brag." In 1765 a visiting Frenchman recounted that there was not a "publick house" without "tables all baterd [*sic*] with the [faro] boxes." Gaming had universal appeal throughout the slave region and among all social ranks almost from the start of settlement in the seventeenth century. Although Mississippi, Louisiana, and Texas were best known for the habit, residents of the Carolinas, Georgia, Tennessee, Kentucky, and Arkansas were also devoted to cards, dice, horse racing, and cockfights. Such diversions had to involve more than simply a chance to turn a profit. The practice had to have social meaning for those participating.

Three aspects of gaming in the South were especially significant in terms of social structure and ethics: its coercive and consensual pervasiveness, its distinctions between the "sporting gentleman" and the professional, and finally its pathological aspects in a patriarchal society. The first feature should be no surprise in light of other factors in the all-male world of planter and yeoman life. Partially at least, the rationale for gambling was the camaraderie it afforded, especially since other forms of entertainment or civic enterprise aroused little interest. One Mississippian summed up his idea of a grand time: "Last Sunday we took 42 people aboard, one sheep and one shoat, two cases of whiskey, hung up two lanterns on cypress snags . . . and had a barbecue. Good fun, poker and crap game, one fight." What more could any man ask of such an outing? he implied.

T. H. Breen, historian of the colonial South, has persuasively argued that betting sports had the function of reducing other kinds of "dangerous, but often inevitable social tensions." Aware of the swift rise and fall of fortunes, the ubiquity of sudden death, the dangers of slave unrest, early colonial Virginia planters solidified their loyalty to each other with cards and quarterhorse racing. So serious was the business that "race covenants" were drawn up ahead of an important event, so that if the outcome was questionable, the injured party had a legal right to sue. "By wagering on cards and horses," Breen says, planters "openly expressed their extreme competitiveness, winning temporary emblematic victories over their rivals without thereby threatening the social tranquility of Virginia."

Certainly the same benefits were enjoyed by the antebellum gaming set, although by then some changes had developed. Love of sport had not declined but instead had become open to more individuals. Men of the same social rank continued to play chiefly among themselves, but there were no longer laws prohibiting lesser folk from betting at public tracks. The larger population of Jacksonian times supported commercial gaming operations of considerable size, whereas before they had been confined to major centers like Richmond or limited to a tavern billiard table. Moreover, cockfighting had become increasingly popular, especially after the new republic began. In 1797, for instance, twenty-one cocks were pitted at Halifax, North Carolina. In fact, state rivalries encouraged large meets. In 1806 gentlemen of several counties of Virginia and North Carolina proposed to organize a cockfight with Maryland planters, meeting at Norfolk, with a $10,000 "main" and fifty cockers participating. Laws had always existed to prevent Sunday sport and even weekday gambling, but they were seldom enforced. It would be difficult to guess the number of gamblers and horse race and cockfight watchers, but one may be sure that they vastly outnumbered male churchgoers. Yet Southern scholars have devoted considerably less interpretive effort to this body of ritualists than to the more easily studied churchmen of the South.

The excitement of the game or race, the crowds that special

events could draw, the absence of other forms of amusement, the ineffectuality of the clergy in suppressing such activities, and the determination of fathers that sons should know manly arts of all kinds—these elements all conspired to make gaming an accepted diversion. Not to play implied cowardice, differentness, unwholesome and even antisocial behavior. To be sure, some men, such as Landon Carter of Sabine Hall, despised the gaming set, never indulged, and sought to immunize the young against the preoccupation. Complaining that his grandson had gone off for a race on one of his fastest horses, Carter ranted that his neighbors, fearful that other planters' sons would get ahead too fast, lured them away "from Duty."

As the Northern middle classes turned against such excitements, pious Southerners also began to lodge complaints and even make serious conversions in the gaming ranks. Samuel Townes of Abbeville, South Carolina, for instance, reported in 1831 that revival enthusiasm at the Mt. Moriah Church just about equaled the jubilance at a racetrack. In fact, since the church was nearby, "every racer, groom and steward, has been converted or seriously impressed." Sadly, "Col. G——" was so overwhelmed with religious zeal that he had sold his training horses "and let out his face as long as a yard-stick." It is hardly a wonder that revivals were popular in the South, more so than religious formalism, since revivals offered the converted something of what they were leaving behind. Even though many in the respectable portion of the population frowned upon gaming functions, the old ways died hard.

Antigambling polemics aroused the sportsmen to defend their practices. In 1862, for instance, "Erskine" replied to "Botetourt," a religious planter, in a Richmond pamphlet. At its worst, he said, gaming was only a small vice, "and all vices are small when the culprit is socially popular and intellectually great." After all, he argued, Southerners were not much inclined to study "Raphael's cartoons" or "Cicero's orations," and gaming provided mental fare in place of such contemplations. Besides, the great men of past and present ages had sometimes been devout gamblers: Charles James Fox; Horace Walpole; Seargent S. Prentiss, the Mississippi Whig;

Henry Clay; and Andrew Jackson, owner of both cockers and race-horses. In addition, gamblers had their place in the political order, and formed an interest group that few presidents had been willing to alienate. Jackson had freed a notorious professional from a Washington jail, disputing that the antigambling law under which he had been tried was in the community's best interest. (James Madison had released Robert Bailey, a faro-box keeper, from the District's prison on similar grounds.) Clergymen "might rant and rave," claimed "Erskine," but men would continue to do as they pleased. Echoing these sentiments from the vantage point of the 1880s, W. H. Sparks, a Georgia memorialist, asked rhetorically if such "rude sports" as quarter race, cockfight, and gander pull had not been "more innocent outlets to the excessive energies of a mercurial and fun-loving people than the . . . shooting-gallery of to-day?"

The very fact that betting was almost a social obligation when men gathered at barbecues, taverns, musters, supper and jockey clubs, racetracks, and on steamboats suggests that Breen's thesis has validity beyond the colonial period about which he wrote. Community loyalties have always found vivid expression in cheering on sportsmen and bettors. There was always a huge turnout in any neighborhood when such occasions arose, crowds that included men and sometimes women of all ranks and conditions. Even slaves could join in the public exhibitions. "Doing-together precipitates a sense of interdependence which is manifest in the ramifying exchanges of services," says Fred W. Voget in regard to such activities. Exchanging money as bets was such a service, with the money almost considered identical with the personalities of winner and loser. As Rhys Isaac, a colonial historian, has perceptively observed, "an intensely shared interest" in a gaming and sporting event, "crossing but not leveling social distinctions, has powerful effects in transmitting style and reinforcing the leadership of the elite that controls the proceedings and excels in the display." In this case, the planters were the priests of the occasion, as it were, and the affair enlisted all the fervor of a religious exercise. In Charleston's race week, for instance, courts, schools, and shops all closed, as if the Sabbath had been extended for seven days. Litanies of oaths, prayers, and other demands for divine or profane intercession were part of the rites of the games. The Southerner was well known for the eloquence of his swearing, and a gaming event provided the opportunity to demonstrate. But most of all, the union of the individual with the instrument of his prowess—the horse, cocker, cards, marksman's gun, or dice—took on a sacred character. That oneness seemed magical, and gave the participant and his supporters the feeling of potential omnipotence in striving for the prize.

Under such circumstances, as Johann Huizinga has observed, games of chance were no less efficacious than ones of skill. By either method, whether by personal ability or sheer luck, "the good powers" triumphed "over the bad." In fact, luck had "a sacred significance; the fall of the dice may signify and determine divine workings; by it we may move the gods as efficiently as by any other form of contest." The emblem of victory—the money won, in most cases—conferred status. It *was* the status, palpable, real, yet supernatural, in the sense that the profane and sacred were joined together. The same exaltation was true for the cockfighter and horseman. The Marquis de Chastellux was struck by the nearly trancelike state of a young man at a cockfight in Virginia who kept repeating, as if in incantation, "Oh, it's a charming diversion!" Others, too, observed the ecstasy that games seemed to arouse. On a tour of South Carolina, Josiah Quincy remarked, "He who won the last match, the last main, or last horse-race assumed the airs of a hero or German potentate. The ingenuity of a Locke or the discoveries of a Newton were considered as infinitely inferior to the accomplishments of him who knew when to shoulder a blind cock or start a fleet horse." The sense of power, heightened by the chance for public admiration, was the appeal of gaming: the congruence of belief and action, symbol and reality, group and individual, outward appearance of moral efficacy and its inner feeling. All these factors inspired allegiance to male ideals of friendly rivalry and good fellowship.

Gambling, no less than hospitality, brought the code of honor into very serious play because of its intimate connection with both personal and group status, which depended so largely upon public perceptions. To abuse the trust of others by cheating was the height of disgrace. For instance, Robert Potter, a state legislator in North Carolina, having lost all his money in a card game, had pulled a gun, seized the winnings, and fled. Indignantly, his fellow politicians waited not a moment to expel him from the state assembly. The investment of honor in games of chance and skill was related to the ephemerality of the glory attached to winning. To delay payment robbed the winner of the immediate gratification of his trophy, the emblematic value of which lasted only as long as public memory of the occasion. As William J. Grayson of South Carolina remarked, echoing traditional English sentiment, "A gambling debt is a debt of honour, but a debt due a tradesman is not."

The distinction deserves some scrutiny. In a cash- and credit-poor economy, ordinary indebtedness was not only unavoidable; it was a means to cement long-standing social connections. In fact, it could be said that the gentry ranks, even more than the yeomanry, were meshed together through intertwined promissory notes, indentures, and other forms of financial entanglements, all duly recorded at the county clerk's office. It would not do to turn down a friend's request for a loan or a signature to stand liable for someone else, a favored kinsman or boon companion. Repayments were, of course, expected, but sometimes, as court records attest, notes were carried for months, even years beyond the date due. A man of wealth gained authority as well as accrued interest by allowing the number of those owing him to increase. Not paying tradesmen and others of lesser social standing was no violation of the code, because honor was very much tied to hierarchy; to manipulate the weak (within some bounds) was no detraction from a man's reputation, and in fact it made the lowly creditor obliged to the nonpaying client in hopes of eventual satisfaction of the debt. In a sense, it was antisocial neither to borrow nor lend. The whole economic and social structure was thus a source of security, of mingled fealties and deferences as well as of anxiety and possible disruption. Of course, not all Southern communities were quite so primitive about finance as this interpretation suggests. Nevertheless, the tendency was to look upon debt as a permanent condition of life and therefore something that should be made to serve other ends than just financial transaction. No doubt a reason for the hostility toward banks in the Jeffersonian and Jacksonian South was the fear that these quasi-political obligations that complemented the economic ones would give way to more impersonal, distant, and invulnerable ways of conducting business. The gaming debt, however, was ordinarily one that could not draw upon these social ties of deference and condescension or sheer friendship; rather it was an arrangement between equals, with triumph and defeat at wager the sole bond. The obligation had to be paid so that the relationship between the players could be terminated.

The place of the professional gambler in relation to the issue of honor and obligation was somewhat problematical and much more complicated than riverboat and frontier historians of an earlier generation once assumed. On the one hand, as legend has long insisted, the professional belonged to the lower orders, outside the social pale. Such clever operators as Jonathan Green, John Morris, George DeVol, and others who plied the Mississippi could scarcely lay claim to high rank. As a Southerner told Harriet Martineau, a man "may game, but not keep a gaming house," just as he might be shabby in money deals "but may not steal." A distinction was drawn between the "high minded liberal gentleman, attached to amusements regardless of loss or gain," as a Virginia gambler explained, and a socially despised "cheating gamester." As a result, laws piled up in the statute books of every state setting high penalties for professional gambling. South Carolina, for instance, banished gamesters, after penalizing them with heavy fines. The punishments had little more than a temporary effect. The tribe was needed to gratify the pleasures of those who did belong to the gentry ranks, sometimes including the legislators themselves. Professionals often arranged the races and matches, set the odds, bought and sold the cocks and horses, furnished the billiard tables, organized the pools, and played with those who would otherwise lack partners.

These sometimes profitable services to the gentry offered a means for ill-educated but shrewd young men to advance in livelihood, if not altogether in respectability. An example was Robert Bailey of the Shenandoah Valley. He came from poor half-Irish folk and never properly learned to read or write. Yet he sent one son to college and law school and a daughter married into the gentry set of Botetourt County, where Bailey's winnings had furnished him with a fine plantation. Nevertheless, his career illustrated the social chasm that sometimes opened up to swallow those who serviced the needs of sporting gentlemen, men "whose motto," Bailey declared, "is honour." On one crucial occasion at the turn of the century, Bailey arrogantly refused some women the use of a hall for a dance at Sweet Springs, near Staunton, Virginia; he had made arrangements for an all-night gaming session there that evening. The next night, at the rescheduled ball, the ladies refused him even a cool greeting, but whispered that he was a "gamester."

Prior to the incident his profession had scarcely been hidden from public view. Bailey held membership in the local Masonic lodge, he had nearly won a congressional seat not long before, and he had just been promoted to captain in the Virginia "Light Blues." These attainments, as well as his efficiency as a gaming impresario, had earned him what might be called a brevet rank of gentleman.

But the incident at Sweet Springs was his undoing, at least temporarily. Once the label of "gamester" was affixed the sporting gentry shunned him; then the authorities felt bold enough to have him arrested for faro dealing. Judge St. George Tucker, then a candidate for a seat on a higher court, sentenced Bailey to three months' labor, the wages to be given to the poor. Mortified, Bailey fled the county, sure that public prejudices, as he later said, "emanated from the name" of "gamester" more than from any of his alleged misdeeds, so long tolerated before the Sweet Springs confrontation. Lamely he tried to ruin Tucker's election plans by charging Tucker with attempted bribery, an accusation so clumsy that even state legislators who had been accustomed to gambling with him refused to investigate. The gamester was forced to move on to Washington. (There his ups and downs—levees at the White House one day and jail the next—continued.)

The labeling process was essential to Bailey's downfall: it clarified at once how the public was to view the fallen gamester, and it was significant that it was women, not men, who exposed him to public contempt. When sufficiently aroused, women could exercise considerable power in determining who belonged in polite company, who was unacceptable, and their husbands had to go along.

Two forces operated on the professional gamester at once. The first was Christian opinion, a growing force throughout the era, especially in the late antebellum years. The Southern clergy, even as early as the 1770s, had begun to speak out forcefully against the whole cluster of male indulgences, although they met with opposition, particularly in the earlier years and always in the newly settled areas of the west. "Fighting parsons," as they were called, proved their manliness by battling sin and sinners. Peter Cartwright of Kentucky was a famous example of the type. No less important, however, was the secular authority of the gentry sportsmen and men of social refinement, not necessarily connected with pious interests. A new sense of gentility was speedily arising.

Even as early as the mid-eighteenth century, those concerned with the orderliness of Southern life recognized that traditional male habits, especially in their own ranks, set a bad example for the rest of society. Aside from admonitions such as Landon Carter's to his grandson and John Randolph's to his nephew, the gentry luminaries had little to offer as social remedy for the violence and corruption that accompanied gaming and other pleasures. Laws were passed. Even in the boisterous river port of Natchez arrests mounted. Out of 249 criminal arraignments between 1829 and 1841, 76, or 30 percent, were for gambling offenses. Yet proportional to the problem the number was very small, Natchez being the headquarters for gamesters, especially after the Vicksburg riots drove the tribe to other locations in 1835. The use of law, however, ill suited gentry notions of how men should be coerced into meeting obligations. Besides, the purpose was not to banish sin entirely but to keep it within proper bounds. As a result, reformation of manners was scarcely an entire success.

Fines, short sentences, social stigmatizing—the penalties Bailey had received—were usually thought sufficient to limit gambling without making such diversions inconvenient by enforced legal prohibition. But when gamblers grew "obnoxious" sterner measures were needed, and the gentry was well prepared to oblige. The most celebrated example, the outbreak of warfare between militiamen and Vicksburg gamblers in 1835, need not be recounted here. Suffice it to say that a military banquet ended up in a general riot in which five gamblers were whipped and hanged, with a wheel of fortune pinned to one of the dangling corpses. Such events were linked in the public mind with rumors of a black insurrection, still more frightening. But these grim events, more complicated than historical studies have so far shown, did finally run their course. Restoration of public morals included the revival of regular gamesmanship, not its expulsion from decent society, the forming of an Anti-Gambling Society in Vicksburg notwithstanding.

Finally, there was the social attitude toward the fallen amateur, the man of substance who despoiled his inheritance in gaming, whether his property was large or small. In the militia set and among those who considered gaming a manly and generous vice, not to play was, like the refusal to share drink-treating, an insult, a denial of equality of standing. Attending a large party of gaming gentlemen, Philip Fithian, the Yankee tutor in Virginia, wrote in his diary, "In my room by half after twelve, & exceeding happy that I could break away with Reputation." Before retiring to bed, a French visitor to early republican Virginia felt likewise under obligation to play a few hands with the insatiable gambler William Byrd III and his company.

Ironically, though, the compulsion to gamble was thought just as unmanly as failure to play. Among modern psychologists, controversies rage about the nature of the gaming obsession, but most agree that the modern victim of this serious addiction is ordinarily someone with feelings of dependence upon the good favor of a father, living or dead, whom he believes deprived him of affection or assistance. The narcissism involved in gambling and the frequently related sexual problems and inability to establish mature relationships all seem part of the magical thinking in which the gambler is engaged, especially when caught up in the passion of play. For some, the greater the loss, the greater the thrill of playing becomes. The punishment of losing provides an autoerotic satisfaction along with the pain and anger of defeat. As in cases of flaunted miscegenation and alcoholism, the antebellum compulsions of the gaming table perhaps had their sources in the rivalries and recriminations between fathers and sons. According to psychoanalytic specialists, the self-destruction involved in compulsive gambling punishes the rebel as well as the parent, though the prodigals seldom recognize that hidden agenda in a conscious way. Richard Minster, a seventeenth-century aristocrat, was among the few to reveal his own anguished delight in self-inflicted shame and humiliation. He declared that when he was winning, "in my recollections there lurked the feeling of a beast, a fornicator suffering a virgin to take his whim," a sense of guilt that mounted with each successful hand. But at last he lost, and a "feeling of relief" overcame him: "It was like a solvent to the harsh world to which I must now return." No doubt pathological gambling was a deviancy to which only a few Southerners were subject. But as with drinking, the occasions for indulgence were everywhere condoned, except among the very pious, very upright male minority. For the individual at war with himself and, most likely, with his family, the addictive world of gambling, in which time, ordinary work, and expectations were all suspended, was both a refuge from reality and a means of acting out resentments. This turmoil and psychic frustration were things that neither the gambler nor Southern society fully understood.

The duel, no less than hospitality and gaming, was inseparable from community evaluation of the individual, although dueling, the most antagonistic of the three strategies for self-enhancement, was alleged to be a defense of personal honor. Actually, that honor was little more than the reflection of what the community judged a man to be. Three ironies emerged from the dueling custom. First, though confined to a segment of the upper classes, dueling served essentially the same purpose as the lowliest eye-gouging battle among Tennessee hog-drivers. Second, because of this congruence between upper- and lower-class concepts of honor, dueling was not at all undemocratic. It enabled lesser men to enter, however imperfectly, the ranks of leaders, and allowed followers to manipulate leaders to their taste. Third, the promise of esteem and status that beckoned men to the field of honor did not always match the expectation, but often enough dueling served as a form of scapegoating for unresolved personal problems.

Southerners themselves recognized that dueling too much resembled the ways of a boisterous, ill-educated society. Not surprisingly, the greatest internal opposition to the practice came from the ranks of the gentry itself. "It is the product of a barbarous age and flourishes in proportion as the manners of the people are coarse and brutal," admonished William J. Grayson of South Carolina. At an 1844 meeting of the Anti-Dueling Society of Mississippi, Judge John F. Bodley disapproved "the anti-moral, anti-legal and anti-ecclesiastical custom," a sentiment which Jefferson Davis and other state dignitaries applauded. Of all the customs of the Old South, dueling was the most vulnerable to the onslaughts of secular and religious nineteenth-century reforms. Yet the proliferation of societies to prevent the tradition had no more impact than the numerous laws that state legislators—duelists included—passed to prohibit the practice.

A recent historian of the *code duello,* Dickson Bruce, follows the earlier lead of Daniel Boorstin in observing that it differed markedly from the combative style of the lower orders. According to Bruce's analysis the duel, institutionalized with "boards" and "courts of honor," carefully orchestrated events prior to the climax. Rules governing the classical fight served to check passion and transform it under the rubric of honor. The crossroads melee, on the other hand, represented a surrender to the passions "which in general Southerners deprecated."

The distinction provides some useful insights. For one thing, there is the relationship between duels and feuds. Bloodthirsty, lengthy feuds—revenge fights among families that were so prevalent in early Celtic and Germanic tribes—were also likely consequences of brawls and killings among American hill-country yeomen in the South. Even among upcoming slaveholders they were not unknown on the frontier. William Faulkner's great-grandfather, Colonel William C. Falkner, for instance, was involved in a family feud that resulted in the killing of two men. The trouble arose over the blackballing of Robert Hindman, applicant for admission to a Tippah

County temperance society. Hindman blamed Falkner, although the young Mississippi attorney claimed to have been Hindman's sponsor. The fight started when Hindman called Falkner "a damned liar" and ended when Falkner drove a knife into his armed opponent. A year later, in 1850, Falkner shot to death Erasmus W. Morris, a Hindman partisan, in an argument over a house rental. He was tried for murder. After the jury rendered a verdict of not guilty Robert Hindman's father Thomas tried to shoot him, but the gun misfired. In 1855 the dispute flared again. This time Hindman and Falkner agreed to a duel, but a third party managed to resolve the conflict without bloodshed. The families did not confront each other again. Like Colonel John Sartoris, a character in *The Unvanquished* based on Falkner, the novelist's great-grandfather stepped out of the Oxford courthouse one day in 1889 and was shot in the throat and mortally wounded by a business and political rival. The jury acquitted the murderer (there were hints of bribery) and the possibility of a new blood feud arose. Colonel Falkner's son, however (like Bayard Sartoris in *The Unvanquished*), decided to end the train of bloodshed. He let the matter rest.

As this story indicates, the duel and the feud were somewhat connected, especially in the socially unstable world of the Southwest. Feuds were generally much deplored, particularly among the gentry, because quite obviously they disrupted community life grievously, and incited conflicts of loyalty among related family members and their friends. Duels, in contrast, provided structure and ritual. Referees assured the fairness of the fight and witnesses reported back to the public on the impartiality of the proceedings. Moreover, the rites of challenge and response afforded time and means for adjustment of differences through third parties. Intermediaries, as in the Falkner-Hindman encounter, were more often successful in peaceably satisfying the injured pride of the principals than legends of duels would lead one to expect. In addition, the duel set the boundaries of the upper circle of honor. They excluded the allegedly unworthy and therefore made ordinary brawling appear ungentlemanly, vulgar, and immoral. In a hierarchical society, all these factors were socially significant. They made violence a part of the social order even in the upper ranks, but at least duels helped to restrict the bloodletting, which otherwise would have been much more chaotic and endlessly vindictive.

It would be a mistake, however, to argue that duels were as much deplored as Southern hand-wringing would lead an observer to believe. Hardly more than a handful genuinely considered duels socially beneficial, although some apologists claimed that the prospect of dueling forced gentlemen to be careful of their language and cautious in their actions. The criticism of outsiders, the clear opposition of the church, the recognition that valuable members of the community sometimes fell for reasons that retrospectively seemed petty—these attitudes placed duelists on the defensive. As a result, most of them explained their general opposition to the *code duello* in almost ritual words, but in the next breath gave reason for its continuation. For instance, Seargent S. Prentiss of Mississippi declared, "I am no advocate of duelling, and always shall from principle avoid such a thing . . . but when a man is placed in a situation where if he does not fight, life will be rendered valueless to him, both in his eyes and those of the community," then the only option was to fight. In fact, men took pride in such vices. All the words against dueling as well as other manly activities made them more appealing. It was a childish but nonetheless powerful motive.

Although duels were confined to the upper ranks of Southern society, the practice cannot be seen as purely exclusionary. The general public was intimately involved (unless the duel occurred on a college campus, a world unto itself). Ordinarily, honor under the dueling test called for public recognition of a man's claim to power, whatever social level he or his immediate circle of friends might belong to. A street fight could and often did accomplish the same thing for the victor. Murder, or at least manslaughter, inspired the same public approval in some instances. Just as lesser folk spoke ungrammatically, so too they fought ungrammatically, but their actions were expressions of the same desire for prestige. Even planters were not above assaulting one another with fists, and sometimes with firearms and dirks. "The violent planter was a deviant," Bruce asserts. "The violent yeoman was not." But in actuality violence pervaded all the white social classes. Whether the combat took a prescribed form or consisted of sheer unchecked fury did not make too much difference, if one or both of the contestants died.

Of course, among Christians and older men who were not expected to show youthful passions excessive violence was considered inappropriate. As Henry Foote noted, devout churchmen could forgo duels or, in fact, any other form of physical redress without incurring public censure. For other men a different standard prevailed. Prestige was the reward for the successful fighter of planter status. After thoroughly beating up a low-class "brawler," James L. Petigru, a young but dignified Carolinian lawyer, "became," as a friend declared, "a favorite with the people, who readily appreciated a strong arm and resolute spirit." Though the forms for defending it differed, the basic concept of personal valor, however displayed, bound the male ranks together even as the distinctions of class remained.

The second irony was related to the first: the effect of general democratic tendencies within the dueling scheme itself. That this should be so, even in rank-conscious Southern society, should come as no surprise, given the origins of the duel. Although introduced to America by British and French aristocrats serving in America during the Revolution, the duel was adopted by regular United States Army officers and, more especially, by the state militia officer corps. The latter was not only democratic in its election of officers but also increasingly so in the kind of men selected from the ranks to be officers. The process of change began even before the Revolution and grew apace. As Colonel John Lewis of Gloucester County, Virginia, reported in 1802 to Governor James Monroe, no "men of the first respectability" were among the officers of his regiment. Yet he had no discretionary power, "as they were the choice of the majority of the company."

In the absence of enormous wealth perpetually held under primogeniture, men in slaveholding states were prone to designate status by titles, and militia rankings were an obvious and useful signification of esteem. Many men, once having gained an elective title, as one Virginia officer complained "care but little about" it and promptly resigned. But once a major or colonel, always one—making these titles especially coveted by those whose property holdings might not otherwise have provided them with status. As one Carolinian wrote his brother in Alabama, "You are right in wishing to get rid of the infernal and eternal title of *Captain*" and become instead "Col. Townes," as "Col. is the prettiest title belonging to the military profession in my opinion." The democratic character of the militia was bound to affect the dueling custom. The duel was not an aristocratic custom that was learned at "mother's knee," contrary to Daniel Boorstin. Instead, dueling was a means to demonstrate status and manliness among those calling themselves gentlemen, whether born of noble blood or not.

Thus it would be a mistake to consider dueling confined to the bluebloods. Aristocracy, as William J. Grayson explained in the 1850s, was far from being an exclusive caste. "We are all *parvenus,* pretenders, or snobs," he admitted. For instance, nothing pleased Robert Bailey, Virginia gambler and captain in the "Light Blues," more than a challenge that he received from a fellow militia officer: the confrontation assured him reception into the world of gentlemen. Yet he knew little about the ritual that lay ahead. (Very few first-time duelists, outside Charleston and New Orleans, probably ever did, and some duels were so poorly conducted that they hardly qualified.) After half an hour of futile instruction, Major Thomas Lewis, his second, advised him simply to feint when his opponent fired, then take careful aim. His opponent was indeed so surprised by his unorthodox motions that Bailey wounded him without receiving a scratch himself.

Not many men of the first rank in society would have deigned to trade shots with an illiterate cockfighter like Bailey, whatever his militia title might be. Yet more duels of that proximate level probably took place than of the more celebrated variety between politicians and editors. In addition, the challenger could always appeal to his peers for vindication if turned down on the grounds that he was socially inferior. Haughtiness was not admired, and the challenger might gain sympathy. Quite clearly, someone like Andrew Jackson could refuse a young civilian like Thomas Swann of Philadelphia without incurring criticism. Less formidable gentlemen often had to fight, because peers had determined that the plea of inequality did not apply and was merely an excuse. Pleas of age difference were generally accepted. Thomas Lesesne of South Carolina noted that a planter had refused to duel a younger man on the grounds that "it would be a degradation of his character to put his life on the footing with so young a Boy." But with social distinctions often difficult to measure, especially in the Southwest, a man was more or less compelled to meet the challenge.

Finally, principals and their seconds were not the only ones involved in disputes leading toward a formal reckoning. Often men of various positions in the local hierarchy acted as a Greek chorus in the Sophoclean drama. For instance, in the famous Jackson–Charles Dickinson duel of 1806, over a dozen men, some of them at the fringes of male society, helped to create a consensus for a lethal settlement that the principals could not ignore. It took nearly six months for the affair to play its course, owing to Jackson and Dickinson's reluctance. Various gossip-mongers, as Jackson himself recognized, had more to do with staging the event than either of the duelists.

A further irony was the role of the "mobbish inferiors," whom the gentry were supposed to ignore when engaged in affairs of honor. Although duels were to be staged away from prying onlookers, the larger male community sometimes determined who should fight and why, particularly so in the less socially rigid Southwest. Militia officers, politicians, and journalists were obliged to prove manhood in order to demonstrate their worthiness as community leaders. Militia officers were most particularly called upon to exhibit prowess with firearms before their troops.

A telling illustration of such pressures from below was the duel between General Felix Huston of the Texan Army and Albert Sidney Johnston, whom President Sam Houston had ordered to command Huston's regiments. A tall, rowdy, and shrewd lawyer from Natchez, Felix Huston had recruited men from Natchez-under-the Hill and brought them to Texas. They proceeded to kill each other, not Mexicans, in Saturday-night brawls. President Houston had decided to replace their commander with a stricter disciplinarian. When Johnston arrived, Huston challenged him to a duel, claiming that his assumption of command had been the result of intrigue and had inflicted "stigma" upon Huston's "prospects in the Texan Army." The charge was false, and Huston knew it full well. But he felt obliged to defend the honor of his troops, who otherwise would have to accept the change in command as criticism of their conduct. Johnston, who had sworn never to participate in a duel and had no experience with small arms, was compelled by circumstance to accept. For six rounds the pair blasted away. (Huston had evened the odds by firing a defective pistol.) Finally, Johnston fell with a ball in his thigh that he carried to his death at Shiloh. According to one officer present, if Johnston had killed Huston or if he had failed to fight, he would have been killed by the soldiers themselves. As it was, Johnston had gained "the moral preeminence" over Huston and the troops that was so necessary for his successful command. The point should be clear. Tyranny of the community, whether simply the participants' peers or the large male fraternity of various social classes, governed Southern society. Leaders, as duelists, orators, and politicians, had to bear that Tocquevillian fact in mind. It was democracy perhaps, but a kind of democracy that placed primary stress on white, manly virtue. Those who failed to set the appropriate standard were soon unseated. Duels were a method for ascertaining who should exercise the power that the community of men was willing to accord the winners.

The final irony was the curious effect that dueling had upon survivors. Most duels were fought by young men (some of them with deceptively senior titles). Quite often their arrogance masked an uncertainty about their place in society and, indeed, about their manhood as well. The inexperienced youth was very likely to take his own measure from public opinion of himself, an inclination that forced a good number to fight—and die—when peers demanded it. Harriet Martineau and William J. Grayson, among others, cited poignant examples to show how young men were compelled to fight each other largely because their equally young peers (and sometimes their seniors as well) insisted that to do otherwise would be construed as cowardice, ruining their future prospects. (Indeed, duels did open up positions in society that young men sought to fill.)

Southerners themselves were sometimes uneasily aware that some duelists seemed driven to violence by inner furies. Such an individual was labeled as "bully," but the term was most often directed toward an unpopular victor, rather than seen as a general problem. For instance, William Cumming, who had gravely wounded George McDuffie in a celebrated duel, was criticized for showing "a Hyena thirst for blood which has lowered him in the estimation of all good men." Partisans of the defeated rival were very likely to take that position when a favorite fell. Nevertheless, the number of fighters who seem to have been harshly driven toward gambles with death is striking—a propensity that puzzled more than disturbed the public at the time. Figures such as William L. Yancey were drawn to this method of acting out bitter feelings because dueling promised not just moral vindication against the "calumniator" who ruined "reputation," but the wonder of all who heard of it. Even though death might ensue, there was supposed to be glory for the defeated as well as the winner. When excoriated for fighting Thomas L. Clingman, a Whig congressman of North Carolina, Yancey replied to the highly critical editors of the *Alabama Baptist* that the laws of God and state and the "obligations" to wife and children all had to bow, "as they have ever done from the earliest times to the present, to those laws which public opinion had formed, and which no one, however exalted his station, violates with impunity."

The appeal of dueling to the restless spirit was exactly that public appproval, a reassurance of self-esteem instantly gratified in victory. Even the victim, declared the Virginia belleletrist George Tucker in 1823, "touches our sympathy and excites our honor," and while, as in a play, the spectators applauded the survivor, they also celebrated the fallen, who "excites more than ordinary regret, and the recollection that his conduct was rash, illegal, impious, and immoral, is lost in the warm and generous feelings of pity and admiration." These Aristotelian emotions of pity and fear were supposed to be aroused and satisfied in the catharsis of the outcome. But the aftermath was not as unambiguous, structured, and glorious as the dedicated duelist presumed.

Although most Southern duelists managed to live through the experience with scarcely a twinge of regret, some both entered and left the dueling ground with their anxieties unresolved. One may speculate that a patriarchal order that left young men desperate for purpose in life was bound to create a scheme whereby self-vindication could be achieved in killing one another. Like gaming, drink-treating, and overt miscegenation, dueling was sometimes the recourse of a failed spirit, or at least of men who feared that consequence. Louis T. Wigfall, for instance, who fought or threatened to fight a number of duels, suffered deeply from "dissipation," remorse, uncontrollable ambition, and total incapacity to reconcile himself to the insolvency that his own aspirations brought down upon him. "Had I been studious & sober instead of idle & dissipated what an immensely high position would I now have inspired in the public estimation," mourned Wigfall. His self-esteem was too low to be retrieved, even through duels. Impatience drove Wigfall from Carolina to try his luck in Texas. Though he there became a secessionist leader and senator, he never matched his hopes.

Other duelists with equal if not greater emotional distresses included William L. Yancey, whose restlessness and alcoholism all but disqualified him from significant participation in the Confederate cause that his eloquence did so much to promote. Seargent S. Prentiss, though popular as an orator, cardplayer, and drinking companion, shared similar states of depression, anguish, and inner rages. Senator Prentiss, declared his friend Joseph Shields, constantly sought the "wild excitement" of alcohol and gaming, a "mysterious and singular infatuation" that he could not overcome. Colonel Alexander K. McClung, age twenty-three when promoted to that title, had already fought one duel as a midshipman. He killed General Allen, about the same age, and fought several others in the course of his life. A man of strange disposition, he was subject to severe depressions that alcohol only made worse. When he was in a drunken state others had to avoid him for fear of arousing his belligerent temper. Alienated from the public he sought to impress, he killed himself. Similarly, General John McGrath, reminiscing about famous encounters in Baton Rouge, remarked that the survivor of one affair "became despondent" in the following years and died "a dissolute character" in his youth. James Stith, another duelist whom McGrath remembered, "also grew morose" and avoided "former associates." Obviously the field of honor was a repository of self-pity.

Although the occasions for duels differed somewhat, almost all arose because one antagonist cast doubt on the manliness and bearing of the other, usually through the recitation of ritual words—liar, poltroon, coward. The stigma had to be dealt with or the labels would haunt the bearer forever. In making such charges or returning them with similar words, the principals might well have been acting out private dramas of their own and asking the public to bear witness that their inner sense of worthlessness applied better to the opponent than to themselves. The parties sought to kill personal anxieties along with the scapegoat who stood ten or twenty paces away. But many discovered, as one Major William F. Pope of Arkansas did, that the duelist carried the mark of death, a kind of evil eye. The promise of immortality that George Tucker made the loser was not always fulfilled. Though he was "pit[t]ed twice," like a cock in the ring, Pope's "sunshine friends" deserted him as he lay in agony from the wounds. He had fought for the sake of family reputation, but even his uncle failed to visit him or pay his medical expenses. Death and abandonment were all too often the outcome for the losers, and even some victors found themselves without the companionship that the duel was supposed to bring them.

These circumstances belied the cult of chivalry. The Southern ethical scheme's personal strategies did not and could not provide the happiness, permanency of status, and degree of authority demanded of them. Hospitality, gaming, and arranging duels to the death all created worlds of adventure in the midst of rural monotony, and the oppressive spirit of rivalry among those who were master to slaves, wives, and fellow men. As George Tucker, the Virginia philosopher, said, if these diversions had been replaced with "literary pursuits" or motions to improve the social and religious order, men of leisure and sensitive pride would have been "spared the necessity of flying from themselves" in search of pleasure and reputation. Whether they really banished fear of apartness and alienation depended upon the resilience of individuals, not upon the society that gave these strategies their romance and appeal.

7

Policing Slave Society:
Insurrectionary Scares

Lynch law, vigilantism, and charivaris were the ultimate expressions of community will. They established the coercive lines between acceptable and unacceptable behavior for all members of the Southern social order. Most especially, these ancient rituals demarcated the separate spheres of racial life, but they also imposed upon the entire spectrum of Southern white ranks the ethical principles to which the consensus of a locale was dedicated: the integrity of family life and the rule of men over women, of "respectability" over the shameless, sometimes of the honor-conscious poor over the rich deviant. Within the rubric of lynch law the slave insurrectionary scare must be most carefully considered—a phenomenon that outlasted, under modification, the "domestic institution" itself. It may seem perverse to categorize the prosecution of the white South's most dreaded crime, black insurgency, as a facet of community action. But the standards of evidence used in court trials were so low, the means of obtaining damaging testimony so dubious, the impotence of constituted authority so evident, that insurrectionary prosecutions at law must be seen as a religious more than a normal criminal process. By such means individual slaves, and sometimes whites affiliated with them, were made sacrifices to a sacred concept of white supremacy. The rite was a celebration of white solidarity, the maintenance of which was reconfirmed by the very disorders and agitations accompanying these exercises in social control.

The issue here is not to decide once and for all whether insurrectionary panics were based upon authentic black conspiracies. The topic cannot be wholly set aside, but it is less relevant to the purposes at hand here than the use whites made of such affairs, real or imagined. For instance, there is no question that Nat Turner's bloody trail across Southampton County, Virginia, 1831, was not a figment of popular hysteria. Outside that southeastern corner of the state, however, scores and possibly hundreds of slaves were whipped, maimed, and killed by one form of justice or another, innocent though all of them were of complicity in the lonely undertaking of Turner and his small number of religiously guided associates.

Nor can there be any doubt that "maroons" or bands of runaways roamed the more isolated reaches of the South, proudly independent of white authority. However, they seldom hoped for more than survival in liberty for themselves, and were not engaged in enlisting others to general rebellion. No condescension is intended in calling them brigands. To endure they had to make forays against solitary plantations, rob travelers, and collaborate, even intermarry, with Indians. They were thought a menace, but Southerners did not consider them guerrillas at war with slavery as such. Their aims were not so lofty. Mrs. Rachel O'Connor reported, for instance, that some runaways robbed Mrs. Pierre's house in 1829. The neighbors in the St. Francisville, Louisiana, vicinity were incensed, and a planter recruited the help of a young slave, who gave information about who the thieves were. Learning of the arrangement, the runaways returned, caught the boy, and "cut his legs and arms off and then pulled out his eyes." He died from loss of blood. The band, it turned out, consisted of twenty-four men, but within a few days a posse of a hundred mounted whites killed eight or ten and dispersed the rest. Incipient revolts could well have sprung from such groups, but trial records do not reveal much connection between outlaw slaves and blacks charged with insurrectionary conspiracies, who were almost always free blacks, black artisans, and domestic slaves.

Under these circumstances slave rebellions, as whites perceived the threat, were much more significant as an abstract, awesome danger from within than an ever-present reality of small parties of runaways and outlaws. Eugene D. Genovese has explained the dynamics of white-black relations generally and has argued that most blacks realistically appraised their situation. Successful insurgency, they knew, was problematic because of the ubiquity of white observers, on and off the plantation; the unfavorable geography, which limited places of refuge and defense to inhospitable swamps and wilderness; the relative inaccessibility of firearms; the lack of a common tongue among imported Africans in which to communicate without risk of white comprehension; and the fear of reprisals against families and friends. These and other factors distinguished North American slave life from the much more volatile situations in the West Indies, Brazil, and Spanish America.

Instead, slave resistance ordinarily took a much more personal and subtly orchestrated form, a mingling of resistance and reluctant, self-protective accommodation that was suited to survival and even a degree of limited autonomy, as Genovese has skillfully demonstrated. Of course, the predominance of one form of resistance scarcely precluded others from taking root as well. Free blacks were more likely to have reading skills, knowledge of the larger world, and a degree of privacy and autonomy, all meaning that thoughts of insurgency could more easily mature into action. Such possibilities did not escape white notice. With every insurrectionary panic the cry went up that something drastic, including deportation, should be done about the free blacks, many of whom, it was noted, had white folks' blood running in their veins and quickening their resolve.

In light of these factors, it may seem paradoxical that the ruling race did not live in constant dread of revolt from below. Instead, masters both early and late boasted of their freedom from such intolerable nightmares. William Byrd, for instance, wrote to an English correspondent in 1735, "Our negroes are not so numerous, or so enterprizing as to give us any apprehension or uneasiness," whereas those who presided over the "poor People of other countrys" had to live in fear. As antislavery criticism mounted in the nineteenth century, Southerners contrasted their lackadaisical habits with those of the wealthy up North. "New York," wrote Judge Thomas Jefferson Withers of South Carolina while on a visit there, "is vehemently exercised in devising laws to hobble the multitude" and provide "locks and bolts to secure the plunder of the few from daily nightly spoliation." He was sure that only in the South was there genuine security from revolution.

Southern plantation dwellers did not live in fear of robbery, rape, or massacre. They left doors unlatched, windows open, gates ajar. Slaves freely roamed in and out of the "Big House" day and night, much to the wonderment of visiting Yankees and foreigners. Her first night in the slaveholding states, wrote Sarah Hicks Williams of New York, a young bride, "we slept in a room without a lock. Twice before we were up a waiting girl came into the room, and while I was dressing, she came to look at me," she said. The slaves "are in the parlor, in your room, and all over." Edmund Ruffin would have found her discomfiture amusing. Said he, "We all feel so secure, & are so free from all suspicion . . . that no care is taken for self-protection," a defiance of fate "incredible to northerners, who have to use every precaution to guard their houses from robberies, & who suppose that every slave in the South wants nothing but a safe opportunity to kill his master." Murder, he admitted, could not be ruled out. But it was rare enough "that no fear is entertained by the most timid of the whites." The consequence was, however, a "blameable & general neglect of all police regulations, & of means for defence against possible violence."

How then was it possible for large-scale, well-educated planters, not ordinarily given to wild fancies, to forsake their usual equanimity and succumb to panic at the prospect, real or imagined, of black-led bloodbaths and the upturning of the social order, with the slaves the new masters, the masters the new slaves? The answer was that two alternating states of mind—apathy and horror—each provided the context for the other. In that fairly institutionless society there was no feeling of permanent mastery of events; instead there were periodic, almost cyclical rallies of white solidarity quickly organized to reassert traditional values, then a lapsing back into somnolence as the fears faded. The slave insurrection scares were analogous to the heresy trials of the Reformation era, the anti-peasant outbreaks that produced the English Black Laws, or the "great fear of 1789," when France was convulsed with worries about vagabonds and rogues. Whether real or not (in Europe the upheavals often were authentic), these perceptions of social imbalance led to frantic demands for group conformity to the traditional moral values. In the Southern situation, the obvious purpose was the allegiance demanded of all to white-race superiority and the obligation of all to ferret out those who threatened the social structure through secret malevolence. Whether there by self-selection, as rebel leaders, or by white scapegoating of innocents, blacks in the dock for conspiracy and treason were despised as symbols of all that was evil. Labeled deviants, they embodied what the community thought to be satanic design.

Obedience and even the semblance of affection were the first requirements of slave conduct; impudence was thought a prelude to insurgency. The method of testing these attributes in a public way was to create what one social scientist has called "degradation ceremonies," a term that has lately been applied to the corporal styles of early American legal punishment. By this means the black rebel became a visible and punishable sacrificial victim. He was the archetypal reverse image of the self-effacing "uncle" that whites liked to think was the ideal servant. Whatever the malefactor's former character might have been, he was thereafter the personification of unreliability, disorder, and nameless horror.

The process took the form of mass ritual: the initial discovery of the plot, the arousal of public opinion to the danger, the naming of conspirators through informers and trials, the setting of penalties, sometimes reviews by state authorities, the final disposition of the prisoners, and the relaxation of agitation. The causes of the periodic explosions may be divided into three categories: general economic, social, and political conditions; the encroachments of slaves and free blacks into forbidden areas of autonomy; and the struggle for community preeminence between two factions within the white world—

a better-educated benevolent element and the more traditionalistic and hard-minded group, which was aided and sometimes controlled by the ordinarily less powerful yeomanry and small planters. One is easily tempted to reduce these rival groups to a simple dichotomy between rich and poor, but economic position alone did not make one man a friend to blacks and another an implacable enemy of the race.

The first set of conditions has been well explored in the historical literature and need only be sketched here. Downturns in the plantation economy often affected the degree of anxiety about the black populace. In 1802 Tidewater Virginia, southern Maryland, and eastern North Carolina, all with large slave populations, suffered from the disruptions of overseas trade arising out of the Napoleonic wars, a state of affairs repeated during the scares of 1808, 1811, and 1812. At the time of the Denmark Vesey plot in South Carolina in 1822, similar economic difficulties appeared. A depression that began in 1819 grew worse in the early 1820s as cotton yields declined precipitously from soil exhaustion. Thousands of planters and farmers migrated west, successfully competing on world markets with their eastern relatives. On a more local level, in 1835 Madison County, Mississippi, was peculiarly aroused to slave dangers, owing in part to the fragile state of the local economy, which was lagging behind more prosperous nearby counties.

Political problems at home and abroad also vexed whites, leading to panics, especially in heavily slave-populated areas. In 1800, 1802, 1808, 1811, and 1812, fears of possible invasion by English and French marauders along the coast and disturbing news of racial struggles in Santo Domingo, Gaudeloupe, and Domenica; in 1822 and 1831, the rise of Northern abolitionist sentiment during the Vesey and Turner tragedies; in 1835, the abolitionists' postal campaign, with widespread anti-insurrectionary reactions. When the Republicans fielded their first national candidate in the 1856 elections, their campaign provoked rumors of an upcoming Christmas rebellion. There was an obvious connection between antislave panics and John Brown's Raid in 1859, and Lincoln's campaign and election in 1860.

The connection of politics and economic and social frustrations to antiblack hysteria continued strong in the postwar era. Insurrectionary plots were uncovered even after emancipation, most notably at Christmas 1865. The last judicial "lynching" for alleged plans for rebellion occurred in Choctaw County, Alabama, in 1881. The paraphernalia of forged documents, a frequent prop in these affairs, helped to convict Jack Turner, a courageous black Republican leader. He was hanged immediately after the trial judge pronounced sentence. But ordinarily, postwar anti-insurgent activity had to adapt to new conditions: the less sanguinary criminal code meant the transference of repressive justice from the courts to lynch law, and the substitution of such charges as rape or impudence for the older one of conspiracy. Nevertheless, the patterns were otherwise similar and devoted to the same ends: the political repression of blacks and the prevention of other whites, at home or elsewhere, from allying with them. Hence in the 1890s lynching activity rose and fell in various localities with the success or decline of Populist party biracial campaigning, most notably in Louisiana.

The second and much less historically visible factor leading to white frenzy was the advance of slaves in ways difficult to halt either by law or everyday custom. Black and white struggles over slave autonomy never ceased. Masters often wearied of trying to impose their will on every occasion that reached their notice. As Genovese and others have shown, slaves in field and kitchen were shrewd observers of "ole massa" and knew how to exploit his grave weaknesses, largely in answer to their grim exploitation at "ole massa's" hands. The irate owner, in helpless fury, could use the whip unmercifully—but mostly with counterproductive results. As John Blassingame has observed, under such conditions slaves became indifferent and worked less effectively than ever before, and some even risked their lives in open confrontations.

On the other hand, tolerant masters watched impotently as each new privilege begged for and granted, at once became plantation tradition and the precedent for further requests. Moses Ashley Curtis of Wilmington, North Carolina, posed these thoughts in his diary as the Nat Turner uprising and subsequent scare unfolded: "No class of beings I ever heard of take such vile advantage of favors as blacks. . . . The faithfulness of a servant who at first brushed my boots as regularly as I took them off was rewarded by occasional donations," for example. But when Curtis tired of offering the gratuity, he discovered that "now I cannot get my boots brushed once a month without issuing an order to that purpose." To neglect strict, undeviating discipline, he advised himself, led directly to poor performance, then to resentment upon correction, and finally to insurrection. Curtis was not at all surprised to hear that Turner had had an indulgent master.

But what Curtis described was a relatively minor infraction, the sort of thing slaveholders took endless pleasure in complaining about to their friends. Far more serious were the perceived signs of a different spirit among blacks. Just as a plantation owner or manager could not hope to regulate every movement and habit of every slave, so much less was white society able to govern the social demeanor of so large a portion of the population. Acts of personal deference—the doffing of the cap, the intoning of the right greeting, the required downward glance, the appropriately modest attire, the lively gait in response to a patroller's order—these were the signals that all was well in the best of worlds. But a glum stare, a brusque reply to a question, a reluctant move—such gestures in face-to-face encounter raised instant worries. Frank Carr of Williamsburg, Virginia, during one scare, wrote a friend that the inhabitants were sure of an incipient revolt. A suspected conspirator, Carr explained, had "addressed Thomas W. Maury in the street yesterday evening" in so rude a fashion that there was "not the smallest grounds for doubting that an insurrection was in agitation." The problem was not, of course, the bad manners per se, but the feeling that whites were helpless to prevent blacks from moving out of accustomed patterns of behavior.

The way slaves dressed could also induce suspicions of the direst sort. According to a black observer writing in New York in 1850 about the Vesey plot of 1822, one young master brought two slaves into court on suspicion of being conspirators. The pair were dressed in their "country rags" and exhibited manners befitting field hands.

The magistrates dismissed them as obviously innocent. Later the same hands, washed and dressed in city clothes, were again brought before the magistrates, who at once "pronounced these very men participants in a scheme of the contemplated conspiracy." However, this sort of protest against kangaroo-court proceedings—for that was the master's purpose in reclothing the two—usually occurred much later in the panic cycle. To have done the trick when fears ran highest would have jeopardized the master himself; he might have been accused of complicity in the slave plot. But as the scare ran its course, detection of false witnesses and other ways of slowing down the slaughter became important. At some point whites had to recognize that the machinery of persecution was beginning to injure the economy.

Black religious advances aroused considerable resentment, too, especially among nonchurchgoing planter and yeoman elements. The intrusion of Christian principles among whites was bad enough. In an attempt at satire Bennet Barrow of Louisiana had painted the "nick Bone of a horse" (the rear end) to look like "a Priest or Preacher praying." He placed the object in the parlor, but kinsfolk did not approve because, he scoffed, they and others had come to "think that a man can't be honest unless a professor of Religion—in other words a church goer, Bah!" Dismayed by the rise of Bible-toting planters, men like Barrow had little sympathy for neighboring do-gooders who sought to advance black religious interests. Thus a planter told Frederick L. Olmsted how a controversy had broken out between a local churchgoing group and those who worked their hands on Sunday. The benevolent faction had started a church at the Louisiana schoolhouse and "made their negroes go to meeting." At the next gathering of the school trustees, the majority voted to deny the facilities to the church. Otherwise, the hardliners maintained, rebelliousness might spring up among the slaves who had to work on Sundays instead of sitting all day hearing sermons and singing hymns. Almost every insurrectionary scare featured complaints about black preachers, especially free ones. "I am convinced that the negro preachers are more dangerous than any other description of blacks," wrote Richard W. Byrd of Smithfield to Virginia Governor John Tyler during the 1810 panic.

In retaliation pious slaveholders would point to the liquor-law violations encouraged by drink-treating masters. "The Saturnalia of the Christmas and other holidays should be suppressed," wrote Calvin Jones to Governor Montfort Stokes of North Carolina in 1830. "Selling spiritous liquors to negroes and permitting their assemblys at musters, elections and other places where they acquire insolence and audacity, should be provided against." But owners had the right to run their places as they liked, and even black tavern-going was hard to stop in a routine way.

Sometimes efforts to control black leisure time figured directly in the insurrection panic itself. In 1810 or 1811 a group of slaves in Georgia bought "a can of grog" and drank it in a garret. As a mounted militia detachment approached on an anti-insurgent mission, one of the hidden slaves drunkenly sounded a bugle, with "electrical effect" upon the troops, who were riding past the site where the slaves were drinking. They caught and whipped a member of the group until he confessed to being part of an insurrectionary plot and named as its leader Billy, a slave belonging to a Captain Key. (His captors probably demanded Billy's name from the frightened prisoner.) At the time, Key was hosting William Johnson, a United States Supreme Court justice. (He recalled the incident for the edification of the panic-stricken citizens of Charleston during the Vesey plot.) Not only was slave Billy in dire trouble but so, though to a much lesser degree, were his owner and the tavern-keeper who had dispensed the whiskey. Billy was hurriedly hanged as the ringleader of an insurrection that was allegedly to be launched by the horn-blowing. The magistrates feared that if they delayed the execution Billy's master and his distinguished guest would gain a pardon for Billy from the Georgia governor. Key's slaves were known to be independent-minded because of their master's deviantly kind treatment, and Billy, "a very worthy fellow," as William Johnson later said, was a prime target for punishment: he was a blacksmith, earning extra money with his skill. The "evidence" in the trial was a bugle, dusty and full of cobwebs, that had been found in Billy's cabin where he and his family lay asleep until he was abruptly awakened to answer the charges. Once the "culprit" was found and punished the community returned to its ordinary repose. Thus, slackness of race discipline, whether in the form of unsupervised tavern-going or permissiveness about black autonomy at work, was part of the anti-insurrection ritual. (Needless to say, Johnson's story, published in 1822, did not have the effect that the justice desired. He had publicized his skepticism too soon in the cycle.)

The white men's objectives in such instances were probably gained for the time being. No doubt for several weeks after Billy's hanging, slaves did not turn up at the local grog shops on Saturday afternoons. Likewise, there was a noticeable change in black habits during and after the Vesey plot frenzy. Following the execution of six Vesey conspirators in the summer of 1822, there was "a wonderful degree of politeness shown to us," a white Charlestonian boasted, "bows and politeness, and—give way for the gentlemen and ladies, met you at every turn and corner." For the citizens of Charleston it was a great relief to see blacks smile deferentially and laugh softly. The world was once again as it should be.

Perhaps the repression of potential revolt was really aimed at achieving just this: the outward appearance of black submissiveness and the restored sense of security arising from white consensus. In addition, the process of repression served to break up any motions toward black unity under a body of leaders like Nat Turner and potentially dangerous figures like Billy, whose self-possession had been interpreted as an unmistakable sign of incorrigibility and "impudence." Several facets of the insurrectionary pattern suggest this reading: first, the curiously self-conscious actions and reports made by those seeking out the guilty parties, and the mixture of skepticism and belief that both slaves and masters exhibited; second, the clear distinction made between the supposed crimes of rebellion and actual offenses committed by slaves, so that seldom was a slave's killing of a master seen as a conspiratorial act but rather as merely a discrete felony; and third, the way in which antiblack zeal would eventually begin to decline so that everyone in the slaveholding society could return to their normal pursuits without further disruptions.

The initial alarm aroused almost universal fright. The rallying of whites extended from the governor to the lowliest woodchopper. Rumors flew about that black bands, numbering in the scores, even hundreds, were fanning out in all directions. Messengers galloped hither and yon to warn villages of approaching rebels. Invariably the rumors proved false—but no matter, an explanation was ready to hand. Black informers, it always turned out, had luckily alerted the white people to their impending doom, days or just hours beforehand, and the ringleaders were now safely in jail, the others having melted into the shadows. Yet everyone was warned to stay vigilant, no matter how normally the slaves were behaving in the quarters and fields. As one militia officer wrote Benjamin Williams of North Carolina, the neighborhood was particularly quiet, but "we still keep a strick patrole [sic]." During the same scare in Virginia, a militia general informed James Monroe that those in his district "can give no good reason for their fears" but "they appear fully satisfied that some attempt will be made by the Blacks." Actually, of course, the situation was the reverse, with whites the first to attack.

Complicating the situation was the fact that slaves themselves both hoped the white fears were justified and also feared that they might be mistaken for conspirators. As a result, rumors spread as quickly through the plantation slave quarters as they did at the courthouse and in the parlors of white residents. Fired by whiskey as well as by the rumors of slave conspiracy, Toney, a slave of Halifax County, North Carolina, for instance, muttered a few slurs against the whites and was promptly hustled off to jail for conspiracy. He was sentenced to hang. (A juryman admitted that only during "such a clammer [sic]" would Toney's offense have warranted so severe a punishment.) Likewise, a slave called Leggett's Sam in nearby Bertie County, North Carolina, heard talk of how Virginia slaves had begun to rise. Though fellow slaves warned him of the dangers, Sam spread the news, thinking, said one slave witness, that "them guns we heard was in Virginia"; actually the sound was the firing of Carolina patrollers, not of slave insurgents. Sam grew so excited by all the drama around him that he told the slaves that he would raise up a band himself: "If I can git a great many to join me which I will try to do then I will let you all know I have a gun. . . ." But if Sam could not find a gun, he said, then he would "try clubs & if theay [sic] wont do I will try to lay stuff at the Doors." His actual rebellion, sadly, turned out to consist of nothing more than the spreading of conjure powders, a sure sign of impotence compared with the military superiority of the enemy. Fellow slaves turned Sam over to the authorities—to save themselves from the magistrates who soon sent him to the grave.

More often than not, the initiating factor in the majority of panics was the work of whites who claimed to have overheard blacks cursing whites and making plots or who had slaves whipped into making such confession because of their apparent insolence or misdeeds. Women, boys, poor whites—people at every level of white society, rich or poor, eminent or obscure—were involved. In 1830, for instance, Mrs. Lewis, the wife of a jailkeeper in Edenton, North Carolina, reported to John Burgwyn, a prominent planter and magistrate, that she had heard black prisoners talking of reprisals upon the white race. Burgwyn, however, discounted the rumor, and the local panic it had provoked subsided. In 1821 Mrs. Frances McDougle reported that she had heard an old white man with "red whiskers" talking to a vegetable seller, an "old tall black negroe man who walked lame," and that the pair had been muttering about the basic equality of the races, before dispersing at three in the morning outside her hotel-room window in Richmond. She admitted to being hard of hearing, and nothing much came of the matter.

In Mississippi, however, Mrs. Latham, a wealthy widow of Beattie's Bluff, Madison County, had tragic success with her alarm. For weeks before the Fourth of July, 1835, rumors of a revolt sputtered and died out. Then several days before the holiday "gentlemen" of the county traced the stories to Mrs. Latham. In an interview she said that the clue was the unaccustomed disobedience and impudence of her house servants. She said she had heard one of the girls say "that she was tired of waiting on the *white folks* and wanted to be her own mistress the balance of her days, and clean up her own house." A genuine, full-scale frenzy was soon underway. It quickly became entangled with the antigambling crusade across the state at Vicksburg and Natchez and with the fright over John A. Murrell's imagined gang of horse and Negro stealers, "abolitionists" in the guise of Thompsonian "steam-doctors" (medical quacks), and other itinerants and transient strangers. On the other hand, in 1829 two white Virginia blacksmith apprentices claimed to have overheard a conversation about insurrection among slave workers at the forge. The neighbors, however, were not in the right spirit for an antislave witchhunt and decided that the trouble lay in a personal controversy between the white and black crews at the forge. No one was tortured or hanged, in stark contrast to the events that Mrs. Latham helped to spark in Mississippi.

There can be no question but that slaves were constantly seeking ways to expand their horizons and, in frustration, risking their lives by talking about insurrections. They well knew, especially after the Santo Domingo revolution and the Turner affair, that not only was freedom a possibility some time in the future but whites elsewhere in the world were protesting their thralldom. White patrols, panics, and intrusions all suggested to them the vulnerability of the Southern scheme of things, but were also the short-term obstacles against internal revolt. Talk was easy, action militarily impossible. Some intrepid spirits—Gabriel and Denmark Vesey, and, of course, Nat Turner—did initiate plots, but even so, these attempts only fed into the massive witchhunts that whites organized. The situation was much more complex, much more subtle than historians, with some exceptions, have so far realized.

Slaves and free blacks hoped that the rumors were true. So obvious was the connection between black excitability about the prospect of liberty and white fear of it that sometimes slaveholders themselves recognized the circumstances. In Hanover County, Virginia, in 1802, slaves Glasgow and Tom came to trial on the strength of an alleged conversation: James, a mulatto slave belonging to Benjamin Oliver, testified that he had heard Tom declare, "You know our masters are very bad to us," and had urged James to join in a fight against the oppressors. Testimony at the trial indicated that Colonel Bathhurst Jones and others on militia patrol had caught James out without a pass. To escape punishment, James had explained that he had just left Glasgow and Tom at the tavern kitchen (Tom belonged to Mrs. Paul Thilman, a widow who ran the neighborhood tavern) because they were planning revolt and he was off to report it to the authorities. Although Tom and Glasgow were at most only guilty of making some casual remarks, thanks to James's quick-witted alibi for his own infraction the two were sentenced to hang. The Thilman family had a curiously unfortunate record; they had already lost slaves in the Gabriel frenzy two years before. In the meantime the husband had died, and his wife was struggling hard to pay off old debts. The loss of Tom would have been especially disastrous, since he was an excellent cook and brought the tavern lots of business. The better element prayed that Governor Monroe would pardon the pair on the grounds that James, the informer, was a "notorious bad character" anyhow, forever running off when it suited him. A petition for Tom read:

We are convinced from recent circumstances that when a meeting hap[p]ens among this description of people that they hold conversation relative to what hath not only already happened, but what may hereafter come to pass, without having a real intention of put[t]ing the same into Execution. This has lately been the case in the County of King William, where a number were taken up & tried, though nothing could be made to appear sufficient to affect their lives. We have no doubt but a conversation was had among those two slaves [Tom & Glasgow] and the Witness [James] relating to something about an insurrection; but the Witness being also a slave, not without his faults, and perhaps the first who mentioned the subject which might lead to their conversation.

In this case, special circumstances worked in favor of the accused. The petitioners, one may surmise, were Mrs. Thilman's friends and creditors, concerned lest she be bankrupted by the troubles. Their pleas were heard, largely because the whole community had cooled off by the time the petitioners launched their efforts. Had there been much opposition to clemency, however, Tom and Glasgow would have hanged. As it was, the community took pity on the slaves and on a woman who might have added to the tax bill if forced to go on the county.

Even at the height of an insurrectionary scare there were occasional doubting Thomases whose voices of complaint about the kangaroo-court proceedings nettled the inquisitors. During the Turner uprising John C. Cabell and John Hartwell Cocke, a retired militia general, earnest evangelical temperance leader, and friend of Thomas Jefferson, bluntly denounced the uproar that the episode had inflamed throughout the state. "We have frequent & no doubt exaggerated reports about discoveries of hostile designs among the negroes, in so much that the white females in this neighborhood, can scarcely sleep at all at night," Cabell wrote Cocke. As a precaution, however, he advised that white ferrymen take the posts of the slave boatmen, to reduce the means of transcounty communication. Cocke, on the other hand, was even more disbelieving, replying to Cabell that an attorney from Petersburg and another friend in Surry County had told him that slaves executed there for conspiracy were totally "innocent," and had known nothing of events farther to the southeast. As for Cabell's plan, "how would it answer to provide by law" that a white should occupy every boat, Cocke asked, in light of "the present State of our miserable navigation" of the rivers? Whites simply would not take the jobs. Cocke advised another course: the education of the public to ignore false, malicious rumors.

The Rev. Moses Ashley Curtis also found the situation much exaggerated near Wilmington, North Carolina, far from the scenes at Southampton. His wife's younger sister, he said, returned from a neighbor's house "sat down, rose—sighed—clasped her hands behind her neck—went out & called to me." She reported that "an express has come" from Wilmington "saying that 200 blacks are within 20 miles," but Curtis dismissed the news and told her to go to bed. Soon, however, he watched as women carrying "trinkets & mattresses" headed for the garrison. Within an hour a hundred and twenty screaming children and hysterical women were sweltering in the tiny, odiferous guardhouse and "under the muzzles of the great cannon in the fort." The next morning, after nothing happened, they all trooped back, somewhat the happier for the fine gathering, though they had had to soothe "their noses with cologne, honey & lavender waters." The whole business was the "silliest" sight he had ever seen, Curtis concluded. Likewise, a wealthy planter in Tennessee exclaimed in 1856, "We are trying our best in Davidson County to produce a negro insurrection, without the slighest aid from the negroes themselves. . . . There is in sober seriousness no shadow of foundation for any belief of domestic plot in insurrection."

For those in official positions the uproar presented the opportunity to display heroism, civic activity, and bureaucratic efficiency. At first militia generals were delighted to have a reason to call out the troops, inspect their military polish, and count the arsenal weaponry. All too often, the militia armaments turned out to have been lost or to have fallen into thorough disrepair, and governors found themselves overwhelmed with requests for fresh supplies of muskets. Thus insurrection scares served the needs of many in a material way, as the clamor itself attested. In fact, in 1856 General Cocke of Virginia was sure that the uproar in that year was owing to the designs of "petty politicians" and others who found some advantage in creating havoc among the slaves. In 1800, the same circumstances took shape around the panic of that year, with officers and politicians lamenting the poor state of defense against insurgency and the need for greater expenditures and new promotions in the military to meet the crisis. Governor James Monroe, a parsimonious executive in ordinary times, reported to the legislature that $10,000 had been expended on new armaments during the Gabriel insurrectionary repression.

The distribution of supplies afforded militia officers and state authorities the chance to solidify political patronage with judicious, selective handouts. In addition, demands accelerated for the formation of new militia units, meaning that whites of uncertain social standing could have the chance to become officers. Such requests challenged the existing regimental commanders. In 1831, for instance, Captain John Price of Danville urged Virginia's Governor John Floyd not to commision Robert W. Williams to form a new company because Williams had just lost an election in the existing unit and was seeking the title through this other means. His troops, said Price, would be composed of the local scoundrels who thought the excitement would gain them free muskets. At the same time, Price himself asked for "75 stand of arms" for the "better informed and more respectable portion of the Town." During the same panic a citizen of Portsmouth, near Norfolk, Virginia, warned the governor that a "Mobb," both "inexperienced" and "undril[l]ed," sought commissions as a new unit, to be called the "Portsmouth grenadiers." Not only was the town already well equipped with regulars, the citizen confided, but the petitioners "would be pritty [*sic*] grenadiers" indeed: most of them "are scarcely five feet high."

Despite these dramatic, if contentious, circumstances, officials felt the winds of contrary forces as the crisis extended from hours to weeks. James Monroe of Virginia (1800 and 1802), Benjamin Williams of North Carolina (1802), and Thomas Bennett of South Carolina (1822), for instance, all became aware during episodes in their respective states that the resources of government were being sorely stretched. Knowing that they would be held responsible for raising taxes after the frenzies subsided, they had a natural tendency to raise doubts about the panics as soon as it seemed feasible to do so without political risk. After several weeks of excitement, Monroe confided to President Thomas Jefferson that "the spirit of revolt" had become so subterranean that it could not be discovered, or else "the symptoms which we see are attributable to some other cause." Like all others involved, Monroe did not understand exactly what the social purposes of the panics were, but nevertheless suspected that something profound was shaking the society: "After all the attention which I have paid to the subject my mind still rests in suspense upon it." Nevertheless, he, like other slave-state governors in such situations, urged his legislature to reform the militia and patrol systems, ponder the future of free blacks, and pass such measures as would eliminate or restrict black preaching, reading, and writing, and other supposed sources of risk. A more important part of the hidden agenda of the insurrectionary scares was the justification of existing race relations and the advancement of white institutional controls.

Although they were a significant part of the rationale behind the scares, mobilizations were costly. In North Carolina, Governor Williams met the needs of the hour with the customary recommendations for reform, but worried lest expenditures outrun the existing budget. When asked to supply arms to Camden County, he argued that all counties "should rest their safety on their own exertions and patriotism," instead of relying upon the state militia, which would necessarily burden all with "the great expence of taxation." In South Carolina, Thomas Bennett also followed the usual pattern in proposing new and harsher laws and improved constabulary efforts. But in contrary spirit he questioned the court procedures of the Vesey plot investigators. In a special message to the state legislature Bennett pointed out these departures from customary rules: star chamber secrecy at the Vesey trials; lack of rights of the accused to confront prosecution witnesses; mingling of prisoners together so that alibis and accusations were harmonized among the parties; and the ready acceptance of testimony of such slaves as Charles Drayton, whose "chilling depravity," Governor Bennett asserted, was obvious. Bennett, however, did sanction the use of torture and other means to "eviscerate the plot." Moreover, he had no doubts that the emergency was real enough. He alerted the federal authorities to the dangers. Though attempting to combine his scruples with stern measures for community defense, Bennett did not by any means escape severe public censure. Both he and Supreme Court Justice William Johnson, his brother-in-law, also a critic of the local inquisition, were suspected of dangerous tendencies. Once his gubernatorial term had ended several years were to pass before Bennett felt that his standing had improved enough that he could re-enter political life in a serious way.

Planters often agreed that "no doubt many innocent ones would suffer," as one of them wrote Justice Thomas Ruffin of North Carolina during the Nat Turner fright. Any forthright animadversions about a particular case, however, threw doubt on the critic's loyalty to community values. Politicians were most circumspect, but prudent men of all ranks held their tongues. Some self-assured individuals boldly spoke out regardless of consequences, a credit to their high sense of honor. For instance, Ruel Blake, owner of the slaves whom Mrs. Latham of Madison County, Mississippi, accused of evil designs, strenuously objected to the torture of one of his own blacksmith slaves. Suspicion turned at once on him, and he was accused of being a ringleader. He fled, but was caught and hanged, slaveholder though he was.

In the Nat Turner tragedy young Edmund Ruffin, later a violent secessionist, nearly wrecked his own career by boldly defending an accused slave against local opinion. Some "fellows of the baser sort, who in times like these always rise to power & influence" had instigated false charges, and "community insanity" had pressed them forward, he fumed. The evidence "at any sober time would not have been deemed sufficient to convict a dog suspected of killing a sheep." Yet Ruffin was branded, for a time, a "favorer . . . of . . . midnight slayers of sleeping men, women and children." Likewise, in 1835, Patrick Sharkey of Hinds County, a leading slaveholder and cousin of Mississippi's Chief Justice William L. Sharkey, freed two whites who had been charged with conspiracy for lack of evidence. Madison County vigilantes were incensed and demanded that Sharkey be delivered to them for punishment. Even Chief Justice Sharkey had to concede the helplessness of the courts. Governor Runnels refused to act at all. Eventually, however, Patrick Sharkey escaped the lynch mob's noose.

Less fortunate was James Allen, near Petersburg, Virginia, who was accused of harboring a suspected slave conspirator during the 1802 panic. Several low-class young men lashed him so relentlessly that "his body[,] his head[,] his legs[,] nay even his very feet" no longer were covered by enough skin to match "a nine pence." The culprits fled to Georgia and never appeared to stand trial for murder.

These demands for conformity to community will were not the work of a planter class in control of events. If there was a slave-holders' hegemony, as some historians have claimed, these elaborate degradation ceremonies cast it temporarily aside. It did not serve rich men's interests to have mischief-makers take advantage of the uproar to make war on the propertied by destroying their most valuable possessions, their slaves, many of them highly trained. The high compensations given to masters for most slaves executed in the scares in Virginia and elsewhere attest to the slaves' economic worth. But wealthy masters, including governors, judges, and militia generals, were often impotent to prevent the losses. Sometimes as many as a score in a county were killed or maimed through lynch action and judicial process. For instance, during the Turner tragedy James Wright, a wealthy planter of Duplin County, North Carolina, found that a cavalry unit had crossed the state line from nearby Southampton County, Virginia, and was about to torture his slaves in order to obtain "confessions." Secretly, Wright urged the slaves to postpone the lashings by admitting complicity and thereby get themselves transferred into the custody of understanding local authorities. The plan worked for all except young Jerry, who told such a good story of a rebel plot that he alone was sentenced to hang. Some weeks later the defense attorney came to believe Jerry's explanation for his false confession, and managed to secure verification from the owner, then on a sickbed. The presiding judge, who was "no friend of the negro," supported the petition for pardon, and the governor agreed. Jerry was quite lucky; few masters would have jeopardized their standing or their lives to save a slave. John H. Cocke, young Edmund Ruffin, and a few others had sufficient honor to meet the danger of public passion. Most planters did not.

Further evidence of the special character of the insurrection scare can be found in the disposition of regular slave criminal cases. If there were genuine revolts one would expect that in most instances the authorities would have regarded any murder or assault on a white as part of the current conspiracy or conspiracies under investigation. Such was not at all the case. In the midst of the frenzies the usual pattern of slave crime persisted. Although offenses included murders of malicious owners, all the careful preparations of evidence and common-law technicalities were observed, or challenged—quite in contrast to the slipshod, hasty insurrection trials. Also, memorials for convicted slaves on whom the community took pity arrived as usual at the governor's desk—at least in states with executive review of capital crimes, notably Virginia, Kentucky, North Carolina, and Tennessee. (Georgia, South Carolina, and Mississippi, however, had no such mandatory provision.) In Caroline County, Virginia, at the height of the panic in 1802, for example, neighbors petitioned for the reprieve of a slave named Cato. His elder brother Patrick had slain their master; Cato had merely helped to place the body under a fallen tree to make the axing appear accidental. The governor and executive council commuted Cato's sentence to life at the new state penitentiary.

More curious was the case of Randall and Cudge of Isle of Wight County. They had quarreled with Reddick Godwin, their master, fired his gun at him, and then pelted with stones the upstairs bedroom in which Godwin locked himself. The governor and council reprieved them both from hanging, changing the sentence to sale and deportation. No doubt the spokesmen for the slaves conveyed orally some scandalous information about Godwin to the Richmond authorities, for the written record does not reveal why such rebellious behavior, in the midst of a supposed rebellion, should be treated so magnanimously. The show of mercy, though, was not unusual, suggesting that the insurrectionary scares were seen as something with a separate and quite deliberate rationale.

The exception, however, was poisoning. Slaves accused of this crime were usually thought to be involved in a widespread scheme of insurgency because, like arson, poisoning was a crime of stealth

which whites could neither control nor understand. Herb and conjure doctors, like preachers, were extremely suspect. Yet at the same
time they were much in demand, not only for the customary love
potions and vengeful tricks that members of both races sometimes
sought to obtain, but also for medical healing. During a Kentucky
scare in 1824, for instance, Sam, reputedly "skilled in 'necromancy,
conjuration, and poisoning,' " was accused of murdering his master
(who had been dead for seventeen years) and, more recently, "his
two promising & lamented young masters," even though the local
physician could explain the natural causes for all three fatalities.
"Perhaps," observed a petitioner for Sam's life, "in no part of the
world does so great prejudice prevail on the subject of negro poison
as in this county. Every disease at all obscure & uncommon in its
symptoms & fatal in its termination is immediately decided to be a
case of negro-poison." Likewise, during the 1802 Virginia "witchhunt" a slave named John belonging to John Hopson of Halifax
County was accused of poisoning a Mrs. Lewis Ragsdale, one of his
patients who had momentarily taken a turn for the worse. The
"evidence" consisted of "palma-christal seeds, dirt-dauber nests, with
dead spiders and snail shells" found in John's box of conjuring
items. (The medicine had a double purpose, John professed. It
could ease sore joints, and also was to be used by Mrs. Ragsdale's
houseservant "to keep peace with" Mr. Ragsdale by blowing it at
him and sprinkling it around the house.) Contrary to all rules of
evidence, General Carrington, a physician named Dr. Walter Bennett, and others mixed these ingredients with powders from another
source and fed it to a cat. The animal promptly died. After John
was convicted and sentenced to die, William Faulkner, the county
sheriff, and others were appalled to learn that John Hopson, the
herb doctor's master, had pled for a gubernatorial reprieve for
John. He had signed the affidavit in a neighboring county, whence
he had had to flee because of the uproar. If the governor was bold
enough to affront the community in this fashion, Faulkner wrote,
he could not answer for the consequences, so determined was the
prejudice of the people against poisoners. Passions, however, did
eventually cool, and Monroe and colleagues, more courageous in

this case than in many others, waived the death penalty and John was sold and deported. Dr. Bennett, the local white physician, however, was no doubt gratified to have his competition reduced by one conjure-man.

The final aspect of the insurrectionary panic that suggested specific community purposes rather than authentic warfare between the races was the general pattern of the trials and the gradual emergence of a consensus in favor of a return to normality. Almost all cases of conspiracy shared common features. First, chief prosecution witnesses were predominantly fellow slaves, although whites participated in a secondary way, having initiated the proceedings. The reason was that by such means blacks were implicated in the destruction of their own leadership, sowing distrust, perplexity, and fear in the quarters. Second, prosecuting attorneys were seldom able to produce any paraphernalia attributable to planned revolt—firearm, pike, sword, incriminating letter, or coded message—directly associated with the accused. Such items were occasionally introduced. Some if not all of the letters were obviously forged, bearing spelling that conformed to white rather than black phonetics. "No weapons," declared Thomas Bennett, South Carolina governor during the Vesey episode, "(if we except thirteen hoop-poles) have been discovered; nor any testimony received but of six pikes, that such preparations were actually made." Six pikes for 5,000 alleged conspirators in South Carolina stretches modern credulity; even for sixty men it would not constitute much of an arsenal. Surely slave brigands or "maroons" ordinarily did better than these conspirators, if such they were.

In this writer's opinion, no substantial evidence presentable in a modern court has appeared to show large stockpiles of arms in any aborted rebellion before the Civil War. Without such weaponry, how could plots have been put into execution? Yet in all these emergencies the exposers of conspiracy claimed to have acted just hours or days before the rising. With so many informers telling on fellow slaves, why would not at least one informer in the scores of uprisings have led his captors to such a hidden arsenal? The absence of evidence is always hard to prove. But surely, even given the crude quality of detective work in that era, the nonappearance of armaments would ordinarily have thrown doubt on whether there was intent to use any.

Third, the damaging testimony was ordinarily an alleged conversation between the informer and the accused, usually without corroboration and often with contrary evidence offered by other slaves who testified to more plausible exchanges. These exchanges were generally so vague that prosecuting attorneys would have been laughed out of court under less compelling circumstances, just as Ruffin attested in his own experience. Fourth, the individual who named the conspirators was usually either severely tortured prior to the revelations or else imprisoned, isolated, demoralized, and deliberately drained emotionally to the point that he would comply with any suggestion offered. (The curious identification of the captive with menacing captors has become a psychological commonplace in recent years.) The slave "medium" who named the victims whom the inquisitors had preselected or who conjured up individuals from his own past to gratify the captors' wishes was the most pitiful victim of all in the degradation ceremony. Once the name was on the confessor's lips, it could not be retracted. Fifth, the confessors were almost always granted the reprieves they begged for as reward. Some received pensions. For such men, perjury was a small price to pay, especially after torture, for rewards ahead.

The most active "medium" for the 1802 rebellion was one Lewis, a runaway caught with a forged pass of his own making. Ability to read and write and a job as a ferryboatman made him a prime suspect. Twenty-four hours of unremitting scourging in the Nottoway County jail elicited from Lewis a detailed and far-reaching story of clandestine doings, though it bore suspicious resemblance to the public accounts of the Gabriel plot of two years before. For the next few months he traveled around the circuit with the judges and attorneys to help the prosecution of those already named. As ringleader he chose an old carpenter from Richmond named Arthur, whom he had not actually seen for nine years. The story that Lewis told of Arthur's plan to burn down Richmond was riddled with contradictions, but it impressed the Henrico court of magistrates. Arthur was to hang. Two white debtors and the warden of the penitentiary where Arthur was temporarily housed before execution were certain of his innocence, and other whites came forward, too. Eventually Arthur was pardoned by Governor Monroe and council, though some whom Lewis named were not so fortunate. Meantime, Lewis received travel expenses to return to his master.

In response to this reading of the slave panic, it could be argued that a prejudiced selection of facts, quotations, and trial verdicts, taken out of context, has unjustly cast doubt upon what in fact was a genuine series of incipient rebellions. Prominent historians such as Herbert Aptheker and Eugene Genovese have approached the matter from quite an opposite point of view. Ideological disagreements are bound to color any such discussion and in any case could not be resolved here. Nevertheless, it may help to offer a more detailed single example of the typical methods employed to convict an innocent slave, one whom Aptheker and others have named as one of the authentic plotters of the 1802 Virginia rebellion.

In this case, Will, a slave of Princess Anne County, accused three others of conspiracy, though only one of them, Jeremiah Cornick, a slave of Norfolk Borough, became the focus of popular tumult. The story Will told was a classic of brevity. On April 11, 1802, he claimed, Jerry Cornick and Walker's Ned, another Norfolk slave, had hailed him on a country road. As they walked, Jerry had turned to Will: "Wont you join us Will? in what said I, in Burning the [Norfolk] town on Easter Monday night, to which I reply'd I will have nothing to do with it in case worse befal[l] me, and Immediately left him and Ned together." Later on the same day, Will explained, he happened on another Ned, belonging to a Col. James Ingraham, and the same exchange took place.

This singularly barren account, a contrast to Lewis's much more fulsome embroideries, triggered an unusual pattern of events: the pursuit of the true circumstances, undertaken by a gentleman of considerable integrity and boldness. The trial and conviction of Walker's Ned, but more especially the proceedings against Jerry

Cornick, aroused the skepticism of George McIntosh, a Scottish immigrant who had married into the powerful Walke and Cornick families of Princess Anne and had a sizable plantation near Lynnhaven on Cape Henry. He had known Jerry for many years as the slave of John Cornick, deceased, one of his wife's relatives. There is no indication that he had any pecuniary interest in Jerry's fate. Respected as a community leader, with his wife's uncle, Cornelius Calvert, on Monroe's executive council, McIntosh was a life-long Jeffersonian. As late as 1848 he was still true to the faith, lamenting the 1848 defeat of the Democratic nominee Lewis Cass and the victory of Zachary Taylor, the Whig candidate. McIntosh not only followed President Jefferson's political credo but also his concern for the precepts of gentility, the ones that insisted on due attention to the protection of the weak by those who had the means and morals to undertake the mission. McIntosh (like Faulkner's Gavin Stevens) understood the responsibilities of gentry rule and, judging from the quality of his thought and prose, he also had the requisite education and good sense to fulfill the old Stoic-humanist tradition regardless of popular opinion. Certainly, as a slaveholder himself and the proprietor of a gun and grocery store in Norfolk he had no quarrel with the institution of slavery as such. But loyalty to the institution had to be accompanied, he thought, by a solicitude for the defenseless. As a result, he undertook an exhaustive search for evidence of what actually occurred, retracing Jerry's steps on April 11, the date of the supposed rendezvous in the country. In every respect Jerry's alibi checked out, with whites and blacks alike verifying the account, though the whites refused to be placed on the witness stand or sign depositions. At no time had Jerry left the town, nor was he ever in the company of Will or Walker's Ned on that day. According to other slaves, Ned and Will had not crossed paths for many months, though, by Jerry's admission, they had known each other for at least twenty-five years. (Jerry claimed that Will had always been a liar and villain.)

Some ten days after Jerry's quick conviction, McIntosh attended the trial of Ingraham's Ned, whom Will had claimed he had met alone later on April 11. McIntosh was surprised that Will's testimony against the slave was word for word the same as that which he had supplied against Jerry and Walker's Ned. Was it likely that conversations held miles apart could be so curiously identical? When asked about the matter after the trial, Will refused to reply. When they had urged him to fire the town, McIntosh asked, did Jerry or the others warn him to silence? No, Will replied. Surely during a scare, with patrols everywhere, an insurrectionist would demand such a pledge. McIntosh realized that something was very much amiss. Moreover, Ingraham's Ned was acquitted. Six justices of the peace were on the bench. Four voted guilty, but James Holt, in handwriting to rival John Hancock's on the Declaration, declared him innocent. The presiding officer refused to vote at all, since a single nay was sufficient to acquit. After the trial McIntosh asked Holt why he had defied the majority. His reply was that Will clearly was "a rogue" and Ned a victim of lies. Even the presiding magistrate, who had refrained from voting, whispered that he thought Will a liar, too. But he had spared himself the frowns, or worse, of neighbors. To Monroe and council, McIntosh reported the discrepancies between Jerry's conviction and Ned's acquittal, both based on the very same testimony.

In addition, McIntosh investigated the character and possible motives of the confessor Will. In the Scotsman's opinion, the key to the episode was Will's capture on April 17. Through interviews with sundry people, he reconstructed events. Two whites, William Boush (owner of twenty slaves) and a man named Jarvis, who had been drinking very heavily, were walking along a road in Princess Anne. They spied Will ahead of them. Jarvis observed that Will was probably running away from John Floyd, a small farmer who had hired him. Jarvis grabbed Will, calling him a "great rascal," in fact "one of the sons of bitches" who had recently assembled near Norfolk for evil designs. Apparently there had been a black revival outside the town. Perhaps Jarvis had heard the unfamiliar sound of Afro-American chanting and assumed that insurrection, not worship, was the purpose. In any event, Boush told his neighbor McIntosh later, Will had denied any wrongdoing, saying "I am shure [sic] Mr. Jarvis you would not have me tell lies. . . ." Jarvis drunkenly kept saying, "You *must tell better than that*." Boush departed, and Jarvis escorted Will back to John Floyd's farm. There the two whites spent the rest of the afternoon drinking. Alternating threats of torture with promises to "let him loose," the pair wore down the slave's resistance as he stood tied to a tree nearby. Finally, by Floyd's admission to McIntosh, Will "sweat large drops for 15 minutes," and then told the story used for the prosecutions.

Further inquiries revealed to McIntosh a clearer picture of what Jarvis was: an unskilled laborer who swilled down as much rum before breakfast as his supply of money could buy. According to the Norfolk court records, he loitered about the courthouse, where, one may be sure, he heard all the exciting news of insurrections and trials. The accounts fired his imagination. Otherwise, Jarvis had no means of making a mark in community life. A former employer thought him no more trustworthy than the lowliest slave in the county. Well might such a man seize the chance to swagger on the public stage. By identifying a plotter Jarvis could not only enhance his own soiled reputation but also contribute to community welfare. After all, society offered him no higher duty than slave patrolling, no chance for acclaim except the discovery of slave wrongdoing. McIntosh discovered that Jarvis had earlier tried to induce another slave to find out "something about the conspiracy," for which testimony the slave "ought to be [set] free." The master overheard the conversation and ordered Jarvis off his place.

Still more remarkable was the disposition of the case. First, McIntosh suffered the inconveniences that too often snuffed out the lantern of reason in such cases. Former friends shunned him in the street. Witnesses who had given him valuable information refused to cooperate in the slightest way. McIntosh complained that "men are afraid to speak or act as they ought, and at this moment I am told a petition is going about for Signatures praying the negroes to be hung, as if examples without public *conviction* of their *guilt* could tend in any way to the Public Good. . . ."

At first Monroe and his council were inclined to accept McIntosh's reconstruction of events. They observed that, "even admitting the perfect credibility of Will," the death penalty was too sanguinary since "the guilt of the said slaves [Jerry and Walker's Ned] does not by any means appear to have been established." The council ordered temporary respites. John Cowper, mayor of Norfolk and presiding justice of the freeholders' court, received a demand for more proof. Cowper was outraged. "I am very much mortified to . . . state that" the executive's intercession "has produced much discontent," in fact, "almost universal discontent." The trial had been a model of equity, he said. Jerry's lawyer "made a most ingenious defence," and the prosecutor "barely expounded the law and summed up the evidence." Despite that advantage, Cowper continued, neither Jerry nor Walker's Ned had convinced a single justice or one citizen among the three hundred spectators that they were uninvolved in an Easter revolt. Furthermore, few were willing to sign McIntosh's petition for clemency for Jerry. Cowper proposed a reprieve for Walker's Ned as consolation, however, since he was "a character of simple cast" duped by his coconspirator. Monroe at once gave the second Ned the reprieve of sale and transportation. For the Norfolk citizens, Ned was an insufficient symbol of the chaos that the social exigencies required.

The outcome was tragically predictable, given the nature of the Southern executive pardon as a ratification of community will. Lacking that public sympathy, Jerry had to die. Monroe did as the mayor insisted and no more respites were forthcoming. The convicted insurrectionary was hanged on June 1, 1802. Until the final hour he had protested his guiltlessness. When asked at the last moment about his crime, he said nothing. Presumably thoughts of his pain and agony over the previous days, of his wife and children, of the kindnesses received from McIntosh and his wife, who had comforted the grieving black family, occupied his last hours. Norfolk residents took his final silence as an admission of guilt. Yet as far as they were concerned he had contributed to the common welfare more in death than ever he had in life. "I have no doubt," exulted Cowper, "but this example will produce the effect that is wished."

An anthropologist examining the insurrectionary phenomenon might well conclude that the purpose of the exercise was the restoration of order through the venting of the society's worst fears. By proclaiming that catastrophe was about to descend, the whites rallied to the banner of white supremacy and sought out victims over whom they could unmistakably triumph. Indeed, the chief result of the scares was the prevention of insurrections. By primitive but effective means, the frenzy reestablished proper race relationships, as whites defined them. In a sense, even the genuine cases of rebellion achieved this end, none being more helpful than Nat Turner's. Authentic and imagined uprisings provided the chance to display the power at white disposal. The subduing of potential rebels (real or not) reassured the dominant race that forcible, concerted means could handle any emergency. The paraphernalia of a judicial system—the county tribunals, the executive review, the sheriff's rope—were the stage props for a performance illustrating that sense of mastery. They were not the essence of the tragedy, but rather the liturgy by which slave society expressed the vitality, racial hierarchy, and oneness of white determination. Instead of signifying the strains of instability, insurrectionary upheavals demonstrated the unity of one race against the perpetually enforced disunity of another. Black was posed against black in these courtroom dramas, forced into betrayals that whites themselves manipulated.

Common interpretations of the ceremony were likewise imposed upon all whites, regardless of class or official position, forcing benevolent and indulgent masters and leaders to remember their duty to the community. By and large, those officials who carried out the will of the white constituency were, by the standards of the time, decent, honorable men. Governor Monroe, as respectable a gentleman as Virginia could produce, was an honest, humane member of the gentry class. If he had had his way, not a slave would have hanged at any time in the course of the 1802 rebellion. (The Gabriel revolt, however, may have had more serious origins in actual sedition and conspiracy.) As governor, and thus as representative of popular will, however, he had no options in the case of Jeremiah Cornick. If because of political misjudgment or a greater sense of integrity—neither of which the review process was designed to encourage—Monroe and the council had granted Jerry a reprieve, the citizens of Norfolk would have responded with a lynching, destroying not only Jerry but also the credibility and authority of the governor himself. In other words, executive defiance of local objectives would have led to instability, and to unsettling results—white perplexity and doubt.

These periodic, seemingly irrational explosions enabled masters and their families, and nonslaveholders and theirs, to express and then master their dread. Moreover, the scares offered a cheap means of public enforcement, one designed for a rural people underpoliced and fearful of taxation. After such an exhibition of white power there was no need to mount expensive guards, constabularies, and standing armies. Policing, like the legal system as a whole, remained rooted in the community. Thus the panics were "fire-bells in the night," as Jefferson once said of antislavery agitation. They were drills to test the whites' mettle and dedication. At the height of the scare, everyone became civic-minded—or else. Patrol captains meticulously followed regulations. Militiamen mustered without straggling. Even the county arsenal, for a while, was stocked with working muskets and shining sabers. It was all very reassuring and impressive to the unsophisticated. Once more the voice of inner terror was stilled.

Almost within days after the last black conspirator had been whipped or hanged, normal routines resumed. Established authorities seized the reins of power again. To them the loss of control of events had been disturbing, especially since the crisis seemed to implicate slaves of high value and loyalty. Planters gradually noticed that the white accusers often belonged to the class without slaves of their own. It was therefore good, most large planters felt, to see slaves returning quietly to the fields to harvest or plow instead of hiding in the woods to escape patrollers foraging for trouble. Even the common folk grew weary of long, dull patrol vigils. A young immigrant barkeeper in Norfolk, Virginia, complained to his father in Scotland at the close of the 1802 panic that he had had "to go out there and wait with my gun" from eight in the evening to five in the morning, before regular work, all during April and May. No wonder he missed muster roll in the summer, costing him a $40 fine. Besides, after Jerry hanged, he said, things had quieted down.

Soon enough, as the Virginia experience between 1800 and 1802 suggested, the same old problems reappeared: quarrels on the muster field, sloppy patrol rounds, broken or misplaced firearms, and other signs of mischief and public lassitude that critics had thought the recent emergency would permanently cure. A resurgence of black encroachments on white regulations (inattentiveness, tavern-going, wearing of fancy clothes, Saturday afternoon horseplay in the village square), increases in masters' largess (indiscriminate pass privileges, unsupervised black church worship), and new symptoms of economic and political woes set the stage for the next panic. Then as the cycle began again the rich and poor, the townsman and countryman, the soldier and civilian, the drunk and sober rallied to the racial banner.

For such occasions, Southern society had to have its ready supply of victims, individuals who were deviants by choice or by public decree. They provided the standard of unacceptable conduct, making clear what rules could not be broken without reprisal. As the insurrectionary ceremonies attested, the powerless and guiltless were most often the subjects of popular sacrifice. In a letter to McIntosh, Jerry spoke to the issue himself: "I have only to imploy [sic] my time in the most earnest manner in endeavouring to make peace with my God whom I call this day to witness my innocence. . . . Perhaps I may never see you more. Therefore Gratitude binds me to return to you my most sincere thanks for the many favours received at your hands. Pray Sir take care of my wife and the dear little ones . . . —and I hope that you and yours may be happy hear [sic] and hereafter[.] [It] is the sincere wish of the innocent but unfortunate Jeremiah." Yet given the passions swirling about the merchant and the slave, McIntosh had reason to be grateful, too. If Governor Monroe had not overruled Jeremiah's defender, McIntosh could also have suffered at the hands of those who were determined to make an example of anyone with discountenanced opinions. In that sense, Jeremiah was put to death, in a manner of speaking, so that McIntosh might live in peace with his neighbors and racial supremacy might prosper.

8

Tar and Feathers: Community Disorder

In a remarkable scene in *Huckleberry Finn* (1885), set before the Civil War, Mark Twain has Colonel Sherburn heap scorn on a mob gathered to lynch him. Sherburn has just killed the unarmed Boggs, a drunken old man whose reckless insults Sherburn had repaid with two shots in the chest. The crowd rages in front of Sherburn's house until he steps out, shotgun in hand, and coolly says, "The idea of *your* lynching anybody! It's amusing. . . . Because you're brave enough to tar and feather poor friendless cast-out women . . . did that make you think you had grit enough to lay your hands on a *man?*" Empty praise from Southern journalists, Sherburn continues, could not hide the fact that lynchers were cowards, no better, no worse than other men, but cowards nonetheless. Otherwise, why do juries acquit murderers? "Because they're afraid the man's friends will shoot them in the back . . . so they always acquit; and then a *man* goes in the night, with a hundred masked cowards at his back, and lynches the rascal. . . . The pitifulest thing out is a mob." The crowd dissolves, each villager slinking off to protect his own skin.

Twain gave his outrage against a common nineteenth-century phenomenon a fictional voice. In reality not many Sherburns materialized in actual history to put a community to shame. Between 1885 and 1903 there were 3,337 mob killings in the United States. (Only Utah and three New England states reported none.) Of these, 2,585 took place in the South, approximately three-fourths of the total. Most of the victims were black. In Mississippi, for instance, between 1882 and 1903 only 40 of 324 lynching deaths were of whites. The statistics reveal the continuing strength of community control of custom against the tides of social change. No single individual, however courageous, could have done much to alter the record.

Three factors ensured the permanence of popular white rule by means of charivari and lynch law. The first of these was the acquiescence, and sometimes the leadership, of those with social and official power. Second, rituals to shame or kill deviants involved the most sacred, ethical rules of the white populace. Third, the lynching rite was socially efficacious. Like the insurrectionary panic, it satisfied participants and spectators that their intent and the result of their actions were one. With no uncertainty, the social and racial values upon which white order rested were thought to be well guarded by such means. Because family purity—in lineage and reputation—was the bedrock of personal and group honor, lynchings and charivari both before and after the Civil War were concerned with misconduct, real or imagined, that threatened familial security and status. Even politically motivated lynchings—to prevent slaves from developing leadership for rebellions or, later, freedmen from voting the Republican or Populist ballots—were ultimately a means to protect white family integrity. Black advances in any aspect of life meant departure from accustomed servitude, endangering the white man's honor. Just as before the war insurrectionary panics provided mechanisms for dividing the blacks and uniting the whites, so postemancipation lynch law set the boundaries beyond which blacks were not to go. For the most part neither mode of social control was a routine occurrence, casually undertaken. By word of mouth the news of a grim summary execution traveled far and wide. A warning was conveyed. No doubt it deterred crime or "impudence," but at a price for both races—in mutual respect, compassion, and economic well-being. For lesser offenses, usually ones committed by whites, the charivari was sufficient. Though different in their levels of violence, both were ceremonies of moral purification through the sacrifice of one or more victims, polluted and profaned. As the antigambling lynchers of Vicksburg put it in 1835, respectable "heads of families, members of all classes, professions, and pursuits" were convinced that " 'order' is the 'first law' " of society, but that society "can sometimes be purified only by a storm." The hanging of numbers of riotous gamesters, averred a chronicler of the events, "will ever reflect honour on the insulted citizens" of that community. It was a common justification for lynchings.

Lynchings, like the quasi-judicial trials and executions in insurrectionary scares, differed from charivaris in the degree of violence attending them. Lynchings consciously defied the law and abstract justice and could result in an explosion of hatred, rage, and anarchy. Certainly such was the case in the aftermath of the Nat Turner Rebellion in 1831. But charivaris and sometimes the firmly controlled extralegal killings of individual (usually black) deviants were often stylized affairs. As anthropologist Victor Turner argues, the use of ritual tends to anticipate deviations and conflicts by channeling crowd actions into long-practiced forms. Ritual only half-loosens social controls; it circumscribes just how far the participants should go, thus upholding stability and order. The last chapter of this book will illustrate how the role of ritual functioned to save the life of a (fallen) member of the planter class. Although the fully unleashed mob and the ritualized charivari aroused strongly hostile feelings, both were ecstatic events. The mingling of justice with bacchanalia; centering about the scapegoat, whether a lowly black or an unpopular member of the ruling class, released social tensions in spectacle. Either the one or other form could sometimes lead to anarchy or rebellion. Most often, though, the ritual itself served to maintain order. The allegedly omnipotent forces of evil existing *within* the society were externalized in bloody reprisal or, more mildly, in the costuming of victims and participants. A recent literary exposition of this theme is John Kennedy Toole's *A Con-*

federacy of Dunces, a story of a madly comic, perversely intellectual and bedeviled protagonist. His rage against himself and his intrusive mother is expressed in wild masquerade and androgynous costume, as if Mardi Gras license characterized the everyday world of policemen, businessmen, tavern-keepers, and whites and blacks in New Orleans.

Whether collective behavior was to culminate in simple ritual or in chaos largely depended on the first issue—official leadership or the lack of it. A festival of misrule such as Mardi Gras was generally contained within bounds because its social leaders provided the authority and ceremonies to ensure a degree of public peace. Lynch law, on the other hand, often lacked these stabilizing components. Officials frequently looked the other way. In 1880, for instance, when four Yankee bank robbers were arrested in Anderson, Indiana, a crowd of over a hundred gathered to storm the jail. The sheriff gave the prisoners advice on how to use their wits to turn away the mob's wrath, but offered them no more substantial aid. As always, particularly in rural and unsophisticated American (not just Southern) communities, the officers of the law saw themselves as mediators between the populace and the institution that they represented. Neither the sheriff nor the lynchers were exceptionally cowardly. So it had always been, ever since Bacon's Rebellion: each man sought his own interests and feared, like Sherburn's mob in Twain's story, to be caught isolated and vulnerable outside the bonds of "brave" men. Honor was thus locally defined as conformity, not individuality.

Sometimes a victim's bold demeanor, a willingness to die game, could modify crowd resolve, precisely because such behavior exemplified conventional ideals. Langdon W. Moore, the leader of the Indiana bank robbers, managed to save himself and his friends with a clever mixture of feigned innocence, generous respect for the mob, and bravado. The sheriff was much relieved that a showdown did not occur. As a later observer of such police behavior noted, it was "less a matter of the individual policeman than of the [community] sanctions behind it."

Sometimes too, a figure of local prominence tried to save the victim, but not always with much success. In the Mississippi insurrectionary scare of 1835, despite his long-practiced courtroom eloquence Henry S. Foote was unable to rescue a young Kentucky boatman from summary execution as a supposed member of the mythical Murrell gang. Not long afterward, at Clinton, Mississippi, he also tried to protect a slave boy falsely accused of rebellion. "I am not willing," he told the excited throng, "that a few generous-minded young men" should have to bear the blame for a wrongful death, once the frenzy subsided. Only eight or ten took the attorney's side. "I left the spot with feelings of sorrow and disgust," Foote recalled. "The boy was swung into eternity in less than fifteen minutes." He warned the slave's owner, a wealthy, respected widow, not to prosecute, but "to bow to the imperious necessity of the hour"—to save her own life.

Although nearly every Southern community had leaders no less capable of firm principles than Henry Foote, those who held local power ofttimes shared the convictions of the neighborhood. For instance, in 1911 Joshua W. Ashleigh, a state legislator of South Carolina, headed a crowd of Greenville residents that dismembered a black accused of raping a white girl. His son, editor of the local paper, not only assisted but announced in print that he "went out to see the fun without the least objection to being a party to help lynch the brute." Though scarcely one who would have participated in such gruesome rites, U.S. Senator John Sharp Williams, a patrician from Mississippi, argued in the same era that "race is greater than law now and then, and protection of woman transcends all law, human and divine." Most political leaders could not for a moment question the general legitimacy of lynchings. A famous twentieth-century example was the struggle between Tom Watson, former Populist leader and editor of the Atlanta *Jeffersonian,* and Governor John Slaton of Georgia. Watson whipped up an impassioned mob to ensure the conviction of Leo Frank, a Jewish factory superintendent who allegedly raped and killed Mary Phagan, a white working girl. Under duress from milling crowds outside, the jury convicted Frank on the slimmest of evidence, to the outrage of the entire Western world. "THE VOICE OF THE PEOPLE IS THE VOICE OF GOD," declared Watson; by Frank's hanging, *"Wom-*

anhood is made safer, everywhere." Then in 1915 the governor commuted Frank's sentence to life imprisonment. Not long afterward a
lynch mob seized Frank at the penitentiary and hanged him in
the dark of night. Like the fictional, hapless Major Molineux,
who had also faced public anger and demand for scapegoats,
Governor Slaton had underestimated the power that common folk
held. To be sure, ten thousand Georgians as well as the presiding
judge at the trial had bid the governor to act with mercy, a showing
unimaginable twenty years before. Judging from the enthusiastic
response to Watson's flaming editorials, however, it must be concluded that the subsequent lynching had widespread approval. On
the other hand, Governor Slaton was disgraced. Only the Georgia
National Guard stood between him and a raging mob, and he had
to flee the state. In this case it was Tom Watson, aging warhorse of
a failed Populist crusade, who cackled in glee over the humiliated
governor's flight, in a way not unlike Hawthorne's "Authority."

The second type of Southern mob action, the charivari, being
a less bloodthirsty, more festive occasion, was more parallel with
church ritual and custom than was lynch law, which was more a
complement to ordinary judicial procedure. (Fine distinctions are
nonetheless hard to draw, and lynchings, at least in the hands of
Ku Kluxers, also had their liturgical aspect, as will be explained
later.) The charivari included a range of crowd activity, from wed-
ding-day jest to public whipping and tar-and-feathering. It was a
means of community policing stretching back to Neolithic Europe.
Examples can be drawn from Portugal to the Balkans, the Levant
to the Hebrides, from Plutarch's *Moralia* in the first century A.D.
and the Old Testament book of Leviticus to news reports from
present-day Belfast and Londonderry. (Not long ago, an Ulster
Catholic girl who fraternized with an English officer was treated to
a dousing in tar and feathers.)

In some cases the crowd prepared effigies or simply made noises
imitating howling wolves, cackling geese, and clucking chickens
while ringing cowbells and beating on pots and drums. In its more
serious form, the victim was not just serenaded in this fashion, but
whipped and forced to wear a disfiguring guise, reducing the indi-

vidual from human to animal order. The goat or ass was often associated with the rite. "And the goat shall bear upon him all their iniquities," reads Leviticus 16:22. On the Day of Atonement, the priest laid hands on a live goat selected by lot, transferring by ritual words the sins of the people to the beast, which "a fit man" would then release in the wilderness. "Scapegoating" was the literal meaning of the rite. It continued to be the essence of charivari—as well as lynchings—through the millennia.

Thus the figure of shame was made to ride a goat or ass. In America or England the one ridiculed was placed on a ladder, pole, or rail. In England this unpleasant means of transportation was called "stang-riding," or "riding the skimmington." Meantime a crowd gathered about, and the marchers were accompanied by "rough music" or, in Germany, *Katzenmusik*. In America, the noisy procession was called a "rogue's march." Tar and feathers were often, although not always, smeared on the offender. As early as in post-Homeric Greece, if not much earlier, tar or pitch was mentioned in connection with the ridiculing of homosexuals, though the emphasis was on their effeminacy rather than on public ceremonies of befouling. In any event, tar was associated with charivari in those locations where the ugly substance was used in quantity for ship caulking—places such as European ports, colonial Boston, or the river towns of the Mississippi Valley. In all these folk customs there was no insistence on particular devices or materials. What mattered was symbolic intent, not punctilious regularity. The prehistoric origin of the ritual may have been connected with Indo-European human sacrifice. The Iron Age European, Celt, or Teuton, apparently pulled a victim, carefully fed and freed from labor, about the countryside in a decorated cart. Then this human votive offering to Nerthus (Fertility), this Scapegoat King as it were, was strangled and thrown in a bog.

Because of the religious significance attached to the rites, the early Christian church tried to eliminate pagan meaning from the custom. In A.D. 1133, for instance, the Monk of St. Trond complained bitterly that villagers still accompanied the Ship of Wheels (*Narrenschiff*, ship of fools) out of its hiding place in the Germanic forest. Human sacrifice had no doubt ceased, but the enterprise disturbed the early church fathers nevertheless. The Statute of Beziers of 1368 denounced such activity as the *ludum iniquitatis,* the evil game. The Edict of Avignon, some years earlier, declared it "obnoxious sport." Nevertheless, the custom endured, chiefly as a young men's frolic. It lived on vigorously as a way for them to enforce community values, whatever the church might do to curb it. To this day, *el vito* (mocking dance), *la pandorga* (the mobbing-up), or *cencerrada* (cowbell-ringing) persists as a means of ridiculing violators of local morality in Spanish rural provinces. Despite centuries of sporadic attempts at suppression, the church as well as civil authorities in Spain have not wholly repressed the folk tradition. It retains, to some degree, its sacred heritage as a scapegoating rite for community evils. When confronted with the opposition of regular authorities, the reply of those engaged has ever been—in America as in present-day Basque districts—"We have given this Charivari because it is our right."

For hundreds of years, ecclesiastical precept and attempts to impose outsiders' law on community life but failed to halt such proceedings, in either the Old World or the New. Only as society became more secular in character, more impersonal in its dealings, and more institutional in its forms of exchange and control did the ancient ideal of community justice erode. In the American South that transformation was somewhat slower than in the rest of the country. There, where a form of primal honor continued to flourish, one could find the same attitudes about aliens, deviants, and social underlings as once existed in very ancient times.

Because of its persistence as a festive as well as shaming rite, the church and even the state adjusted their practices to accommodate the popular mode. For instance, common-law punishments prior to the great reformation of penal policies in the late eighteenth century consisted largely of folk tradition carried out under the aegis of the law, itself a ritualistic and supposedly divine institution. The penalty for thievery on Richard I's crusade in 1189 was, by royal edict, the tar-and-feathering of the felon before he was set upon land and abandoned. In England as late as 1722, Eleanor Elson, who had killed her husband, was first covered in tar, with "a tarred bonnet put on her head," then hanged before she was enveloped in flames. In 1779 a fourteen-year-old girl, a member of a counterfeiting ring, was to be burned after being covered with tar, but a nobleman prevented the ritual from being carried out.

In America many of the common-law customs were allowed to die out or were never introduced. Yet as late as 1796, to take one example, South Carolinian statute still provided that a woman illicitly with child was to be not only fined for bastardy but also forced to walk behind the "cart's tail," as the phrase went, as it was drawn through the streets of Charleston. The objective was to encourage citizens to join in the customary charivari, pelting the woman with stones and sticks and accompanying the procession with the requisite "rough music."

Just as the law found ways to incorporate community rites, so the church adopted the rituals. Many of them made their way into morality plays in comic, cuckold characterizations. In A.D. 837 Pope Gregory transformed the Druids' rites of the dead on November 1 to All Souls' Day, or Hallowe'en. Most popular of all was the Feast of Fools, derived from the Roman Kalends, one day of which has come down to us as the New Year's celebration. In the slave South, as in ancient times, it was a time of holiday, with much drinking, dancing, and even some loosening of the bonds of slavery. The mummeries of the Old World were continued particularly in Catholic Louisiana, where whites and blacks fashioned the decorated carts (the modern-day floats) and paraded with music through the streets of New Orleans. A "Rex" was chosen and honored in mock deference. In Scotland the figure was called the Abbot of Unreason, in England the Lord of Misrule, but the object was the same: the brief throwing off of the ordinary monotonies and restrictions of institutional life, customarily corrupt and unpredictable even in the best of times. The participants were chiefly young people, especially unmarried young men. (In New Orleans, however, old aristocrats took the coveted masked role of "Rex.") In Mobile, leaders of the Mardi Gras, mostly young militia officers and planters' sons, called themselves "the Cowbellions." In revels, as in lynchings, male youths served, with their elders' blessing, as the "conscience of the community by making" themselves "the raucous voice of that conscience"—and of pleasure, as an early modern European scholar has pointed out.

Although the religious-festive aspects of Mardi Gras in the Catholic Deep South are too well known to require examination, it is possible to find similar traditions in Protestant sections of the Old South. Slaves sometimes acted out fantasies of power by wearing masks, dancing nimbly in the streets, and subtly ridiculing their masters. In 1830 the Rev. Moses Ashley Curtis described a saturnalia in Wilmington, North Carolina:

> The negroes have a singular custom here . . . of dressing out in rags & masks, presenting a most ludicrous appearance imaginable. They are accompanied by a troop of boys singing, bellowing, beating sticks, dancing & begging. Three or four of these John Cooners as they are ycleped [called] made their appearance to day. One of them was completely enveloped in strips of cloth of every color which depended in the most ragged confusion from every part of his ebony hip. Over his face was drawn the nether part of a raccoon skin from the center of which hung the tail signifying that "nasal attributes are meant here." On each side of the tail appeared two holes through which shone the whites of his eyes. . . . Then dancing & his rags flying & his flexible nose gamboling about his face, singing with a gruff voice in concert with his satellites, I was ready to burst with laughter.

Curtis thought that the custom had been introduced by visiting Frenchmen some years before. African origins were more likely. But in traditional societies the world over mask and revelry, religion and entertainment were universal combinations, though the specific forms differed from one society to another. What mattered to the Episcopal clergyman, however, was the eventual disappearance of such heathenish practices as the saturnalia, especially since he observed that some of the young blacks involved had ended their revel with a session around a jug that left them insensible.

Special religious events aside from the seasonal occasions were also subject to the boisterous jest of charivari, most particularly a marriage celebration. Vance Randolph, for instance, described the "shivaree" as practiced in the twentieth-century Ozarks. The day of a wedding a company of bachelors first selected a captain who led the way to the newlyweds' home and removed the obstacles—hidden wires and the like—placed in the young bachelors' path by the bridegroom. The new husband was supposed to treat the visitors for as long as they wished to make merry—all night if need be. (The newly married couple was not supposed to have intercourse the first night; marriages were as much public as private events in Southern folk society.) If his hospitality fell short of expectations, a mock shivaree with a riding to a nearby creek and dunking usually followed. In 1830, at St. Louis, a thousand to twelve hundred ruffians *"charivaried"* the wealthy Colonel John O'Fallon on the evening of his second marriage. In customary fashion, the colonel sent word to the cowbell-ringing, chicken-crowing throng that he considered them a "respectable company of gentlemen" who were his "friends," and promised to pay for all their entertainment that night. The pledge cost him a thousand dollars but, said a city chronicler, he had no choice; "such was the honor and respect" that had to be "paid to power" of the "loafers and rabble."

The significance of this kind of charivari, even in its most jocular vein, was its mixture of fun and hostility, an ambivalence about the marital event itself. In rural backwaters where these games were prevalent as late as the early twentieth century, the bridal couple celebrated not only love but also freedom from the yoke of parents and the beginning of independence. For the bachelor friends of the groom, however, there was joy, jealousy, and a sense of comradely loss. Moreover, for the small neighborhood itself the new status of the nuptial pair meant a change in family arrangements and alliances, perhaps for the better, possibly for the worse. The purpose of the tricks and jokes was to act out these mixed emotions in a structured though unruly way, without serious jeopardy to the marriage. In small-scale societies, anything that required abrupt readjustment in community relations entailed uncertainty. The charivari helped assuage that anxiety. It also provided a way to resolve it: the groom and bride eventually regained privacy, and the revelers had to go home to solitary beds.

As the benign form of "shivaree" in the example of wedding jollity suggests, the central concern among the common folk of the South was to preserve family reputation and inviolability. By and large, the social impact of gossip sufficed to keep family members true to communal values. In some honor-shame cultures, most notably in Spain, North Africa, and the Levant, women were held in close confinement. Men, indeed all members of society, dreaded the possibility of sexual misbehavior and maintained strict means of guarding against it. In the Old South, although chaperones in the upper ranks were common, young girls and women generally enjoyed much greater latitude in this regard. Anglo-American tradition permitted women a wide range of acquaintances, associations, and even occupations, at least by comparison with the Mediterranean mode. As a consequence, gossip was the mechanism used to enforce restraint and hold everyone in the grip of public scrutiny. Also, it gave meaning to the lives of those who had little standing themselves. In 1622, for instance, William Gouge, an English writer on manners, remarked, "When servants of divers houses men or maids meet together, all their talke for the most part is of their masters and mistresses, whereby it cometh to pass that all the secrets of the house are soone knowne about the whole towne or city."[16] So it was, too, in rural America, where democracy opened all to the public gaze, and most especially in the slaveholding South. Despite the isolation, slaves in field and house soon spread the word of goings-on among the whites, conveying information faster, sometimes, than masters thought possible.

As a result, talebearing was not an "idle" pastime, though the gossipers in fact may have had little better to do. The exchange of speculations and opinions among the whites served to guide all members of the community toward a common set of standards for sexual and marital behavior. True, in church circles, of which there was a growing number throughout the antebellum years, church members and elders in rural settings did not hesitate to warn male-factors publicly or even to expel them if they were impenitent. Gossip, however, was used by churchgoers and nonchurchgoers alike as the least disruptive and most effective way to impose social sanctions. It helped to name who belonged and who should be excluded. The power of rumor may be seen in the fact that there were so many suits for defamation, particularly in the early years of American settlement. False reports from unbridled tongues had to be regarded as a social and certainly a personal menace. Such irresponsible behavior threw doubt on legitimate gossip. Sometimes charivari or, in colonial times, the "cucking" or "ducking" stool of ancient folk and common-law custom was the remedy for excessive and divisive rumor-mongering. Despite constant complaints about the danger of idle speculations, especially women's, Southern folk society was accustomed to use gossip as the first line of community defense against individual waywardness. When that resource or church admonition failed, then, it was thought, more stringent measures should be invoked.

A grim destiny awaited the serious violator of family and gender ethics. Among the deviants singled out for charivari were promiscuous unmarried women—prostitutes or otherwise; wives adulterous or violent toward their husbands; and both women and men who made marriages deemed incongruous. The charivari was also used for certain kinds of male offenses, from chronic inebriation to political or religious unconventionality. By no means were these rough exercises confined to the South. Charivaris, usually for sexual offenses, could be found in late nineteenth-century New York, New Hampshire, and other New England states, but they had all but disappeared from the more populous and sophisticated Yankee areas. The punitive "shivaree" flourished most widely in the Mississippi Valley, from Iowa to New Orleans. The reason was not the inadequacy of frontier justice, but rather the continuation of primal modes of social control that farming and pastoral folk still found useful as their ancestors had before them. Primitive conditions, not simply the dislocating process of settlement alone, held men and women true to these customs. In new settlements of sophisticated planters in the West one was unlikely to find these ancient traditions, but among common folk, whatever their location might be, there the old heritage lived on.

Not surprisingly, charivaris were very popular among the Creoles and Cajuns of the coastal Southwest, from the late seventeenth century to the 1940s. Probably the most celebrated one—over an incongruous marital union—took place in New Orleans about midway between those dates. In 1798 the young widow of the enormously wealthy Don Andres Almonster y Roxas remarried too soon. The bridegroom did not suit the New Orleans populace. For three days large crowds surrounded the house of the bridal pair. "Many were in disguise dresses and masks," wrote a foreign observer, "and hundreds were on horseback; and all had some kind of noisy musical instrument, as old kettles, shovels and tongs, and clanging metals." The masqueraders drew carts containing effigies of the former husband in a coffin and the second lover, while another mummer impersonated the widow. Refusing to respond in the required spirit of gracious submission, the widow found herself ostracized and rudely treated in the streets for weeks thereafter. Finally, she gave three thousand dollars "in solid coin" for an outdoor mass to mollify opinion. In the 1940s it was still customary in isolated bayou country to carry out this relatively harmless but hostile sort of charivari, with nightly appearances lasting as long as thirty days.

High on the list for still more serious doses of community ridicule were girls who violated the code of chastity. The evidence was the appearance of an illegitimate child. Charivaris in Europe most often centered on such unwelcome events. The shaming rite was also used for this purpose in the South, Old and New. Vance Randolph recalled from his Ozark experiences in the 1920s that in one Arkansas settlement a girl had caused so much trouble for other men's wives that the neighbors "decided to 'drum her out.' About thirty men and women appeared at her cabin one morning, firing pistols, beating on tin pans, and yelling at the top of their voices." Without a word she ran out the door and was not seen in those parts again.

Her relations were utterly "humiliated rather than belligerent." They made no attempt to protect or avenge her. In fact, they accepted the community verdict and acted as if she had never belonged to the family. Yet exceptions should be noted. In the far backlands, according to another investigator as well as to Vance Randolph, mountain girls were allowed to produce a child before wedlock. In this way a girl's fecundity would be assured. (Herbert G. Gutman, a leading authority on the black family, has discovered the same phenomenon among slave girls and in modern black culture as well.) Ely Green, a mulatto from Sewanee, Tennessee, recalled a most unusual example of sexual practice and family reaction in the isolated Lost Cove valley near there sometime in the 1890s. A daughter in the Cannon clan, a large "covite" family, was living with a black partner, Alf Cannon, her father's former slave. When whites from Sherwood came to drive the couple out, her brothers took up arms. The mob wheeled off. "The Cannons were a tough sort. They made them scram," Ely Green concluded admiringly. However, in most parts of the Southern hill country, as elsewhere, the "shameless" woman was a local byword, one who risked public humiliation.

Women who beat their husbands or entertained gallants at the expense of their husband's reputation were another category of miscreants. At Turkey Hills, Massachusetts, in 1761 a Mrs. Phelps was seized for both offenses. A crowd of young people "carried her on a rail, blowing horns and ringing cow bells" in the traditional fashion. In the American South such customs persisted well beyond the more disorderly eighteenth century. Following the First World War, believers in traditional ethics, whether they were city dwellers or countrymen, were horrified at the secular ways of the new America. They undertook organized missions to repress an upsurge of age-old vices, as well as new ones such as gangsterism and bootlegging. In Muskogee, Oklahoma, for instance, a defender of old-fashioned community retribution in all its forms declared, "I have not seen a case . . . that all the leading good people of the town have not said, 'It's a good thing, push it along.' It moves out the gangster, bootlegger . . . fast and loose females, and the man who abuses and neglects his wife and children." Moral offenses—adultery and fornication among them—were part of the repertoire of the post–World War I Ku Klux Klan, with whippings, tar-and-feathering, and sometimes branding the usual penalties during that era of community anxiety and dread of a sort of social change that was beyond popular comprehension.

Defense of womanly virtue and family standing was always a prominent motive for community action, one that sometimes involved the victimizing of adulterous, abusive, or philandering men. For instance, in 1730 a visitor to North Carolina found that the last Anglican clergyman in the region was known for his sexual proclivities. He "Importun'd a Woman to give him a Nights Lodging but no sooner had the parson his Cloths off" than a party of irate women came with horsewhips "& Chastized the poor naked Parson to that Degree that He took his Horse next Morning & has never been seen since. . . ." (The notion that women could act in this way, in violation of their submissive role toward any male, moral or immoral, surprised the observer. In 1707 a similar incident took place in Boston, where an assembly of both sexes hauled a man from his house, tore off his clothes, and beat him with rods for harsh treatment of his wife. The local magistrate was so alarmed that he had the women in the crowd whipped in retaliation.) Likewise, both an adulterous wife and a cuckolded husband might be given mob punishment, on the grounds that he was as recreant as she in meeting the duties of gender. Moreover, townsmen did not take lightly affronts to their virgins. In Charlotte, North Carolina, in 1845, for instance, three young men had made up enormous posters directing obscenities against "some of the respected young ladies of the community," the local editor said, and had nailed the signs to the courthouse door. Early the next morning the villagers were highly agitated. The town's young men found the culprits out, gained confessions, and rode all three on a rail, each covered in the customary feathery garb. The newspaper piously denounced the rough work, but excused it on the grounds that all townsfolk had agreed about the imperative for "summary punishment." After all,

the pranksters had defamed their own sex by casting unjust asper-
sions on the good name of the girls and their families.

Punishments on behalf of family regularity and social control of
female behavior were always prominent in American as well as in
foreign charivaris. Yet in this country there was a second category
of offenses that were not to be tolerated and for which popular justice was the favored remedy. These were, first, the fairly petty in-
fractions that the law overlooked or punished more lightly than the
community judged proper, and second, misdemeanors that only became a public nuisance because of their number, not their character. An example of the first was the irritant of small thievery and
trading with slaves—two offenses that were almost synonymous in
parts of the South. Ofttimes the malefactor was thought to be a
Yankee peddler, a figure usually regarded with deep suspicion. (He
might be an abolitionist spy "tampering" with the slaves.) Even if
an outbreak of purloining might actually have been traceable to
some local poor white who was trading whiskey for a master's stolen
provender, nevertheless the peddler was a convenient scapegoat. In
1839 in Elizabeth City, North Carolina, for instance, one Charles
Fife from Connecticut was suspected of trading with blacks. The
offense could not be proved in court, so some young men of the
village gave him a pole ride through town, followed by the tar-and-
feather ritual. When the peddler, claiming innocence, refused to
leave town, the rowdies repeated the ceremony the next Sunday.
Fife then sued his enemies before Judge John L. Bailey, a young
planter, but in the midst of the proceedings the ruffians leaped on
the plaintiff and his lawyer and beat them up before the bench.
Judge Bailey acquitted the defendants and fined Fife $100—without
evidence or prior indictment—for trading with Negroes. Fife, at last,
left town.

Sometimes poor whites actually were caught at "Negro-trading."
In 1829 Mrs. Rachel O'Connor's slaves stole some corn and sold it to
a yeoman near Jackson, Louisiana. The young village braves gathered and, she reported, made the suspected tradesman ride a pine
pole all through the town. "His wife clamored all the while for

them to stop," but instead "they put her on the same pole, and gave them a ride together." The slaves meantime fled homeward.

An illustration of a minor infraction that required "shivaree" was a rash of riotous drinking. Towns and crossroads were sometimes plagued by yeomen and laborers who came to grog shops on Saturday and ended up in the jailhouse for the night, paying only a light fine. Residents wearied of the noise and stench. In 1838 matters were so out of hand in Windsor, North Carolina, that young villagers seized those "staggering about the streets" and gave them due warning "by blacking and painting their faces and putting them in boxes." As in many such charivaris, the perpetrators had disguised themselves. Although fear of retaliation from the abused parties was a factor, as Twain's Sherburn had observed, anonymity served to give the impression of complete community solidarity— making the ritual a more sobering experience than punishment at the hands of particular individuals would be. William D. Valentine of Windsor, who recorded these proceedings, was delighted with the results. Lawyer though he was, he considered "wretches" all those who demeaned "their family's standing" by public drunkenness. They had committed "an unpardonable sin," he believed, for which the shaming penalties were almost insufficient.

Finally, the shame ritual was appropriate for the political or religious deviant. "Rough music" had accompanied the departures of Tories in many of the colonies during the American Revolution. Many years later, in the 1880s, when Mormons began their missionary efforts in the South they were often subjected to tar-and-feathering, even mob shootings. Needless to say, they had previously suffered such persecutions in the North and West in the days before the Civil War. Efforts to prosecute the mobsters through the law failed utterly. A Georgia court reminded the complainants from Utah that the state "recognized no law for Mormons"; their polygamy was thought to be a particularly heinous sin.

Defense of sacred notions of family purity was even more applicable to advocates of abolitionism. The Southern *cordon sanitaire* descended on all forms of public antislavery agitation after the Missouri Debates in Congress (1819–21), and even more so after Turner's Rebellion and the appearance of William Lloyd Garrison's *Liberator* in 1831. Nor was the initial popular hostility confined solely to the slaveholding states. Although tar-and-feathering had diminished since the triumph of the Patriot cause in 1781, the practice revived in Yankee political affairs over the slavery issue, which proved no less divisive than the Revolution. For instance, in 1837 the Rev. Marius Robinson, a youthful Ohio member of Theodore Weld's antislavery band, was kidnapped by a dozen or so men, stripped naked, tarred, and feathered. At dawn a Trumbull County, Ohio, farmer found him in a nearly incoherent state, lying in a ditch.

Needless to say, such incidents occurred with greater frequency in the South. A one-legged Yankee clock mender in Dothan, Alabama, for instance, talked too openly about the merits of "free soil." His penalty was a session of repeated duckings in a nearby waterhole and a boisterous escort to the edge of town, riding a rail and accompanied with the usual "rogue's march" of cacophonous music. Native Southerners also had to be very circumspect about airing their feelings on the touchy subject of race emancipation. At Columbia, South Carolina, recalled an old-timer, a stonemason named Powell had spoken up for the freedom of blacks. His fellow workers and others seized him, ran him to "Fisher's Pond," and removed his clothes; then "he was well smeared with tar, then a pillow-case was opened and he was feathered."

In essence, lynching was a charivari with deadly as well as shaming intent. Like the charivari, it was often associated with community efforts to protect family security and conventions, but the perceived menace was not as manageable as a girl's wandering affections, a mistake in marital choice, or an oversupply of local drunks. Instead, the problem was often regarded as a gross violation of race custom or rule. Frequently, a black victim was alleged to have raped a white woman. The charge was often patently fraudulent and other motives, such as fears provoked by black tendencies to independence, refusal to be servile, or signs of economic advance, were involved. Particularly after the Civil War these "violations" were a hidden factor beneath the more sensational accusation. In any case, the two were linked: black economic parity with whites would, many believed, encourage "amalgamation." From the point of view of the lynchers it scarcely mattered whether the sexual offense was real or not. Family defense and white racial supremacy were so inextricably mingled in the public mind that the victim's "crime" boiled down to the sheer effrontery of remaining alive after he had been accused of whatever it was that aroused popular fury.

In proceeding with a lynching, the Southern white mob did not necessarily show much sense of ritual. Rumors circulated about a crime and its perpetrator, and then the accused was seized from his home or place of work or the jail and tortured, humiliated, and hanged or burned. But even that simple, grim rite had overtones of religious meaning. It was carried out in the name of Christian rule—the maintenance of divine as well as human order, which decreed the separation of black from white, the honored from the forever honorless.

At times of unusual social and racial stress, however, lynchings were carried out with some attention to liturgy and magical paraphernalia. The Ku Klux Klans and other secret fraternal orders (chiefly made up of young men) arose after both the Civil War and the First World War. The commercialism of the second Klan was based on the impulse for pomp, masquerade, and religious ceremony. The Klan of the 1860s and 1870s, however, indulged in such fantasies in a less artificial, moneymaking way than the manufactured machinery that "Doc" Simmons and Hiram Evans hawked throughout the country in the 1920s. With post–Civil War Emancipation and then congressional intervention in Southern "home rule," all the most horrible nightmares of Southern whites, rich and poor, suddenly seemed to burst upon their society in satanic retribution. The supernaturalism of the Klan rituals, dress, and language deserves more attention as windows into the Southern white soul than historians, preoccupied with the political aspects of racism, have been willing to give.

The early robes of the Klan, reminisced the chroniclers of the Klan's founding at Pulaski, Tennessee, in 1866, were white, "the emblem of purity for the preservation of the home and for the protection of the women and children. . . ." The trimmings, sewed by Pulaski matrons, were red, "emblem of the blood which Klansmen were ready to shed in defense of the helpless." But there was no uniformity. Some Klansmen of that era wore robes of black trimmed with white, with a red cloth to mark the mouth. Some robes were entirely red. Hawthorne's bizarrely costumed militia leader would have been properly attired for a Klan rally. The headgear varied as well, but the customary symbols of charivari were certainly unmistakable. Caps were tall and conical or crowned with horns, a phallic representation as old as the charivari itself. The cowbird's or cuckold's horns, the horns of the Devil, were chosen for the Klansman's headpiece with no self-conscious or contrived intent: such gear was simply a tradition.

In the early Reconstruction Klan rituals, after the usual oaths of allegiance the blindfolded initiate was covered in a "royal robe" and had a "royal crown" placed on his head and a "sacred sword-belt" strapped to his side, recalled William B. Romine of Tennessee. Then the blindfold was removed and the new recruit saw "in the altar (a mirror) that his robe was a donkey skin, his crown an old torn hat bedecked with donkey ears, and his sword-belt a common saddle-belt." The horseplay mingled the customary seriousness of fraternal ritual with a mocking spirit. So it had always been in the *ludum iniquitatis* so typical of young men's games since prehistoric times. To be sure, the eclectic nature of the Klan's title for the organization (from *kuklos,* the Greek word for circle) and for officers—Grand Gyclops, Grand Exchequer, Lictor, "Hydras, Furies, Gobbins [*sic,* Goblins?], and Night Hawks"—indicated borrowings from Masonry and college Greek-letter fraternity usages. In turn, these clubs, too, in many respects, reflected honor-shame traditions.[28]

No doubt for many members of the post-Emancipation Klan and its revived successor these were mere trappings, with little inherent meaning. The main objective was to frighten the allegedly gullible blacks who, whites thought, were subject to unsophisticated fears of ghosts, monsters, and other apparitions of the night. Costuming, then, was secondary to putting the black in his place by whippings or worse. Nevertheless, we must remember that the common white folk were themselves not immune from dread of supernatural manifestations. The impulse to overcome the evils of the world by donning a fantastic mask and other regalia was indeed still thought to be a way to master events and drive off evils, seen and unseen. The Klan "magic" made men feel unconquerable, with purposes blessed by God.

At a revival service in Blount County, Alabama, in 1870, the relationship between supernaturalism and Klan activity was particularly evident. During the service the wife of the presiding preacher gave birth to a stillborn, deformed baby, at her home near the campground. A witness before a congressional hearing into anti-black atrocities later declared that the malformed baby "was a perfect representation and facsimile of a disguised Ku Klux": the infant's forehead was square and flat and about "three times the height of an ordinary child"; near the temples two small horns appeared; "around the neck was a scarlet red band; and from the point of the shoulder, extending down each side to about the center of the abdomen, was all scarlet red." Displayed before the fifteen hundred worshippers at the revival, the chimera created a great sensation. It was regarded as a judgment on the preacher, a white who had twice been beaten for failing to join the Klan and for preaching against it. During the congressional hearing the congressmen asked for a description of Klan attire and witnesses described it in terms resembling the child's appearance. Indeed, the violent mummers often claimed supernatural powers for themselves. One North Carolina witness at the hearings said that the Klansmen boasted "in my county that a man could not kill a Ku-Klux; they said that they could not be hit; that if they were the ball would bounce back and kill you. I thought though that I would try it. . . ." He had in fact wounded a Ku-Kluxer.

Blacks knew better than to be as fearful of Klansmen's supposed magical powers as they were of the Klan's real power to inflict immediate, ghastly pain. For all the Klansmen's bragging that they had "come from the moon," ridden with ghosts on the wind, and consumed gallons of water without a swallow, their truly fearsome aspect was the ethical certitude of divine command with which they meted out the Klan's punishments. Half-belief in magic gave the Ku-Kluxer all the assurance he needed to treat violators of his sacred principles as if they were less than animals. In this spirit, Klan work included all the humiliating rites against sexual offenders—whites guilty of common-law mating with black women, supposed black rapists, prostitutes of both colors—and petty thieves (mostly hog stealers), plus unnumbered punishments and killings of political activists in the Republican parties of the Southern states.

The work was quasi-judicial and quasi-religious at the same time, at least by the standards of the primal ethic. Yet as in Hawthorne's story, the grimmest of lynchings, whether carried out by Klansmen or by an aroused throng, had its celebratory side. At Maysville, Kentucky, in 1899, for instance, Robert Coleman, a black who confessed to having killed his employer's wife, was marched to the outskirts of town by a crowd numbering in the thousands. Tied to a tree and surrounded by a pile of dry brush, the victim screamed for mercy. His pleas only increased the will of the mob that he should die as painfully and slowly as possible. The murdered woman's husband was given the honor of applying the first match. Her brother lit the second. Then a third relative gouged Coleman's chest with a knife. His eyes had already been burned when an onlooker threw acid in an eggshell into them. Somehow he lived through these ordeals for at least three hours, while the fire, deliberately made to burn slowly, consumed him. The newspaper account declared that "all the leaders of the mob were well known and . . . some are the leading citizens in all lines of business and many are members of churches. . . ." To visit upon the sinner the fires of hell was simply to carry out on earth the fate awaiting him on the other side. Such a rite of complete exorcism—the total obliteration of the victim's remains—was seldom if ever performed on a white, but a member of the alien race was not even to be allowed the burial of a dog. For those outside the sacred white circle no absolution, no opportunity to live, even in disgrace, was considered fitting if the crime supposedly committed was judged fiendish. But mockery and amusement were still part of the ritual. For all its inhumanity, it was—sad to say—a very human event. The community rejoiced that an evil had been avenged. There was no wrenching sense of guilt. The tortures and death expelled guilt; they did not incur it. The festivities signaled that feature. Even children were allowed to share the pleasure. "All afternoon," noted the *New York Times* report of the Coleman murder, "children, some of them not more than six years old, kept the fire blazing around the blackened body by throwing grass, brush, bits of boards, and everything combustible that they could get together. This they kept up until dark," when mothers called them home for supper.

The festive character of the Southern charivari and lynching suggests the efficacy of these tragic rites. The chief aim was the protection of traditional values and conventions against forces outside as well as within the community. They were simple group dramas in which evil was defeated, good was reinstated. By that means virtues were reconfirmed, boundaries of conduct set, and allegiances to the *deme* revitalized. The execution of lawful sentences could do the same, so long as spectators were present to see that the will of court and community was carried out. But particularly after Reconstruction governments abolished public hangings and whippings, that sort of popular participation in the enforcement of decisions was no longer possible. Yet the ethic of honor and shame lived on for another half-century, through the system of summary justice. People thought they needed to see the actual triumph of right over wrong, not just be told about it in a newspaper summary of how the felon looked and acted in his final moments.

Like Robin Molineux, the witness to an official hanging or a popular action felt the alternations of "pity and terror," the twin Aristotelian responses to tragedy, feelings often followed by hilarity. This primal psychology had begun to disturb the sensibilities of some thoughtful reformers in England and America early in the nineteenth century. A movement to abolish public hangings, if not the penalty itself, gradually won victories in the Northern states and finally, in 1867, in Great Britain. It was thought preferable to make the death penalty a private business, behind walls, impersonal, no longer a public drama, or carnival, of savagery and death. In the Southern states the end of public executions did not come until Reconstruction. Until then, however, the practice excited common folk, whites and blacks alike, who streamed to the site. William Faulkner's great-grandfather, William C. Falkner, upon first arriving in Mississippi, wrote up a condemned murderer's confession in 1845 and sold it to the thousands attending the execution at Ripley. Similarly, hawking penny sheets and broadsides, "last confessions" and doggerel verse was in the best of English tradition at Tyburn and later at Newgate. Public displays, of course, did little to deter crime, but they brought home to spectators—most often men and women who were at the edge of the law themselves—their luck in being alive. The misery of another made life a little sweeter.

George J. Holyoake, a British observer in the 1860s, explained the crowd's feelings at Newgate—emotions no different from those of the spectators at an American hanging or lynching. "The wretch," he said, "stands face to face with inevitable pitiless premeditated death. Not the scythe, but the strange cold cord of death strikes against his ear, and the crowd knows he knows it. They see the neck. The noose is adjusted, the click of the drop is heard . . . and the wretch descends still in sight; and then the rain, the cold, the damp, the struggling of the night is all forgotten in the coveted gratification of that . . . moment."

For the American writer Mark Twain, however, justice of this kind was hard to comprehend, particularly if the community will, not the law, was being served. He could not bring himself, skeptic though he was, to think that "people at a lynching enjoy the spectacle and are glad of a chance to see it. It cannot be true; all experience is against it." In reaction to the atrocities that blacks suffered at the turn of the nineteenth cenury, Twain declared, "We are out of moral-courage material; we are in a condition of profound poverty."

The problem was still more tragic than that. Moral courage is always in short supply, and it could scarcely be expected that some cavalier would try to prevent even the most palpable injustice against the powerful consensus that usually set these rites in motion.

Hawthorne understood the issue better than Twain. For the heart of the matter was the primal ethic. Until the code of honor was itself destroyed, such practices were bound to persist as the means of moral enforcement. Under such circumstances there was no difference between the legal public hanging and the communal rite of lynching. Both were the same insofar as they exercised the spectators. For them the violence of the gallows was just retribution for the prisoner's misdeeds, but it had to be witnessed, not hidden away, brutally explicit, not antiseptic.

The malefactor not only suffered for his crime in such rituals, legal or otherwise; he also served as an offering to the primal, sacred values of common folk. This is evident from the trophies seized on such occasions—for instance, swatches from Leo Frank's clothes and bits of the rope that hanged him. Like the Indians' scalp locks, these mementos signified triumph over villainy and deception, and gave proof that the once live enemy was no more a threat. The humiliation and death of perceived miscreants served as a "suppurating device," as one scholar has called it. It was a means of bringing evil to a head so that it could be lanced like a boil, purifying the ailing social body. If the rites of charivari and lynching seemed profane to outsiders, that profanation, if such it should be called, also had its purposes. As Mary Douglas, the English anthropologist says, pollution is often used to provide atonement and rededication to traditional ideals. The punishment of transgressions and the separation of the villainous from the virtuous community members "have as their main function to impose order on an untidy experience." Life itself was untidy, unclean; to smear tar, blood, and feathers or to employ flame or scaffold purified those who belonged. They rested easier for having eliminated fellow men who had been transformed in their eyes into beasts.

Like the Germans whom Tacitus observed, like the milling throngs of Englishmen outside the Debtor's Door at Newgate, American whites took satisfaction in the wretchedness of others because the shaming rituals dispelled abiding fears of their own loneliness, vulnerability, and inevitable demise. Every society has its own forms of insensitivity, of communal practices and strategies for dealing with the unwanted, the powerless, and the damned. In later life Sigmund Freud was struck by the intractability of primal traits in man, a conviction made the more poignant by his flight in old age from Hitler's Teutonic Reich. "Psychoanalysis," he wrote after World War I, "has concluded from a study of the dreams and mental slips of normal people, as well as from the symptoms of neurotics, that the primitive, the savage and evil impulses of mankind have not vanished in any individual, but continue their existence. . . . They merely wait for opportunities to display their activity."

The good that primal honor could arouse in men was equally matched by the tragic horrors that it produced. But sinister as those very personal rituals of degradation were, it is not enough simply to take comfort in the fact that they are gone. Remember that in modern times murders, rapes, and crimes of terrorism have far outpaced the number killed earlier by lynching or unfair legal judgment, even when differences in size of populations are taken into account. Today a gun, rather than a flimsy sheet, makes men, criminals and policemen alike, feel omnipotent. The moral boundaries are much wider today than then, in deference to personal liberty and in condemnation of ascriptive and communal prejudices. Yet, with impersonal means of destruction more available than ever before, the impulses of which Freud spoke still abide, with tragic consequences. Though none would wish to reinvoke the Iron Age sanctions that once flourished in this and other lands, the exchange of old for new ways of judging men and character has had its ironical costs.

9

Anatomy of a Wife-Killing

The end of this study, like the beginning, concerns violence, family expectations and disappointments, male-centered community life, and elemental popular traditions. The killing of Susan Foster near Natchez, Mississippi, in March, 1834, was not a notable crime. Neither the deed itself nor its aftermath was well publicized nationally, regionally, or even locally. Unlike Lilburne and Isham Lewis, Thomas Jefferson's feckless nephews and literal butchers of a slave boy in Kentucky in 1811, the Fosters, husband and wife, had no famous connections to lend their lives notoriety. Folklorists will recover no ballads, broadsheets, or ghost stories commemorating the tragedy. Moreover, in contrast to a parricide in France of the same period (1835), the Foster affair aroused no public stirrings about the insanity plea. Unlike the celebrated Manning case in 1849 London, the Natchez killing did not attract a writer of Charles Dickens's stature seeking to use it as material for a novel (*Bleak House*) and as an argument against public punishments that simply indulged the popular taste for blood. Even Yankee abolitionists missed the chance to savor the incident as yet another example of Southern atrocity. Yet although the Fosters were not famous and their troubles lacked both political and literary significance, the events surrounding Susan Foster's death and the public reaction to it function as illustration. Many of the themes that have arisen in these pages were woven into the circumstances, a tapestry that brought together real emotions, mythic qualities, and grievous results.

Here the case will be used as the people of Natchez used it—as text, a moral scenario in which actions spoke a language that revealed inner passions and intensely felt social values. The "deep play" of the drama reproduced, on a small, manageable scale, the ageless contradictions of honor when disorder was paradoxically employed to reconfirm collective order. And on an individual level, the rites of humiliation to which Susan Foster's killer was subjected gave the individual participants a momentary sense of mastery over death, as if the bloody shaming of their victim extended and gave rich meaning to the lives of his tormentors. In that exercise, the Natchez participants in the charivari mocked human mortality, just as Hawthorne's symbol of Authority gloated over his own survival by means of Molineux's disgrace, and just as Corydon Fuller's Arkansas tavern associates danced drunkenly around the dying inebriate.

What occurred in Natchez could, of course, have happened elsewhere—in the semirural North or even in some other part of the Western world. Nineteenth-century Southern whites were not unique in upholding the ancient ethic, but they did so with a primal spirit that elsewhere in the transatlantic community was under steady attack. This was a consequence, in part, of their reliance on the institution of slavery and race-based caste proscriptions. In 1834 Natchez, Mississippi, was ethically not very distant from the world that Hawthorne described in his classic story "My Kinsman, Major Molineux."

At seven in the evening on Friday, March 14, 1834, James Foster, Jr. took his wife Susan for a walk near his widowed mother Sarah's house at Foster Fields. The large plantation stretched almost a mile along the winding St. Catherine's Creek, a treacherous stream that eventually runs into the Mississippi River a few miles below the town of Natchez. Though it was only three miles from the Adams

County courthouse, those living at Foster Fields considered themselves residents of Pine Ridge, a neighborhood on the Natchez Trace. At ten o'clock Foster ran back to the homestead in a state of agitation. There were twelve adults and a number of small children asleep at the house. But the planter roused only his sister, Nancy A. Wood, a woman old enough to have been his mother, and his niece, Nancy Ligon.* Hastily they put on wraps as he stammered out his story. (When under stress, Foster had a tendency to stutter.) He and his wife, he told them, had been down by the bayou, about a thousand feet from the house. There he had "switched" his wife for being "unchaste," and she had confessed her guilt. Somehow, though, the inflictions had "frightened her into a fit." Grabbing Mrs. Wood by the arm, Foster led the women to the slave quarters. He had carried Susan to one of the cabins.

Inside, Mrs. Wood and Mrs. Ligon found the body laid out on a low bed. Prince, Will, and Bridget, slaves belonging to the widow Sarah, stood by. Prince was a son of Abd al-Rahman Ibrahima, the African ruler whom Thomas Foster, Sr., late owner of Foster Fields, had finally allowed New York colonizationists to transport home to Africa. Both the senior Foster and his aged black servant Ibrahima had been dead some five years. They had not escaped the misery that Thomas Foster, Jr.'s liaison with Ibrahima's daughter Susy had caused, but at least death spared them the disgrace into which the family was plunging in 1834.

Frightened and confused, Mrs. Wood and Mrs. Ligon glanced quickly at Susan's body. Foster excitedly begged the women to apply camphor to her face. But resuscitation was impossible. The body still felt warm, but the hands, Mrs. Wood recalled later, had already turned cold. Susan's dress had been removed, and she was covered only with an underdress that had no bodice. The body had been washed; her hair was still damp. The slave Bridget, Prince's wife, had done her task tenderly, and so well that the women did not notice much evidence of violence. They could only see a small bruise near the temple—or so they later claimed. On Mrs. Wood's

* Because the family was so large and the relationships so crucial to understanding the case, a genealogical table has been appended at the end of this chapter.

orders, Prince and Will, another slave, carried Susan Foster to the main house. They placed her on the bed in the couple's bedroom.

The following day Sarah Foster, Thomas Foster Sr.'s invalid widow, summoned William Foster from his neighboring plantation. William was her husband Thomas's elder brother. A childless but long-married kinsman, he had always taken a special interest in his brother's thirteen children at Foster Fields. Aged though he was, William recognized more signs of violence on Susan's body than a flickering lamp in a slave hovel had revealed the night before. As far as he could tell, "the neck and shoulders from one point to another were all black and blue." On later inspection, he noticed "a grip" on her neck and blood and froth "oozing . . . slowly . . . out of her left nostril." Meanwhile David McIntosh, the husband of Caroline, one of James Foster's nine sisters, hastened over. The McIntosh place was on the opposite bank of the creek, not far away. With Susan lying dead in his own room, James Foster had spent the night at David and Caroline's house. At breakfast on Saturday Foster had told the pair that his wife had died, but had not elaborated on the circumstances. McIntosh came to Foster Fields seeking more information, but could not seem to get a straight story from anybody. The women were too shocked and distracted from the sight they had seen the night before. When Mrs. Ligon and her mother Nancy Wood asked him if Susan should be buried "publickly or privately," McIntosh answered, "Publickly of course as she had died with a Fit there could be no danger." For the first time the two women faced up to the truth, at least partially: they replied, "She did not die in a Fit." Mrs. Frances Ann Wells, another Foster sister in residence, and Mrs. Wood admitted to McIntosh that the night before they had "advised James Foster to escape." Yet they denied having any suspicions of wrongdoing when they were informally questioned later by Woodson Wren, the Adams County clerk of court. Captain Samuel K. Sorsby, husband of Elizabeth, another sister, who had died in 1831, was present in the house on the fatal weekend, but apparently neither took command nor even volunteered advice. The women had had to face the situation as best they could.

At four o'clock on Saturday afternoon, as soon as a coffin could be hammered together and a hole dug, a small retinue of whites and a pair of slaves accompanied the remains to the Foster burial site, about a hundred feet or so from the bayou where she had fallen. One can only guess who attended the burial: Mother Sarah, if her health or inclinations so directed, Mrs. Wood, Mrs. Ligon, Mrs. Wells, and old William Foster. James was not present. Being a religious man, Uncle William may have said a few appropriate words. The Rev. James Smylie, a well-known Presbyterian clergyman and the author of an early apology for Christian slaveholding, lived within easy reach; he was not, however, asked to preside or attend.

David McIntosh left Foster Fields for home before the interment, to keep an eye on James Foster. He found his guest fast asleep; James did not awaken until long after the burial had been completed. As the sun disappeared, Foster expressed his regret over losing his wife so early in their marriage. Uneasily, he inquired if any "suspicions" had been voiced at the house. McIntosh, his best friend, had collaborated with James on many a business deal; four years earlier the pair of them and Levi Foster, the family's first son, had tried to gain control of slaves belonging to James's alcoholic brother Thomas Foster, Jr. McIntosh would not let his old drinking companion down now. He lied that he knew of no "suspicions." The family was not much given to facing matters straight on.

After breakfast at the McIntosh place on Sunday morning, Foster saddled his horse, put fifty-two dollars of McIntosh's money in his pocket, and left. His host accompanied him as far as the Pine Ridge meetinghouse where the Reverend Smylie held forth. Upon parting, McIntosh suggested that Foster not go through Natchez as he intended. Rumors might have traveled there already, he implied. But McIntosh may have known that Foster was in bad odor in town for other reasons, too. In any event, Foster did as his partner advised, following a back route into Wilkinson County, where the family owned another plantation. At Foster Fields the family rested easier upon hearing of Foster's flight.

Rumors originating from the slaves or some talkative family member circulated quickly. Yet not until the next Wednesday did the wheels of Southern justice begin to turn. Ferdinand L. Claiborne, a leading squire, magistrate, and militia officer—he had captured Aaron Burr many years before—presided over a jury of inquest at the gravesite. (A coroner's jury could convene even though a physician was not present.) Claiborne's examination was thorough. He failed to confirm William Foster's report of fingermarks at the throat, but even so, other reasons for death besides strangulation were evident. Lifting the body out of the coffin, the jurors discovered that "on the back of the neck and shoulders, and on the small of the back there were marks of great violence, so that the skin was sloughing off of these parts. That there were many whip marks over her back and her thighs red, suposed [sic] to be produced by whipping. That her left arm was broken near the shoulder and that every part of her body had blisters . . . produced by a whip." Moreover, the bottom of the coffin was covered by a thick film of blood, and "the clothing [was] bloody." Claiborne surmised that "the blood seemed to have terminated very much to the head, and the clothes that were laid under the head to raise it were saturated with blood." Susan's agony had been prolonged.

Judging from the report of the coroner's jury and William Foster's deposition, one may conclude that Susan Foster's killer had acted in a frenzy, probably without deliberation and possibly without any premeditation. Though no one at Foster Fields mentioned James's condition the evening Susan died, he was probably thoroughly drunk. Foster was a "stout, athletic" man, over six feet tall; he did not know his own strength. Although a complete description of Susan Foster cannot be found in any record, she, in contrast, was likely to have been small. In any event she was barely full grown, being still three months short of her sixteenth birthday at the time of her death.

Two days after the exhumation, Woodson Wren, neighbor, justice of the peace, and county clerk, came by the Foster house to interview witnesses. Mrs. Ligon, Mrs. Wood, and David McIntosh recited some of the bare facts informally, but generally were tight-lipped. Wren ordered them to appear at the courthouse for fuller, sworn statements on Monday, March 28, before himself and state prosecutor Daniel Greenleaf. Joining them there were William Foster and the family lawyer, Felix Huston, a neighbor on Pine Ridge. Under more searching scrutiny, the witnesses expanded their testimony somewhat. Yet they shed no light on why Foster had acted as he did. They did not say that he was insensibly drunk that night, nor, curiously, did the interrogators ask them. The witnesses simply noted that the couple had arrived sometime before Christmas 1833, but said nothing of the way Foster supported his wife. He was not, however, gainfully employed. Winter was a slack time on the plantation anyhow. Probably he and McIntosh occupied themselves with hunting by day, drinking by night. The unhappy group facing Wren and Greenleaf divulged none of these particulars. Reticence came naturally to these country folk. Their chief loyalty was not to some abstraction of duty or justice, nor were they really concerned to protect James, a family disgrace the sooner forgotten the better. Instead, it was the family itself that was under threat of unraveling. Only William Foster fully cooperated with the investigation. But the old man knew little of affairs at Foster Fields, much less than when his brother Thomas had still been in charge there.

If there was something furtive about the Fosters' behavior throughout the episode, the reason was not hard to find. In a society where patriarchal leadership was so greatly needed and usually forthcoming, they sorely felt its absence. How the Fosters' difficulty—one seldom treated historically—came about deserves some explanation.

The Foster clan had not always been as demoralized as it was in the early spring of 1834. In fact, for some forty years Thomas Foster, Sr., and his brothers had fared extremely well. Like so many Southwestern settlers of their generation, they had struggled from obscurity to local prominence and wealth. Yet the substantial claims for reputation laid by the first generation were squandered away by the next—a pattern we have encountered before. The original Foster settlers arrived in Natchez about 1783. They were so undistinguished that recent efforts to trace them in South Carolina, their point of departure, have been unavailing. The immigrants—an aged mother

named Mary, four brothers, their wives, one sister, and some neighbors, probably from South Carolina's Abbeville ("Old Ninety-Six")
District—arrived in Mississippi and took out Spanish land patents.
Without slaves (or at most only one or two among them all) at first,
they began to clear the forest along St. Catherine's Creek. John
Foster, who was either the eldest or second eldest of the brothers,
not only prospered over the next two-score years, but following
American annexation of the region in 1798 he took public philan-
thropy seriously as an expression of his republican zeal. He helped
to found the village of Washington a few miles from Pine Ridge.
The little center for a short time rivaled Natchez in growth, and
the Mississippi territorial legislature met there briefly. John Foster
also provided some of the land and set in motion the plans for Jefferson College, housed in a federal-style structure, now a state monument and park site. Of all the brothers he was the most civic-minded;
he had even served as a constable during the Spanish period. John
Foster was one of the three brothers (James and Thomas being the
other two) who all married into the Zachariah Smith family. The
Smiths were the Fosters' Pine Ridge neighbors, and may have been
from the same South Carolina district whence the Fosters had come
in 1783. This pattern of brothers marrying sisters was a common
occurrence among Southern yeomen families. Unfortunately the
genealogical and court records do not reveal much information
about John Foster, aside from his philanthropies and land transactions. However, he may have been the John Foster who in 1822 left
the overcropped soils of St. Catherine's Creek for Texas. Possibly
this John Foster was the pioneer's son, but in either case the decision to emigrate was a wise one if the upcoming generations were to
flourish as well as the first settlers did. In any event, John Foster
(father or son) was one of Stephen Austin's famous "Three Hundred" when he settled at Fort Bend, Texas, on the Brazos, near the
future city of Houston. There the clan thrived, in contrast to the
cousins left behind at Foster Fields.

James Foster, who was perhaps the eldest brother, also succeeded
in tobacco farming and later in cotton growing on the alluvial lands
of Pine Ridge. Unlike Foster Fields, which has long since been aban-

doned and obliterated, Foster's Mound, James, Sr.'s, homestead, still stands on the site of an ancient Indian barrow. Joseph Ingraham, a teacher at Jefferson College on Pine Ridge and prolific writer on the Southwest, thought Foster's choice of site was tasteless: "A strange dwelling-place for the living, over the sepulchres of the dead!" But even a slight elevation made life a little more comfortable in that insect-infested region. Although a man with little education, James Foster, like John, dispensed charity, giving liberally to the institution where Ingraham taught. Perhaps James was Thomas's favorite brother, for he christened James Foster, Jr., for him, the only brother so honored. At the time of Susan's death, James Foster, Sr., was still alive, but had recently sunk into apathy, and possibly into senility. Not much guidance or command could be expected from Foster's Mound.

William Foster, the next in line, was the only male member of the first generation to assist widow Sarah and her family in the crisis. His interest showed a fidelity to family and Christian precept that his brothers either lacked or confined strictly to their immediate kin. William put little faith in things of this world. He had a comfortable property and twenty-four slaves, but he made no pretense of wanting or working for more. In fact, in wry comment on his brothers' vast holdings on Pine Ridge, William called his place Poverty Hill. He was different in other ways, too. He loved the Bible and the Methodist order, serving the faith throughout the region. He entertained circuit riders, organized new churches, and healed factional wounds. Though not as rich or distinguished as the nabobs in Natchez, William was honored with a seat on the board of trustees of the Mississippi Bible Society and led the subscription list for the building of the first charity hospital in Natchez. In 1834 the kind of devout, mission-minded, and benevolent planter that William Foster represented was not very easy to find in the Southwest. Such folk were in greater supply in the east. And William differed from most planters in the region in another respect. Unlike his brothers, he entertained doubts about the morality of slaveholding. He willed his slaves their freedom, on condition that they emigrate to Liberia. A church historian and beneficiary of his kindnesses later recorded that "Mr. Foster was taciturn, and not much gifted in exhortation . . . but he had important and useful talents as a financier, and they were solemnly dedicated to God and the good of the Church." In fact, his loans to preachers accounted for his relatively sparse resources. Not all of them were paid back. William and Rachel, his wife, were just as generous toward the family as toward the church. Though illiterate, Rachel raised a number of orphans in the clan, and William faithfully protected their inheritances. Yet despite his useful characteristics, William did not serve as example to the younger males of the Foster clan. Besides, he too was old and worn. He died before the ordeal of 1834 had fully run its course.[12]

If Thomas Foster, Sr., the youngest in the first generation, had come west alone instead of in so large a family, one would be tempted to imagine him as the inspiration for Faulkner's Thomas Sutpen. They shared some characteristics. Like Faulkner's character, Thomas was highly ambitious and ruthless in his drive to found a dynasty. Moreover, like Sutpen he had to witness family commotions over which he had little control. Nor was he, any more than Sutpen, able to set the family securely on an upward course. But Faulkner's figure was much larger than life, while Thomas Foster, Sr., was something less grand than either hero or villain: he was a conventional farmer who did well and hoped to see his sons and daughters do likewise. As was noted in an earlier chapter, though, he did not much believe in learning. His boys were simply to get along as he had. Not even Levi, the eldest, was sent off to college.[13]

Unlike William, Thomas Foster, Sr., hardly ever went to church. His wife Sarah could not even persuade him to read her the Bible, which she could not read for herself. William and Rachel sometimes took her to their Methodist meetings at the Presbyterian church on Pine Ridge. But whatever his failings as a Christian might have been, Thomas Foster was certainly an ample provider for his family. On some occasions, especially after the War of 1812, he deposited as much as $9,000 in the Bank of Mississippi at one time—a fund of cash that freed him from the expense of high interest rates. Before his death, his slave work force grew to 102, despite various disbursements to sons and dowry gifts to daughters. He even owned a coach, mostly for his daughters to parade up and down the streets of Natchez in. (Mother Sarah was not much interested in such pleasures.) In addition, Foster owned a large number of horses, necessary for his overseers and young sons on the 16,000-acre properties that he owned. Money was useful for family needs and luxuries but little else, according to Thomas's philosophy. He failed to contribute to Jefferson College, though the struggling school was almost a family fiefdom. Certainly he wasted nothing on a library. In contrast, his brother William owned twenty books of sermons and history. When Thomas Foster, Sr., died, he still owed eight years' subscriptions to the *National Intelligencer,* a Washington paper. Thomas Foster, close-mouthed, rugged, and commanding, did not bequeath his strengths to the next generation, nor did he give his progeny the educational means to find other inner resources.

At one time Sarah Smith Foster, his widow, might have ably filled her husband's shoes. Widows often rose to such occasions, and she was as hardy as most. According to family tradition, she was a young girl in Revolutionary South Carolina when British troops swarmed over the farm where she was then living. They were hunting for loot that the family had hidden away. Young Sarah knew where the cache was but refused to tell the soldiers. The commander of the unit ordered her to be hanged by the neck until she talked. As historian Terry Alford tells the story, "Sarah had no more to say dangling above the floor than she had had standing on it." Choking and only half-conscious, she was finally cut free from the noose, and the troops left no richer than they had come. Another story also gave insight into her character. Early in Ibrahima's life at Foster's place, the proud slave had run away in response to a beating by his master for refusing to work with his hands. (He was born of royal blood and in his own land had been exempt from menial toil.) Several months passed, but then one night Ibrahima returned, gaunt from his failed effort to reach his homeland. Sarah was alone in the earth-floor hut that later became the large house on St. Catherine's Creek. Though startled as the ragged apparition emerged from the shadows, she held out her hand in welcome and smiled.

In keeping with this determined temperament, Sarah fulfilled the wishes of her husband. She had borne him four daughters in succession (Ellen, Cassandra, Sarah, and Nancy), then a son, Levi. Three more girls followed—Mary, Frances Ann, and Elizabeth. The ninth child was another son—Thomas Foster, Jr.—and then came a daughter, Barbara. James Foster, Jr., born in 1804, stood eleventh. Caroline, David McIntosh's wife, completed the roster of daughters. Isaac, child of Sarah's old age, was the last of the sons, though he scarcely fulfilled the biblical hopes that his mother had in mind at the christening. Scattered as they were through an overwhelmingly female family, the three sons must have felt at times quite alone in the midst of so many women. What Sarah was able to do to counteract the effect upon her boys cannot be known. With thirteen children to handle, no doubt she found the burden increasingly wearisome over the years. After Thomas, Jr.'s, escapades with Susy, she might have greeted the scandal of Susan Foster's killing with some apathy. She was herself not far from death.

Failing even a single fragment of family papers, we can only speculate why no one in the second generation of Foster men measured up to the role of patriarch. Only Levi, the eldest, had much talent and self-confidence and, unwilling to wait for his father to retire, he had left Natchez and established himself in Franklin, Louisiana, as a planter, lawyer, and speculator. In June 1834 he too died, quite unexpectedly, thus depriving the clan of his counsel in its time of need over the next several months. Thomas and James were both family black sheep; Thomas had died a drunkard in 1831. Isaac, it seems, was either totally unreliable or mentally defective. By her will of 1835, mother Sarah had to place Foster Fields under a trustee; Isaac was apparently incapable of managing the plantation by himself.

It sometimes happened that a daughter filled the role of family leader in the absence of a male with the necessary qualities. Traditional societies seldom acknowledged such deviations openly, but widows with sufficient property, for example, could inspire enough awe and hope for future reward to work their will. Such, however, was not the case in the Foster household. Thomas Foster, Sr.'s, daughters lacked the requisite drive. Perhaps Mary (Carson) Foster, Uncle James's daughter-in-law, set the tone for her young cousins by marriage. There was not much social life at Foster Fields; old Sarah had a fine pioneer spirit but was hardly a woman to relish a fast social pace. Mary Foster, however, did her fluttery best. Margaret Wilson, a Yankee governess who met her at Foster Fields a few years later, reported that Mary looked "like a jolly milk maid" but, aware of her own lack of polish, compensated with "as many fine airs as she could manage, but without any effect but that of disgusting me." The Yankee observer may have been unfair. But certainly there was nothing very commanding about any of the women in this Foster generation. Their Southern, half-genteel upbringing freed them from the milk pail perhaps, but they were not comfortable issuing orders to menfolk from the parlor.

Cassandra, alone among the nine daughters, might have been able to assume the headship. She most resembled her father Thomas; she had always been his favorite. As her name suggests, Cassandra was not born to happiness, despite her father's special regard. First she married a wastrel named Ephraim Foster, possibly a cousin. Not only was he a poor plantation manager on Pine Ridge but he was a very abusive husband as well. Cassandra, an independent soul, returned to her father's house and, in 1824, sued her husband for divorce to escape his "severe, cruel and dangerous blows." Before the matter could be adjudicated, Ephraim died in a Natchez boardinghouse. Within days of his passing, Cassandra, wasting no time on bereavement, married John Speed in early 1825. The family was delighted that Cassandra, thirty-seven years old and childless, had so quickly rescued herself from the solitude of a single life. Six years later, in 1831, she too died. At Cassandra's request, mother Sarah relinquished her burial spot next to her husband Thomas so that Cassandra could once more be close to her father. Almost at once the family, including James Foster, Jr., sued Speed as Cassandra's heir. The litigants claimed that Speed was a bigamist and argued that therefore Chancellor John A. Quitman should restore Cassandra's sizable holdings to the Foster survivors. No doubt one reason for James Foster, Jr.'s, lengthy stay at Foster Fields the winter of 1833–34 was the expectation of a ruling on the case. Quitman, however, took his time. The following year he dismissed the suit, on the grounds that Speed's prior marriage had never been proved. Rather than helping matters, Cassandra, even after death, had helped stir up a bitter dispute over an outsider's possession of property once belonging to the clan.

In the absence of direct kin able or willing to assume patriarchal burdens, sons-in-law sometimes filled the role. Once again, the Foster family was hapless. Either the best of the number, like General William Barnard, Barbara's husband, had already died, or they lived too far away. The most likely candidate was David McIntosh, but he was not the kind to take on extra responsibilities. He was known as a "bottle man and proud of the fact." He had encouraged James Foster's unfortunate habits, so much so that widow Sarah had little use for him. Some years after this family crisis, McIntosh crossed St. Catherine's Creek at high water. Drunk, he stumbled and began to drown. A slave woman heard his cries and struck him on the head with a plank, which split his skull. He went down for good. She claimed that she had only meant to save him; there was no way to prove otherwise.

Quite clearly the Fosters were the antithesis of the model patriarchal family, which was well ordered, with a clear purpose and clean lines of authority. As this recounting suggests, however, death as well as the vagaries of gender order and number could sometimes play havoc with the usual expectations. The conditions of life often showed the vulnerability of patriarchy, but for centuries there seemed no other way to organize matters. The Foster clan represented that sometimes-overlooked historical factor—family failure— even as its members also typified the dilemmas of the planter nouveaux riches. There was a desperation in the Fosters' battle to retain wealth that they had not become wholly accustomed to having. No doubt pressures over money, his place in the family counsels, and his own wretched failings led James Foster, Jr., to make a scapegoat of his wife. Just a week before the murder, Sarah had made clear her feelings about him. She had distributed some additional lands to her favorite, widowed daughters, including Nancy Wood, whom Foster called upon to help resuscitate his dead wife. But the aged widow had not given James a single acre. Without land and capital, Foster could hardly support himself, much less a wife as well.

James Foster, Jr., had no way out. His fury, for a time, was out of control. Perhaps the tragedy would not have occurred if Thomas Foster, Sr., had still been alive. But in the absence of some formidable or calming authority, James had let his resentments and self-hatred take command. For all of the recently deceased Thomas Foster, Jr.'s, alcoholic and sexual compulsions, he had only threatened to destroy Susannah, his wife, and their children, but he had never actually harmed them. In a sense, the old patriarch had stood in the way. Perhaps he had somehow stunted his sons, but once he was dead Thomas Foster, Sr.'s, presence seemed more necessary than ever. Despite their bravado, Thomas, Jr., and James were not complete men, but quivering bundles of contrary feelings. Like so many young planters' sons caught under the patriarchal yoke, they threw their aggression outward from a garrison that had no walls.

The killing and the family's ineffectual reaction to it illustrated the anarchy that threatened a traditional household when the patriarch had no successor. It also pointed to issues of honor and shame. Had Foster simply been a wife killer, the public response might have been milder than it proved to be. But in the community's view he was not just a wife beater who had let his feelings get the better of him. To the epithet "murderer" the people added the label "blackleg," that is, professional gambler. It was therefore a matter of public satisfaction when Constable Norwood found Foster passively waiting, like Faulkner's Wash Jones, for the arrival of the law at the plantation doorstep in neighboring Wilkinson County. Quite probably James was apathetic because he was not fully conscious of what he had done that night. It was almost as if he half-sought a public judgment to ascertain who he was. The tendency to find one's reflection in the mirror of public praise or blame was much a part of the old ethic.

The prisoner returned with his captor sometime in the early summer of 1834. For six months or more he was to languish in the Adams County jail awaiting trial for murder. Sheriff Gridley, a good Methodist and a friend of Uncle William Foster, would not have permitted Foster's gaming friends from Natchez-under-the-Hill to help him idle away the hours. In fact, they too were currently subject to heavy public criticism, which Foster's crime only made more severe.

James Foster, Jr., had not been a gambling addict at the start of his adult life. Like his eldest brother Levi, who had left years before to make a fortune in the Attakapas District, James had been impatient for the old man to die. What was a young fellow to do while waiting for his father to distribute his properties? Tiring of the slow pace of the declining port of Natchez, James left town in 1825 and headed for Franklin, Louisiana, where brother Levi and his in-laws, the DeMarets, had established themselves as land, cattle, slave, and cotton dealers. James was a welcome addition to society in St. Mary. Black-haired and wild—like Nathaniel Bacon—he led no cause but his own claim to glory. Some called him the best-looking man in the Southwest. Certainly he was popular with the men, thanks to high animal spirits and a willingness to open his purse for another round of whiskey. When old Thomas Foster, Sr., finally died of a stroke in 1829, James bought some land from Levi, next to Levi's plantation on Bayou Teche. He raised "pretty fair crops," young Daniel Lacy, Levi's overseer, declared. One year he brought in enough cane to make over sixty hogsheads of sugar. Generous as always, he grandly lent the widow Lacy, Daniel's mother, over $500.

From the moment of his arrival in Franklin, James was willing to take risks that Levi, his elder by ten years or so, ordinarily passed by. In those very litigious times, Levi had only found occasion to sue seven individuals from his arrival in 1812 to 1824. After brother James appeared in 1825, he and Levi, his new partner, were plaintiffs in forty-three cases between 1825 and 1832. (After that date, matters grew worse.) By 1833, Levi discovered that he had lent over $5,000 to various people. The collateral that they offered was no more valuable than the borrowers' reputations.

Levi had always been one to speculate without too much regard for business proprieties. The evidence is in the records of his manipulation of his wife's estate, an inheritance from her father, the aristocratic head of the DeMaret family. But the frenetic activity that Louisiana court records reveal suggests that James Foster, Jr., had inveigled his brother into lending money to gaming friends. With capital in short supply, Levi fell behind in debts he owed suppliers for his store and other enterprises. Sometimes the gamblers, usually cowpokes, also appeared in the suits, making claims that they had been plied with liquor and then forced to sign notes to cover losses at the table. James, a master card player, easily assumed the role of the genial planter at leisure. He owned a handsome faro box and bet sums as great as one hundred dollars at a time. (Few of these devices were not rigged.) Games made him feel omnipotent, an arbiter of destiny. Neither the ordinary routines of planting nor even money itself offered comparable excitement. Besides, the other big men in Franklin often cut the decks with him—Judge John Moore, planter Edgar DeMaret, Helair Carlin, attorney Benjamin R. Gant, Attorney Alexander Splane, and Captain Winfrey Lockett. It was a fast society, and James Foster, Jr., moved with the best.

Levi Foster also played hard, and he admired James for being much like himself. But in 1832 the press of lawsuits and James's increasingly erratic behavior, noticeable ever since Thomas Foster, Sr.'s, death in 1829, threatened to break up their close relationship. They quarreled over who owned which of Thomas Foster, Jr.'s, slaves. But the crop of 1832 was so enormous that James Foster, Jr., saw still greater vistas for making a name for himself and outdistancing his elder brother. Instead of paying off outstanding debts, he bought himself an eighty-foot schooner, the *St. Mary,* sported "fine clothes," traded for "fine horses," and even found time for a trip to Texas to look over a half-league of land that he had bought with money borrowed against his father's bequest. In early January

1833 he grandly announced a special trip to New Orleans to sell his remaining crop. Widow Susan Lacey, the mother of Levi's overseer, entrusted her crop to his care. That excursion proved to be James Foster, Jr.'s undoing. At a later trial for fraud, initiated by his creditors, evidence about his habits during this period came to light. As several witnesses remarked, Foster boasted of picking up five to six thousand dollars for the cane sold in New Orleans. He would produce a bankroll "as big as your wrist" to prove the point. After a visit to a theater, declared Edgar DeMaret, a Franklin planter, James Foster, Jr., entered a New Orleans "gaming house where they had rolette and Farrow [sic]." DeMaret watched him bet and drink until Foster went off and "frolicked" (whored) for a while. Later DeMaret came upon Foster at a coffee house, and Foster boasted that he had been betting "fifty dollars at a time" and that he was only pretending to be as drunk as he appeared. DeMaret's testimony was particularly impressive; he was one of Levi Foster's brothers-in-law and belonged to one of the oldest families in the district. However, other witnesses claimed that Foster was not so penniless as DeMaret and several other witnesses claimed. William B. Lewis, a Franklin resident, implied that Foster was very successful at cards throughout the time he was in New Orleans, and had even won at "veint-un" on the way back to Franklin. The issue was important; creditors suspected that Foster had hidden away his profits to escape their demands. Helair Carlin, a well-regarded planter, maintained that Foster was "verry [sic] much addicted to gamboling [sic] . . . drank a good deal . . . and had become more and more embarrassed until the time he left" for Mississippi in November 1833. Carlin's opinion seemed to be the common view in Franklin, however much Foster's creditors hoped that he had not completely "busted."

When James Foster, Jr. returned to Franklin from New Orleans in January 1833, he certainly acted as if he had no cash at all. He put off an emissary from Susan Lacy, eager to have her crop money. Loading up his schooner with cargo, still unpaid for, Foster set sail for the Gulf. He was spotted, however, and the sheriff of St. Landry Parish seized him on behalf of creditors in the Opelousas area.

Though he was forced to walk from Franklin to Opelousas on a leash attached to the sheriff's saddle, James Foster, Jr., had not yet run out of luck. Brother Levi hastened to the Opelousas courthouse and stood bond for him, whereupon he was released from jail.

In March James was to be found aboard the *Calcasieu,* a vessel about which there is no information at all. Witnesses reported seeing James Foster, Jr., aboard with Captain Bundick, the master, playing cards and drinking. The vessel was apparently a floating casino, although it carried flour and other kinds of cargo, too. It was during the sojourn on the *Calcasieu* that Foster met and perhaps solemnized the union with Susan. (No marriage record can be found.)

The honeymoon was not long. In September the sheriff of St. Mary Parish arrested James Foster, Jr., for fraud. This time all his creditors, some eighteen of them, joined their suits together. While Alexander Splane, the prosecutor, prepared his case, James spent the fall in the Franklin jail. Meantime, Susan lived at Levi Foster's place. She had come in June "decently dressed," but by fall her husband, "shabby and ragged" himself, had gambled away her clothing, too. She did not even have a bonnet left, making her look "common," said the Foster brothers' cousin John Smith of Franklin. Nothing could have been more mortifying for the bride, or indeed for the family as a whole. At James's urgent request from jail Levi supplied a new bonnet.

With the always pliable Judge John Moore to help, Levi arranged Foster's bail in November, with gaming friends Lockett, Boyce, and Hungerford posting bond. Wheedling money from cousin John Smith, Foster and Susan fled to Natchez, much to the outrage of Prosecutor Splane and the planters who had forfeited the bond money. Ironically, when the trial was held in James Foster, Jr.'s, absence the following year the jurors found him innocent of fraud. But all his assets, including the schooner, a dirk, a pistol, a cowhide whip, card decks ($1.38), saddles, and horses, were sold. The total came to $10,895.75, far short of the sums owed. From being a "sporting gentleman" James had become a mere "blackleg," a status among men equivalent to that of a prostitute among women. For a young wife, he was not much of a figure to admire.

Nothing is known about Susan, his bride. Her maiden name may have been Alphin, Alphari, or possibly Alpha. Since neither the people of Franklin nor those of Natchez knew her or her family, she remains, from the historical vantage point, a wraith. All efforts to trace her have failed. But one fact is readily clear: whoever she was, she had no kinfolk to avenge her death or to hire an attorney to help the prosecutor, a common and welcome addition to state cases in those days. The lack of curiosity of those in Franklin and Natchez said something about the attitude of Southern society toward kinless womankind.

As a rule, a young married girl preferred to be within reasonable proximity of kinspeople. Susan was not given that option, probably because she came from poor or unsettled people. She brought nothing to the marriage but herself. Like Susannah, Thomas Foster, Jr.'s, young wife, she was particularly vulnerable to her husband's whims. Married before her fifteenth birthday, she was hardly mature enough to judge her handsome spouse in a critical light, at least at first. Mrs. Wood, Mrs. Ligon, and Mrs. Wells, the widows at Foster Fields, befriended the young girl, but she certainly made few acquaintances on Pine Ridge—not enough to give any substance to Foster's charge of unfaithfulness. Had there really been some liaison or flirtation, the Fosters would have quickly pointed it out to county officials.

The Pine Ridge neighborhood was shocked that one of its residents had so cruelly killed his wife, a friendless, kinless waif, a mere child. The gentleman who took it upon himself to serve as her guardian *post mortem* was Spence Monroe Grayson, a thirty-one-year-old lawyer just gaining local prominence. In 1839 he was to oppose the passage of the Mississippi Women's Property Act in the state senate, arguing eloquently that woman's purity had to be kept free from the corruption of business transactions. In keeping with these chivalrous views, he volunteered to assist the state's attorney, Daniel

Greenleaf. In fact, Grayson had himself listed as the prosecutor of record in the court docket. Known for his speaking abilities, Grayson no doubt expected to make the chief plea to the jury, leaving to Greenleaf the paperwork and investigation of the circumstances.

Grayson's associations with Pine Ridge ran deep. His uncle and guardian, Beverley R. Grayson, had raised him. William Grayson, congressman, planter, and Revolutionary hero of Prince William County, Virginia, was the head of the clan. Spence Monroe Grayson had lost both parents in 1803 when he was an infant. His uncle Beverley removed to Mississippi, where he hoped to reduplicate the glories and prestige of the family's Virginia forefathers. Beverley Grayson raised his nephew as his own son, and set his young charge a very high example, in the best Southern tradition. Beverley Grayson was long active in civic affairs in Natchez and on the Ridge. With the Foster brothers, James and John, he had helped establish Jefferson College and Elizabeth Female Academy on Pine Ridge. Far from what Southwesterners regarded as the typical Virginia gentleman, impractical and overcivilized, Beverley Grayson operated sawmills, cotton gins, and stores as well as the requisite plantation. Spence Monroe Grayson followed suit. Though just about the same age as James Foster, Jr., whom he must have known since boyhood, Grayson had long before charted his course and knew his mind. He had studied well in school and at Jefferson College, and at age twenty-three he had already joined the Natchez bar through the sponsorship of Senator Thomas Read, his mentor. In 1830, unlike James Foster, Jr., he married a woman with unimpeachable Virginia and Philadelphia connections, Sarah R. Chew, whose father was a leading Natchez nabob. The couple settled down not far from the Fosters' district. It would be interesting to know if there had been bad blood between James Foster, Jr., and his prosecutor when they were growing up together. In any case, Spence Monroe Grayson, as his obituaries in 1839 later attested, was a flower of Southern gentility. Susan Alpha (?) Foster was to have a bold knight after all, though only as avenger of her death.

If Grayson was to serve as representative of Southern civilization, Felix Huston, Foster's attorney, epitomized Southern tradition. Scots-Irish by extraction, Huston was as tall as an ancient Frankish king; the troops in Texas whom he led a few months after Foster's ordeal called him "General Long-Shanks." He and Seargent S. Prentiss, his partner for a time, had the most lucrative practice in Natchez, and Huston's wife, Mary E. Daingerfield, had a plantation directly adjacent to Foster Fields. There Huston entertained lavishly—hunting parties, balls, picnics, shooting matches—but whether the Fosters were ever invited is not known. Sophisticated though he was, Huston was much less genteel than Grayson. Proud of his marksmanship, he fought more than one duel, although his encounter with Albert Sidney Johnston during the Texas Revolution was the most celebrated.

Felix Huston had no second thoughts about taking up the defense of James Foster, Jr. He was already representing him—and many other Foster relations—in the dispute with John Speed over Cassandra's will. Fortunately for Huston's legal strategy, confusions over the impaneling of Mississippi juries under common law were then obstructing judicial procedures. Therefore, Prosecutor Greenleaf quickly responded with a brief upholding the methods by which Woodson Wren, the clerk of court, had established the array. Since no other attorney had utilized the same challenge in that court session, Judge Alexander Montgomery, recently defeated for reelection to the bench, decided to postpone the Foster trial. In the October term Montgomery had felt obliged to throw out all jury cases on the same grounds—that the grand jury that presented the indictments had been improperly convened—and did not wish that to happen again. Therefore he set Foster's trial for the very last day of the term, so that the Foster indicment could be dismissed without cleaning out the docket for the entire term. Although Montgomery did not announce his intentions regarding the Foster trial, its postponement gave a hint that the townspeople did not at all like. It suggested that Huston's motion to quash the venire would probably be accepted. However, they would have to wait until January 2, 1835, the final sitting, to learn whether the wife-killer was to be tried or not.

By the time Montgomery was ready to give his opinion, the Natchez public had been entertained with a full session of cases—four Negro-stealings, an embezzlement, thirteen assault and battery charges, two fornications, and other assorted crimes.[39] Excitement mounted as the only murder trial that term approached. Moreover, there were other tensions in Natchez, indeed in Mississippi and in the nation at large. Devastating cholera attacks had already shocked the region and the country as a whole. Poor weather conditions had unsettled expectations in the Mississippi Valley. In national politics, partisan warfare over President Jackson's determination to destroy the Bank of the United States had grown increasingly bitter. In prior months both Felix Huston and Spence Monroe Grayson had been in fist fights at local rallies of Jacksonians and their opponents, soon to be called Whigs. Still more alarming to friends of the Union was the appearance of organized abolitionism. In October 1833 Northern evangelicals and Quakers had formed the American Anti-Slavery Society in New York, with a local riot to give their efforts national notoriety. At that time, Felix Huston had written to the New York *Courier and National Enquirer,* a fiercely anti-abolitionist paper, saying that if, as a result of the new organization's agitation among slaves, "one female had been violated by that unhallowed union of white and black desperadoes, no man in the State" with antislavery sentiments "would have escaped—they would have perished to a man."

In broad terms, some kind of public sense that moral boundaries and expectations were no longer so precise and sturdy as they once had been seemed to afflict the nation at large. In New York City there were sudden outbreaks of riots, not only against abolitionists and free blacks, but also among political factions. Mobs from Boston burned the Ursuline convent and school at Charlestown, the first of many attacks throughout the northeast in protest against Irish immigration. The epidemic of civil disorders was to grow still worse in 1835. Particularly was this so after the abolitionist postal campaign, which aroused much indignation, North and South, when antislavery pamphlets reached their destinations. Even in 1834, Mississippians feared for public safety when Alonzo Phelps, brigand and murderer, escaped from jail, though he was killed when cornered. The dramatic revelations of Virgil Stewart about a widespread conspiracy of similar highwaymen, "steam doctors," and professional gamblers under John A. Murrell was to reinforce those worries in 1835. White Mississippians readily believed that abolitionists had joined with these villainous elements to overthrow the social order and pillage, murder, and tyrannize law-abiding citizens. There was not a word of truth in the public fantasy. The terror, however, served a customary purpose, notifying all whites of the need for solidarity.

All these eruptions, North and South, were directed toward the reestablishment of traditional popular morality: the supremacy of the Protestant "good" over the Catholic "menace," the white man over the rebellious black, the gentleman of leisure over the lying gamester, the patriot over the subversive abolitionist, the honest citizen over robbers, medical frauds, and anyone else who sought to snatch away the citizen's hard-won cash. These simple themes of alien menace reduced complex circumstances to masterable proportions, so that even the most illiterate yeoman or worker could understand and participate in the rites of exorcism, expulsion, and purification.

James Foster, Jr., it might be said, was one of the early victims in this recurrent but variously motivated "inflammation of the popular mind," as Hawthorne called it. The rituals of sacrifice, by shaming one individual, thereby "proved" the worth, purity of purpose, and security of those beset with evils not so readily apprehended. Such actions thrust the pain of self-recognition upon the victim and what he or she represents. In a sense Foster was to be punished not for his crime alone, but for the anxieties of the citizenry.

There was nothing class-conscious or very modern about any of the mobs of the 1830s, particularly the one that milled about Natchez's handsome, porticoed courthouse on January 2, 1835. The crowd was there to participate in a ritual no less stylized and mythic than that which Hawthorne depicted in his story. Believing that Foster's indictment was likely to be quashed, the citizens told each other, as people had in similar situations in America since the seventeenth century, that the system of justice was defective, unreliable, that technicalities conjured up by the wizards of the law protected rich clients like Foster, leaving the public at the mercy of fiends. The waiting crowd, one of its members later recalled, expected that the judge would soon let the prisoner "loose upon an outraged community, unscathed, unwhipped of justice." Foster's hands would be "reeking with the blood of his virtuous and butchered wife," and he would be free "to exult and gloat over his infamy, and, like a wild beast *once* fed on human flesh and blood, acquiring an insatiable love for such food, to hunt for other victims." Colonel James Creecy, who later wrote these words, expressed the less grandly articulated feelings of the mob. The ceremony of degradation itself would translate those visceral sentiments into symbolic actions.

Yet, as in all such enterprises, anger was not the sole emotion to sweep that assembly in Natchez. There was also the sense of joy and celebration that a charivari ordinarily elicited. After all, it was January 2, a Saturday in the New Year's holiday. It was a time when, traditionally, bells were rung and noisemakers twirled to scare off a community's old sins and spirits and to welcome in a new beginning, pure and innocent—when ancient Authority, Father Time, was deposed and the new-crowned child was exalted.

Sheriff Gridley and his deputies marched the accused the short distance to the courtroom. Pale and faltering after months of close confinement in shackles, Foster met Felix Huston before the bench. Judge Montgomery, the first native Mississippian to serve as a state common pleas judge, wasted no time. It was his last case before vacating the office. The venire was quashed, he ruled. Foster was free, at least momentarily.

The crowd outside swelled to three hundred or more as word of Montgomery's decision spread. It was as diverse a throng as could be imagined—planters' sons in town to promenade and carouse, Choctaw Indians and their squaws, riverboat men, steamboat passengers, prostitutes, gamblers, town urchins and apprentices, slaves and ordinary white folk visiting on court day. None were dressed for outlandish masquerade. Their regular attire was motley enough, however, according to "Thimblerig," an observer and participant. Thimblerig, who was a professional shell-game artist, later told his story to Colonel David Crockett, whom he joined on a steamboat bound for New Orleans not long afterward. Crockett, on his way to Texas, included the account in his famous autobiography.

Officials of the court and the better sort of folk were not visible. However, they certainly were aware—and tacitly approving—of the events that would ensue. Judge Montgomery, prosecutor Greenleaf, and Sheriff Horace Gridley were nowhere in sight. The Duncans, Holmeses, Quitmans, and others of high station would never have led the rites. The task belonged to upcoming young men not yet weighed down with honors and dignities. Grayson, the prosecutor of record, and Huston, Foster's attorney, remained to accompany him as he stepped into the light of the winter noonday sun. At once "two gentlemen" seized Foster, who fell in the ensuing scuffle. Huston intervened. Urging the pressing throng to move back, Huston helped Foster up and gained permission for them both to pass up the street a hundred yards or so. As they walked away from the catcalls and angry fists, Foster, sobbing abjectly, begged Huston to save him. There was not much the attorney could have done, even if he had wished to do so; by acting like a wheedling coward Foster merely aroused mob disgust all the more. Then, as Huston and the mob had arranged, Huston gave Foster the signal to run. If Foster could have outrun the crowd, he would have gained his freedom. But the prisoner was paralyzed. Depression, shame, and dread sapped his will. The mob grabbed him once again.

According to one account, a line then formed in near silence. "The word 'march' was pronounced finally by the tall man in front," Colonel James Creecy later remembered. He was referring to Felix Huston, who was no longer the prisoner's lawyer but now his chief tormentor. Grayson also joined the head of the procession as it moved toward the ravine near the toll bridge. It was the place where Thomas Foster, Jr., and the slave Susy had met to make their escape together a few years before. The hollow was the customary site for community rituals of this kind in Natchez. The leaders lashed Foster to a tree. For the next several hours—from about noon to sundown—the citizens laid on the strokes with a cowhide whip, "until," said Thimblerig, "the flesh rung in ribands from his body." Each lash was a reminder of the agony that Foster had perpetrated upon Susan, a biblical retribution indeed.

As the sun began to set, the lynchers heated up the tar, while debating whether Foster should be branded on both cheeks, have his ears slit, or be scalped. (The first two choices were penalties current on the state's statute books. Not for another decade did the penitentiary mode replace corporal exactions in Mississippi.) The decision was for a partial scalping; a complete one would have been fatal. After this was done, tar was poured over Foster's head, shoulders, and back, followed by a dousing with the traditional feathers. Dressed in this manner and otherwise wearing only "a miserable pair of breeches," Foster was led back to town. On the way he fainted several times. As he lay groaning, no one attended him. He was, recalled Thimblerig simply, "an object of universal detestation." After Foster was seated backwards to the cart's tail, the lynchers accompanied the "common dray" with the sounds of pots banging, lids clashing, boys whistling, and drummers beating unrhythmically—the "rough music" of the antique "rogue's march."

By this time the crowd was a happy thoroughly drunken New Year's throng. As Sheriff Gridley helped Foster climb the jail steps, a howl went up. "Take him to the river, tie him to a log, and set him adrift," some yelled. "Hang the villain!" "Never turn such a fellow loose to butcher another wife," cried others. These bowdlerized threats from Colonel Creecy's account do not capture the gutter language that was no doubt really used. But Grayson, who addressed the mob from the steps, was probably accurately quoted. He was said to have replied, "My friends, we have *done* our duty as good citizens, and I now propose that we all go quietly to our homes!" The "common dray" was rolled off. The bulk of the mob dispersed. Gridley took Foster inside, for Foster's own protection. Only a few stragglers remained, but they had murderous intentions. Some were muttering that Foster should have been branded and his ears cut off, back at the hollow. They were waiting for a chance to act on their own.

James Creecy, in his memoir, claimed that he had not seen Foster clearly until the victim was led up the steps. In awe and fear, he exclaimed, "Almighty Father, what a picture! He was more like a huge shapeless fowl, covered with masses of feathers, all turned the wrong way, than anything else." Thimblerig also described him: "The blood oozing from his stripes had become mixed with masses of feathers and tar, and rendered his aspect still more horrible and loathsome." Finally, the editor of the Natchez *Courier* aptly remarked, "So far from recognizing Foster" as he had appeared in court that morning, "we could scarcely realize that he was a man. The mob believed he was a monster at heart, and were determined that his external appearance should correspond with the inner man."

The mob had sought to purge the community of a deviant judged so beneath human attribute that tar—a kind of representational excrement—was fitting apparel. Instead of acting as the protector of his wife (who was also a child), he had had no "fear of God before his eyes" and, as the common-law indictment read, had been "moved and seduced by the instigation of the Devil" to slay her maliciously. In a patriarchal world, one might chastise a loved one, but few crimes were worse than intrafamilial killings. In addition, Foster was a gamester—in debt, accused of fraud, and so addicted to gambling that his habits aroused contempt even in that gambling-obsessed age and region. Like an alcoholic who could not hold his liquor, Foster repelled other men who were drinkers and gamblers themselves. His excesses caricatured their own inclinations in frightening ways. He was the mirror of what they might become. For these reasons Foster had to be transformed from what he was, an ordinary, even physically attractive young man, into a creature with whom no one needed to identify himself. Clad in feathers, he became the male-turned-female, a humiliated cowbird, the symbol of the cuckoldry that he had sought to escape in his furious assault upon his wife. From a superhuman beast "hunting for other victims," to borrow from Creecy, Foster was translated into a puny-brained, two-legged, feather-covered capon, as harmless as the bird whose neck was habitually wrung for Sunday dinner.

One may be sure that such humiliations had the desired psychological effect on the victim. Hawthorne's description of Major Molineux's reaction was very accurate. Foster's state of mind was even more abject. His agony can best be compared with the violation felt by a man or woman subjected to unremitting gang rape. Later that night, at about two in the morning, two men on horseback led an unmounted horse to the jail. Thimblerig, who watched, recalled that "Foster was with difficulty placed astride." The mob's lookouts tried to grab him, but Foster found strength enough to shake them loose. One fired a pistol, but the shot only grazed Foster's hat, and the three rode off into the night. The party stopped at Foster Fields, only a few miles away.

One of the two men who rescued Foster was one of his brothers-in-law, Daniel MacMillan of neighboring Franklin County, Mississippi, a justice of the peace and a hard-driving man. Perhaps the other horseman was MacMillan's son. On May 21, 1835, almost five months later, Foster had sufficiently recovered to assign his share of whatever remained of Thomas Foster, Sr.'s, estate to that son, Calvin MacMillan, his nephew. No doubt this was the reward for the rescue. The Foster clan of James, Jr.'s, generation, it would seem, seldom did much for each other without some monetary exchange. Once his signature was on that indenture, Foster disappeared.[50]

The Fosters seldom spoke of him again, but one member of the clan thought that he had gone to Texas. Allegedly, he never remarried and died at the close of the century. According to the same unsubstantiated report, he left a large estate in Houston town lots to his grandnephew, Governor Murphy Foster, the grandson of James's former partner in Franklin, Louisiana, Levi Foster. The legacy, so the story goes, would have been a public embarrassment during the reform governor's reelection campaign against the infamous Louisiana Lottery gang, then a powerful political machine, and so Murphy Foster, fearing that the ancient murder would hurt his election chances, refused the inheritance. The whole tale seems implausible.[51]

Nevertheless, it appears that Foster did survive, as Grayson and Huston had intended. Certainly recuperation from some 150 lashes required a strong constitution, but Foster owed his life to the attorneys who had allowed his humiliation but had prevented a sentence of death. The reasons for this mercy were several. First, Grayson was a gentleman who took the title seriously. It would have been barbarous for a Virginian and Christian to let him die after a court had rendered a contrary verdict. Second, both Grayson and Huston were lawyers sworn to uphold the sanctity of the court with which they were affiliated. Third, they were members of the planter class, and Foster had once been so regarded, too. Though his rank had been lost, it could not be forgotten. To let a mob of the poor and powerless kill someone of superior original standing would violate convention and order. The ordinary cheating gamester, the rebellious slave, the lowly ne'er-do-well were fit objects for a death sentence under lynch law. But a planter, even a wife-killer, was not to be hanged summarily. The second generation of Fosters might have forfeited their place in local estimation with two divorce cases, adulterous miscegenation, and then murder. Nevertheless James Foster, Jr., reasoned Huston and Grayson, should be allowed to survive.

Yet these factors do not explain why the crowd so promptly obeyed Grayson's call for a return to order. All but the handful who lingered in hopes of more excitement accepted his plea and left the scene. The reason they did so was that Grayson and Huston had also served another purpose. As leaders of the mob, they had given sanction to what was done. For the duration of the charivari they were exploited by the crowd as much as they used it for their own ends: the punishing of a planter who had violated the class code and the code of honor attached to it. The attorneys lent legitimacy to deeds that were clearly illegal, even reprehensible if undertaken by a single actor. Through them the rite became "holy aggression," in contrast to Foster's distinctly unholy offense. Someone had to initiate the action in the name of all, and at once such an individual became more than a leader: he was regarded as a hero by those following him, as one whose strength of will and sense of rightfulness could set aside all doubts and fears. The crowd shared in his glory even as they were the instruments by which the hero acquired it. If the individual who instigated the first acts against the scapegoat had no prior prestige but arose from the mob itself, matters could quickly get out of hand. But leaders like Huston and Grayson were men already held in respect. They had the authority to control both the beginning and the ending of the episode, so that studied "misrule" did not degenerate into wild disorder. If that had occurred, Foster would doubtless have perished. To folk ill equipped for deeds of special courage, the power of the respected leader assumed almost a magical character. He made possible, as Ernest Becker put it, "the expression of forbidden impulses, secret wishes, and fantasies." As father and elder brother in the phalanx of honor and heroics, individuals such as the two attorneys condoned and supervised the appetites of conventional men for power, or rather the semblance of it. If anything went wrong, the leaders, not the anonymous participants, would have to bear the burden.

Yet it was important for the leaders' own self- and group esteem to restrict the action, much as a father would in dealing with a child dangerously close to a frightening loss of control. Too much power makes men afraid. It opens floodgates of passion not easy to shut. It destroys the crowd's unanimity, beneath which hide the ever-present anxieties of life and of death. Grayson thus demanded what the crowd really wanted: release from their own dreams of omnipotence, dreams too intense to sustain for very long. At the same time, his words of restraint implicitly reminded the listeners that those who initiated such awesome proceedings had the authority, derived from the crowd and from their own local prominence, to end them. The fantasy of heroism that fellowship evoked had to cease. The squeaks of Foster's empty cart, receding into the night, signaled the return to mundane human concerns and transciencies.

It was therefore hardly surprising that the Foster affair led to no reexamination of public policy. No journalist or judge called for the strengthening of the police and judicial systems. No preachers—Adams County boasted very few anyhow—climbed the rostrum to denounce the charivari or the ethic that made it so serviceable a device. The very opposite occurred: the launching of lynch law crusades throughout the state to hunt down other deviants from conventional standards of behavior. Even the Fosters may have thought it all had turned out for the best. The wastrel son relinquished his legal claims to Cassandra's fortune and whatever else might come to him from his father and mother's estates in future. The succeeding generations buried the memory of his disgrace as they had Susan, who still lies in the sod of Foster Fields, without a marker. People who rely upon oral tradition have very selective memories.

What was true of the clan's amnesia about James was also true for the South as a whole. The darker aspects of honor were seldom to be questioned, then or for many years to come. Individuals and sometimes groups spoke out against popular forms of injustice and honor—duels, summary hangings, mob whippings. These efforts at reform seldom received public acclamation and support. Even historians, whether native to the South or not, have not seen these expressions of public will and private esteem as part of a total cultural pattern. Instead they have been labeled tragic aberrations, or techniques by which the planter class manipulated lesser, more virtuous folk. Gentility, the nobler, brighter feature of Southern ethics, has been a more congenial topic. Certainly it was the model that Southerners have publicly revered and exalted. The selectivity was natural. Nonetheless, the higher claims of chivalry, Stoic and Christian, were put to the service of primal honor. Gentlemen like Spence Monroe Grayson often found themselves carried along on the tides of multitudes, or were driven to silent acquiescence with no chance of guiding the public into calmer moods. The choice that Grayson made in standing at the head of Foster's enemies was exactly the same one that many others would later make when "honor" cried out for secession. The prudent man was wise to stand aside, saving doubts for afterthoughts when passions died away. Thus the "innocence" of primal values, as Faulkner made clear, was an imperfect shield against misperceptions, contradictions, and thoughtless cruelty. It could even be their very source. As Hawthorne had observed, men had many voices, and more than one mask. Honor had always had many faces.

THE FOSTER FAMILY GENEALOGY*

Mary Foster of Abbeville, S.C.?
b. ?
m. ? (husband d. before 1784)
d. 1819

John of Old Oaklands	James of Foster's Mound	William of Poverty Hill
b. ?	b. Aug. 2, 1752	b. 1759
m. Rachel Gibson	m. Charlotte Brown	m. Rachel?
m. Sarah Gibson (sister)	m. Elizabeth Smith	d. 1834
m. Mary Smith	d. Nov. 14, 1835	no issue
d. Fort Bend, Texas, 1836 (?)	c. 8	
c. 4		

Ellen (Elinor)	Levi	Frances Ann
b. mid-1780s	b. 1790?	b. 1795
m. Isaac Nierson	m. Zeide DeMaret	m. Samuel W.
(1802)	(1816) of Franklin,	Wells (1814) of
m. Joseph Carr	La. (d. 1852)	Opelousas, La.
(1815)	d. June 13, 1834	d. Dec. 1837
	c. 4 (incl. Gov.	
	Murphy J.	
	Foster's	
	father)	

Cassandra	Nancy
b. 1787?	b. 1791?
m. Ephraim	m. Ethan Wood
Foster (1807)	(1810)
m. John Speed	d. ?
(1825)	dau. Mrs. Ligon
d. March 21, 1831	
no issue	

Sarah (Sally)	Mary
b. Feb. 1787	b. ?
m. Daniel MacMillan (1810)	m. William K. Collins
of Franklin County, Miss.	d. (1814)
d. 1852	c. 1?
c. Calvin MacMillan	
(James Foster left property	
claims to him, 1835)	

---

* The names of the family members important in reference to this account are
italicized.
This genealogy is partly an adaptation from a table in Alford, *Prince among
Slaves*, pp. 194–95; it is reprinted by permission of Terry Alford and Harcourt
Brace Jovanovich.

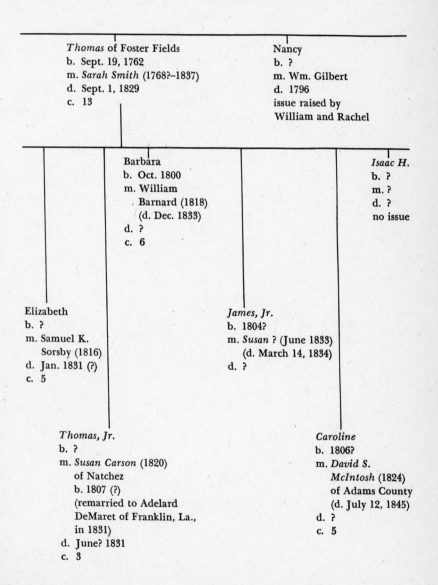

Thomas of Foster Fields
b. Sept. 19, 1762
m. *Sarah Smith* (1768?–1837)
d. Sept. 1, 1829
c. 13

Nancy
b. ?
m. Wm. Gilbert
d. 1796
issue raised by
William and Rachel

Barbara
b. Oct. 1800
m. William
  . Barnard (1818)
   (d. Dec. 1833)
d. ?
c. 6

Isaac H.
b. ?
m. ?
d. ?
no issue

Elizabeth
b. ?
m. Samuel K.
  Sorsby (1816)
d. Jan. 1831 (?)
c. 5

James, Jr.
b. 1804?
m. *Susan* ? (June 1833)
   (d. March 14, 1834)
d. ?

Thomas, Jr.
b. ?
m. *Susan Carson* (1820)
  of Natchez
  b. 1807 (?)
  (remarried to Adelard
  DeMaret of Franklin, La.,
  in 1831)
d. June? 1831
c. 3

Caroline
b. 1806?
m. *David S.*
  McIntosh (1824)
  of Adams County
  (d. July 12, 1845)
d. ?
c. 5

Suggested Readings

I.   Honor, Culture, and Religion

For those interested in honor as described here the best sources of enlightenment are more often anthropological and literary studies than works of history. In definitional terms, the places to begin are "Honor" as defined by Julian Pitt-Rivers in the *International Encyclopedia of the Social Sciences*, David L. Sills, ed., 18 vols. (New York: Macmillan, 1968), VI, 503–11, and the essays in J. G. Peristiany, ed., *Honor and Shame: The Values of Mediterranean Society* (Chicago: University of Chicago Press, 1968). Because imaginative literature, including the classics, has often assumed a didactic function, such literary investigations as these are pertinent: Sir Kenneth J. Dover, *Greek Popular Morality in the Time of Plato and Aristotle* (Berkeley: University of California Press, 1974); Moses I. Finley, *The World of Odysseus* (New York: Penguin, 1979 rev. ed.); Curtis B. Watson, *Shakespeare and the Renaissance Concept of Honor* (Princeton: Princeton University Press, 1960); and George Fenwick Jones, *Honor in German Literature* (New York: AMS Press, 1970 [1959]).

Works covering the Anglo-American world of the nineteenth

century include: Shirley Robin Letwin, *The Gentleman in Trollope: Individuality and Moral Conduct* (Cambridge: Harvard University Press, 1982), a discussion broader in scope than the title suggests; John Fraser, *America and the Patterns of Chivalry* (New York: Cambridge University Press, 1982); and Mark Girouard, *The Return to Camelot: Chivalry and the English Gentleman* (New Haven: Yale University Press, 1981). Much can also be learned about the style and character of the American gentleman in Edwin Cady, *The Gentleman in America: A Literary Study in American Culture* (Syracuse: Syracuse University Press, 1949) and Stow Persons, *The Decline of American Gentility* (New York: Columbia University Press, 1973).

The best of the older works related specifically to Southern forms of honor is still Wilbur J. Cash, *The Mind of the South* (New York: Knopf, 1941). It had an influence in the development of the concepts used here. Noteworthy are these older but still informative works: John Hope Franklin's seminal study, *The Militant South, 1800–1860* (Cambridge: Harvard University Press, 1956); Rollin G. Osterweiss, *Romanticism and Nationalism in the Old South* (New Haven: Yale University Press, 1949); Clement Eaton, "The Role of Honor in Southern Society," *Southern Humanities Review*, 10 suppl. (1976), 47–58; and William R. Taylor, *Cavalier and Yankee: The Old South and American National Character* (Cambridge: Harvard University Press, 1979 [1961]). Taylor portrays Southern honor as a literary illusion, but *Cavalier and Yankee* remains a monument in intellectual history. For a newer, vigorous approach to Southern letters and cultural factors, consult Michael Kreyling, "The Hero in Antebellum Southern Narrative," *Southern Literary Journal*, 16 (Spring 1984), 3–20. Although specific in focus, Phyllis Vine, "Preparation for Republicanism: Honor and Shame in the Eighteenth-Century College," in Barbara Finkelstein, ed., *Regulated Children/Liberated Children* (New York: Psychohistory Press, 1979), 44–62, has wider implications for understanding the eighteenth-century code of ethics. Representing a break with many past assumptions about colonial social life and culture, Rhys Isaac, *The Transformation of Virginia: 1740–1790: Communications, Re-*

ligion and Authority (Chapel Hill: University of North Carolina Press, 1982), provides a wide-ranging set of social and religious issues in an elegant manner. For a different but intriguing approach, consult Timothy H. Breen, *Tobacco Culture: The Mentality of the Great Tidewater Planters on the Eve of the Revolution* (Princeton: Princeton University Press, 1985).

With regard to Southern religion, there are many excellent recent publications. Chief among them are: Donald G. Mathews's seminal study, *Religion in the Old South* (Chicago: University of Chicago Press, 1977); John Boles, *The Great Revival in the South* (Lexington: University of Kentucky Press, 1972); Anne C. Loveland, *Southern Evangelicals and the Social Order, 1800–1860* (Baton Rouge: Louisiana State University Press, 1980); Fred Hood, *Reformed America: The Middle and Southern States, 1783–1837* (University: University of Alabama Press, 1980). Finally, Jon Butler, author of "Enlarging the Bonds of Christ: Slavery, Evangelism, and the Christianization of the White South, 1690–1790," in Leonard I. Sweet, ed., *The Evangelical Tradition in America* (Macon, Ga.: Mercer University Press, 1980), 87–112, is the only church historian to deal effectively with the problems of religious indifference.

The theme of the South's distinctiveness and its continuity, with large implications about popular ethical concerns, is explored most subtly in C. Vann Woodward, *Thinking Back: The Perils of Writing History* (Baton Rouge: Louisiana State University Press, 1986). A contrast may be drawn between Woodward's position and that of Carl N. Degler, *Place Over Time: The Continuity of Southern Distinctiveness* (Baton Rouge: Louisiana State University Press, 1977). Particularly notable is Edward Pessen's essay, "How Different from Each Other Were the Antebellum North and South?" *American Historical Review,* 85 (December 1980), 1119–49, supplemented by stimulating rejoinders from leading critics (pp. 1150–66). John Shelton Reed, *The Enduring South: Sub-Culture Persistence in Mass Society* (Lexington: University Press of Kentucky, 1972) and *Southerners: The Social Psychology of Sectionalism* (Chapel Hill: University of North Carolina Press, 1983) bring up to date the enduring features of the ethic of honor in the contemporary South.

II. Southern Political Culture

Still the most comprehensive interpretation of the early secession movement in South Carolina is William W. Freehling, *Prelude to Civil War: The Nullification Controversy in South Carolina, 1816–1836* (New York: Harper & Row, 1965). In contrast to Freehling, James B. Stewart, in " 'A Great Talking and Eating Machine': Patriarchy, Mobilization and the Dynamics of Nullification in South Carolina," *Civil War History,* 27 (September 1981), 197–220, suggests that fears for lost honor rather than worries over slave plots agitated the Nullifiers. Based on deep research and quantitative analysis, J. Mills Thornton, III, *Politics and Power in a Slave Society: Alabama, 1800–1860* (Baton Rouge: Louisiana State University Press, 1978), supports the interpretation presented here, though using a different terminology. Another exemplary study is William L. Barney, *The Secessionist Impulse: Alabama and Mississippi in 1860* (Princeton: Princeton University Press, 1974). William J. Cooper, Jr., *The South and the Politics of Slavery, 1828–1856* (Baton Rouge: Louisiana State University Press, 1977) and *Liberty and Slavery: Southern Politics to 1860* (New York: Knopf, 1983) are reexaminations of Southern political life before the Civil War. Older but still valuable is Ulrich B. Phillips, *The Course of the South to Secession* (Gloucester: Peter Smith, 1964 [1939]). David Potter, *The Impending Crisis, 1848–1861* (New York: Harper & Row, 1976) gives the overview of political events leading to the war.

III. Biographies and Contemporary Personal Accounts

The most interesting eighteenth-century diaries for studying popular ethics and personal attitudes are: Jack P. Greene, ed., *The Diary of Colonel Landon Carter of Sabine Hall, 1762–1776,* 2 vols. (Charlottesville: University Press of Virginia, 1965); Louis B. Wright and Marion Tinling, eds., *The Secret Diary of William Byrd of Westover, 1709–1712* (Richmond: Dietz Press, 1941); and Hunter Dickinson Farish, ed., *The Journal and Letters of Philip*

Vickers Fithian: A Plantation Tutor of the Old Dominion, 1773–1774 (Williamsburg: Colonial Williamsburg, 1957 [1943]). Robert Dawidoff, *The Education of John Randolph* (New York: W. W. Norton, 1979) interprets in stimulating fashion the peculiarities of one of Virginia's leading gentlemen of the old school.

For the later years of the pre-Civil War period, Elisabeth Muhlenfeld, *Mary Boykin Chesnut: A Biography* (Baton Rouge: Louisiana State University Press, 1981) and C. Vann Woodward, ed., *Mary Chesnut's Civil War* (New Haven: Yale University Press, 1981) present the life and reflections of the Old South's most acute social commentator. A similarly interesting pair of works deals with James Henry Hammond, another Carolinian: Carol Blesser, ed., *The Hammonds of Redcliffe* (New York: Oxford University Press, 1981), a collection of family letters with commentary, and Drew Gilpin Faust, *James Henry Hammond and the Old South: A Design for Mastery* (Baton Rouge: Louisiana State University Press, 1982), a beautifully crafted study of a conservative planter from needy beginnings obsessed with matters of power, wealth, and reputation. Hammond's intellectually gifted friend William J. Grayson wrote an autobiography which was edited by Samuel G. Stoney in the 1948 issues of the *South Carolina Historical and Genealogical Magazine* (vol. 49). One of Hammond's friends suffered from mental depression and irascibility: his journal has been edited by William K. Scarborough in two volumes as *The Diary of Edmund Ruffin* (Baton Rouge: Louisiana State University Press, 1972, 1976). Craig A. Simpson, *A Good Southerner: The Life of Henry A. Wise of Virginia* (Chapel Hill: University of North Carolina Press, 1985) deftly portrays a Virginia governor and gentleman of the state rights school. Robert E. May, *John A. Quitman: Old South Crusader* (Baton Rouge: Louisiana State University Press, 1985) recounts the life of a Mississippi governor of Northern upbringing who, like Wise, prided himself on his gentility. A valuable reinterpretation of General Lee's role in the public mind is Thomas E. Connelly, *The Marble Man: Robert E. Lee and His Image in American Society* (Baton Rouge: Louisiana State University Press, 1977).

IV.   White Social Structure

There is much about interclass relationships to be learned from Carl Degler, *The Other South: Southern Dissenters in the Nineteenth Century* (New York: Harper & Row, 1974) and from that treasury of information about one locale: Orville Vernon Burton, *In My Father's House Are Many Mansions: Family and Community in Edgefield, South Carolina* (Chapel Hill: University of North Carolina Press, 1985). Most persuasive is Michael P. Johnson, "Planters and Patriarchy: Charleston, 1800–1860," *Journal of Southern History*, 46 (February 1980), 45–72. Depicting Southerners as middle-class folk little different from Yankees of the same class, F. N. Boney's lively *Southerners All* (Macon, Ga.: Mercer University Press, 1984) makes an interesting contrast to the interpretation offered here.

Partly because of a paucity of personal records related to the white lower classes, Southern historians have favored the activities of the planter elite. Accounts by contemporary observers traversing the backcountry provide some first-rate accounts, most notably, Frederick Law Olmsted, *The Cotton Kingdom*, Arthur M. Schlesinger, Sr., ed. (New York: Modern Library, 1984); *A Journey in the Seaboard Slave States* (New York: Negro Universities Press, 1956), and *Journey in the Back Country* (New York: Schocken Books, 1972). Another acute observer is Joseph Holt Ingraham, author of *The South-West. By a Yankee*, 2 vols. (New York: Readex, 1966 [1835]).

Utilizing court documents and the statistics that can be gleaned from them, Steven Hahn, *The Roots of Southern Populism: Yeoman Farmers and the Transformation of the Georgia Upcountry, 1850–1890* (New York: Oxford University Press, 1983) and William J. Harris, *Plain Folk and Gentry in a Slave Society: White Liberty and Black Slavery in Augusta's Hinterlands* (Middletown, Conn.: Wesleyan University Press, 1985) draw somewhat separate conclusions about class and geographical relationships in Georgia, but both are worth examination. For a third approach see Robert C. Kenzer, "Family, Kinship, and Neighborhood in an Antebellum

Southern Community," in William J. Cooper, Jr., Michael F. Holt, and John McCardell, eds., *A Master's Due: Essays in Honor of David Herbert Donald* (Baton Rouge: Louisiana State University Press, 1985), 138–60. Two older sociological works on the upcountry folk hold interest: Horace Kephart, *Our Southern Highlanders: A Narrative of Adventure in the Southern Appalachians and a Study of Life among the Mountaineers* (Knoxville: University of Tennessee Press, 1976 [1922]) and John C. Campbell, *The Southern Highlander and His Homeland* (New York: Russell Sage Foundation, 1921). Frank Lawrence Owsley, *Plain Folk of the Old South* (Baton Rouge: Louisiana State University Press, 1949) endures; no scholarly work has yet replaced it.

V.   Slavery and Racial Prejudices

The literature on slavery has been so enormous that limiting selection to just a few authorities is not easy. First, there are the prolific and stimulating inquiries of Eugene D. Genovese, the Marxian interpreter of the Old South. Among his studies are: with Elizabeth Fox-Genovese, the unfortunately neglected *Fruits of Merchant Capital: Slavery and Bourgeois Property in the Rise and Expansion of Capitalism* (New York: Oxford University Press, 1983); and *The World the Slaveholders Made: Two Essays in Interpretation* (New York: Pantheon, 1969); *The Political Economy of Slavery: Studies in the Economy and Society of the Slave South* (New York: Random House, 1965); and *Roll, Jordan, Roll: The World the Slaves Made* (New York: Pantheon, 1976). Other works worthy of citation are: George M. Fredrickson, *The Black Image in the White Mind: The Debate on Afro-American Character and Destiny, 1817–1914* (New York: Harper & Row, 1971) and *White Supremacy: A Comparative Study in American and South African History* (New York: Oxford University Press, 1981); Winthrop Jordan, *White Over Black: American Attitudes toward the Negro, 1550–1812* (Chapel Hill: University of North Carolina Press, 1968); Herbert G. Gutman, *The Black Family in Slavery and Freedom, 1750–1925* (New

York: Pantheon, 1976); Leon F. Litwack, *Been in the Storm So Long: The Aftermath of Slavery* (New York: Knopf, 1979); and the latest of many works by David Brion Davis, *Slavery and Human Progress* (New York: Oxford University Press, 1984). Willie Lee Rose brilliantly explores the evolution of masterhood in "The Domestication of Domestic Slavery," in *Slavery and Freedom*, William W. Freehling, ed. (New York: Oxford University Press, 1982), 18–36. Peter Kolchin's two articles, "Reevaluating the Antebellum Slave Community: A Comparative Perspective," *Journal of American History*, 70 (December 1983), 579–601, and "American Historians and Antebellum Southern Slavery," in Cooper et al., eds., *A Master's Due*, 87–111, offer unsentimental perspectives on life in the quarters and how historians have described it.

Often overlooked is James H. Johnston, *Race Relations in Virginia and Miscegenation in the South, 1776–1860* (Amherst: University of Massachusetts Press, 1970). Joel Williamson, *New People: Miscegenation and Mulattoes in the United States* (New York: Free Press, 1980) is the most recent study of sexual intermixing. Readers of this book will be interested in Terry Alford's fascinating *Prince among Slaves* (New York: Oxford University Press, 1986 [1977]) because "Prince," heir to the throne of a West African kingdom, belonged to the Foster family whose story is related in the last chapter.

With fluency and comprehensiveness, three books explore black cultural life on large and small scale: John Blassingame, *The Slave Community: Plantation Life in the Antebellum South* (New York: Oxford University Press, 1972); Lawrence F. Levine, *Black Culture and Black Consciousness: Afro-American Folk Thought from Slavery to Freedom* (New York: Oxford University Press, 1977); and Charles Joyner, *Down by the Riverside: A South Carolina Slave Community* (Urbana: University of Illinois Press, 1984). Jacqueline Jones, *Labor of Love, Labor of Sorrow: Black Women, Work, and the Family from Slavery to the Present* (New York: Basic Books, 1985) surveys a neglected topic. A work that complements the thesis of this book is Orlando Patterson, *Slavery and Social Death: A Comparative Study* (Cambridge: Harvard University Press, 1982).

It is discussed at some length in my review essay in *Society,* 21 (March/April 1984), 92–94.

The degree of fantasy and substance involved in insurrectionary plots and scares has been the subject of much controversy. An excellent example of the debate emerges from a comparison of Richard C. Wade, "The Vesey Plot: A Reconsideration," *Journal of Southern History,* 30 (May 1964), 144–61, and William W. Freehling, "Denmark Vesey's Peculiar Reality," in Robert H. Abzug and Stephen E. Maizlish, eds., *New Perspectives on Race and Slavery in America: Essays in Honor of Kenneth M. Stampp* (Lexington: University Press of Kentucky, 1986), 25–47. Other works on insurrections and scares include Herbert Aptheker, *American Negro Slave Revolts* (New York: International Publ., 1973 [1943]); Eugene D. Genovese, *From Rebellion to Freedom: Afro-American Slave Revolts in the Making of the Modern World* (Baton Rouge: Louisiana State University Press, 1979); and, perhaps the best so far, Gerald W. Mullin, *Flight and Rebellion: Slave Resistance in Eighteenth-Century Virginia* (New York: Oxford University Press, 1972).

VI. Women and Family Life

The best source for studying domestic life is, of course, the memoirs, diaries, and correspondence of nineteenth-century Southern families. Foremost in the genre is Robert M. Myers, ed., *Children of Pride: A True Story of Georgia and the Civil War* (New Haven: Yale University Press, 1972). Other examples include: Mary D. Robertson, ed., *Lucy Breckinridge of Grove Hill: The Journal of a Virginia Girl, 1862–1864* (Kent: Kent State University Press, 1979); the recently reprinted Susan Dabney Smedes, *Memorials of a Southern Planter,* Fletcher M. Green, ed. (Jackson: University Press of Mississippi, 1981 [1887]).

Long an interpretive classic in women's histroy, Anne Firor Scott, *The Southern Lady: From Pedestal to Politics 1830–1930* (Chicago: University of Chicago Press, 1977) provides an excellent point of departure. A number of other studies, however, have expanded our understanding of women's life and work in the Old South but also have opened up a major dispute. On the one hand, Jan Lewis in *The Pursuit of Happiness: Family Values in Jefferson's Virginia* (New York: Cambridge University Press, 1983), Jane Turner Censer, *North Carolina Planters and Their Children, 1800–1860* (Baton Rouge: Louisiana State University Press, 1984), and Daniel Blake Smith, *In the Great House: Planter Family Life in Eighteenth-Century Chesapeake Society* (Ithaca: Cornell University Press, 1980), all propose that Southern courtships and marriages were individualistic and companionate, untroubled by the interferences of family or fatherly involvement. Catherine Clinton's *The Plantation Mistress: Woman's World in the Old South* (New York: Pantheon, 1982), on the other hand, stresses women's subordination. Meantime Suzanne Lebsock, in her prize-winning *The Free Women of Petersburg: Status and Culture in a Southern Town, 1784–1860* (New York: W. W. Norton, 1984), sees both patriarchy and change, resilience and retreat, in complex combinations.

Childrearing has been a neglected topic, but see Philip Greven, *The Protestant Temperament: Religious Experience, and the Self in Early America* (New York: Knopf, 1977). Also there are two thoughtful articles on the theme: Michael Zuckerman, "William Byrd's Family," in *Perspectives in American History*, 12 (1979), 255–311; John F. Walzer, "A Period of Ambivalence: Eighteenth-Century American Childhood," in Lloyd DeMause, ed., *A History of Childhood* (New York: Harper & Row, 1974).

VII.   Social Life and Graces

One of the best early studies of Southern character and social inclinations was written by a Southerner of Northern residence: Daniel R. Hundley, *Social Relations in Our Southern States*, William J. Cooper, Jr., ed. (Baton Rouge: Louisiana State University, 1979), with a forceful introductory essay by the editor. For another but less complex analysis of Southern social life, see Joseph G.

Baldwin, *Flush Times of Alabama and Mississippi: A Series of Sketches* (New York: Sagamore Press, 1973). A fascinating document from many points of view is Edwin A. Davis, ed., *Plantation Life in the Florida Parishes of Louisiana, 1836–1846, as Reflected in the Diary of Bennett H. Barrow* (New York: Columbia University Press, 1943).

Attitudes about hospitality provide insight into the way a group reacts toward the outside world. F. G. Bailey, ed., *Gifts and Poison: The Politics of Reputation* (Oxford: Basil Blackwell, 1971) and Julian Pitt-Rivers, "The Stranger, the Guest, and the Hostile Host: Introduction to the Study of the Laws of Hospitality," in J. G. Peristiany, ed., *Mediterranean Rural Communities and Social Change* (Paris: Mouton, 1967), 13–30, show the complexities behind decisions regarding visitors and newcomers. For more conventional views, read Joe Gray Taylor's lively *Eating, Drinking, and Visiting in the South: An Informal History* (Baton Rouge: Louisiana State University Press, 1982). Old but still useful on social matters are: Rosser H. Taylor, *Ante-Bellum South Carolina: A Social and Cultural History* (Chapel Hill: University of North Carolina Press, 1942); Guion Griffis Johnson, *Ante-Bellum North Carolina: A Social History* (Chapel Hill: University of North Carolina Press, 1937); Everett Dick, *The Dixie Frontier: A Social History of the Southern Frontier from the First Transmontane Beginnings to the Civil War* (New York: Capricorn Books, 1964); and Thomas D. Clark, *The Rampaging Frontier: Manners and Humor of Pioneer Days in the South and the Middle West* (Indianapolis: Bobbs-Merrill, 1939).

Southern historians have generally neglected such matters as horseracing, cockfighting, gambling, drinking, and other nineteenth-century male recreations. But these are some resources: Philip Alexander Bruce, *Social Life in Old Virginia* (New York: Capricorn Books, 1965 [1910]); Jane Carson, *Colonial Virginians at Play* (Williamsburg: Colonial Williamsburg, 1965). Timothy H. Breen, "Horses and Gentleman: The Cultural Significance of Gambling among the Gentry of Virginia," in *Puritans and Adventurers: Change and Persistence in Early America* (New York: Oxford University Press, 1980), 148–63, offers a significant interpretation. Stephen Longstreet, *Win or Lose: A Social History of Gambling in America* (Indianapolis: Bobbs-Merrill, 1977) fills a need. Despite current interest in ecology, no historian has yet studied the role of the hunt in Southern history, surely an issue that could divide as well as unite the propertied and unpropertied elements in a locale. Instead we must rely on literary scholars: see Louis D. Rubin, Jr.'s title essay in *William Elliott Shoots a Bear: Essays on the Southern Literary Imagination* (Baton Rouge: Louisiana State University Press, 1975), 1–28, which compares the world views of a Carolinian sportsman and a twentieth-century hunter and novelist, William Faulkner.

VIII.   Violence: Personal, Legal, and Communal

Much work remains to be done on the history of Southern jurisprudence, crime, and community justice. Dickson D. Bruce, Jr., *Violence and Culture in the Antebellum South* (Austin: University of Texas Press, 1979), however, treats the topic with much penetration. For comparative purposes Douglas Hay et al., eds., *Albion's Fatal Tree: Crime and Society in Eighteenth-Century England* (New York: Pantheon, 1975) casts light on Southern law and ritual. Peter Shaw deals with the traditions of crowd behavior in *American Patriots and the Rituals of Revolution* (Cambridge: Harvard University Press, 1981). More directly appropriate is Edward L. Ayers, *Vengeance and Justice: Crime and Punishment in the Nineteenth-Century South* (New York: Oxford University Press, 1984), which, like Shaw's work, uses the ethics of honor and shame as a point of departure. Not to be neglected is Michael S. Hindus, *Prison and Plantation: Crime, Justice, and Authority in Massachusetts and South Carolina, 1767–1878* (Chapel Hill: University of North Carolina Press, 1980).

Lower-class personal violence has received recent examination in Elliot J. Gorn, " 'Gouge and Bite, Pull Hair and Scratch': The Social Significance of Fighting in the Southern Backcountry,"

American Historical Review, 90 (February 1985), 18–43. Grady McWhiney finds Celtic sources for Southern mayhem: "Ethnic Roots of Southern Violence," in Cooper et al., eds., *A Master's Due,* 112–37. In a more conventional vein, Jack Kenny Williams is both entertaining and enlightening in *Vogues in Villainy: Crime and Retribution in Ante-Bellum South Carolina* (Columbia: University of South Carolina Press, 1959). James C. Klotter, "Feuds in Appalachia: An Overview," *Filson Club History Quarterly,* 56 (July 1982), 290–317, presents the most recent findings on the Southern feud. On class relations, law, and felony, see also Bertram Wyatt-Brown, "Community, Class, and Snopesian Crime: Local Justice in the Old South," in Orville Vernon Burton and Robert C. McMath, Jr., eds., *Class, Conflict, and Consensus: Antebellum Southern Community Studies* (Westport, Conn.: Greenwood Press, 1982), 173–206.

With reference to the inner dynamics of nineteenth-century lynch-law, there are no recent studies worthy of the topic's significance, but one essay, E. P. Thompson, " 'Rough Music,' Le Charivari Anglais," *Annales: Economies, Sociétés: Civilisation* (Mars–Avril 1972), 285–312, suggests the almost universal character of the phenomenon, and another, Charles L. Flynn, Jr., "The Ancient Pedigree of Violent Repression: Georgia's Klan as a Folk Movement," in Walter J. Fraser, Jr., and Winfred B. Moore, Jr., eds., *The Southern Enigma: Essays on Race, Class, and Folk Culture* (Westport, Conn.: Greenwood Press, 1983) applies Thompson's findings to the Southern species. Readers may be interested in *Col. Crockett's Exploits and Adventures . . .* (Washington, D.C.: Thomas McGill, 1837) because in it he recounts at second-hand the tarring and feathering of James Foster, Jr. The Reconstruction Klan as an arm of vindication and honor, as well as of race control, must be reexamined, but see Kermit L. Hall, "Political Power and Constitutional Legitimacy: The South Carolina Ku Klux Klan Trials, 1871–1872," *Emory Law Journal,* 33 (Fall 1984), 921–51.

The duel is the most visible but least well treated of Southern forms of violence. The only recent book on this subject is Jack R. Williams, *Dueling in the Old South: Vignettes of Social History* (College Station: Texas A & M University Press, 1980). Steven Mac

Stowe, "The 'Touchiness' of the Gentleman Planter: The Sense of Esteem and Continuity in the Ante Bellum South," *Psychohistory Review*, 8 (Winter 1979), 485–510, is a perceptive essay. Kenneth S. Greenberg's work on slavery and the planter class, soon to be published by the Johns Hopkins University Press, will no doubt offer new findings and interpretations. Older works include Don C. Seitz, *Famous American Duels with Some Account of the Causes That Led Up to Them and the Men Engaged* (New York: Thomas Y. Crowell, 1929); Thomas Gamble, *Savannah Duels and Duellists, 1733–1877* (Spartanburg, S.C.: Reprint Co., 1974 [1923]).

Although no one has yet examined the role of common law in Southern legal history, the field shows signs of new vigor. See especially David J. Bodenhamer and James W. Ely, Jr., eds., *Ambivalent Legacy: A Legal History of the South* (Jackson: University Press of Mississippi, 1984), in which may be found a selective bibliography with references to essays on collective violence and criminal justice. One must not overlook an older but still excellent summary: Charles S. Sydnor, "The Southerner and the Laws," *Journal of Southern History*, 6 (February 1940), 3–23.

Index

Abbott, Abiel, 67
Adams, Henry, 43–44, 52, 76
Adultery, 35–38, 95–115, 199, 202.
    See also Cuckoldry; Fornication;
    Gallantry (sexual)
Affability, concept of, 41–42, 45, 50.
    See also Hospitality; Largess
Alexander family, 69
Alford, Terry, 224
Allen, James (of Virginia), 173–74
Alston, J. Motte, 125
"Amalgamation," 206. *See also*
    Miscegenation
Ancestors, 59–60, 64–67
Anticlericalism, 83, 162
Antigambling, 134, 140–41
Anti-intellectuality, 46, 50–51
Antislavery, 27–28, 108, 159, 167, 203–4,
    214
Appearance, as moral determinant, 26,
    27. *See also* Ascriptions
Apprentices, 16, 167
Aptheker, Herbert, 179
Arete, 61
Aristotle, 47
Arson, 175
Asceticism, Christian, 47
Ascriptions, 26, 33–35, 188; community
    evaluations of, 26, 30–32, 154.
    See also Bloodlines
Authority, 7–10, 46. *See also* Leader-
    ship; Patriarchy

Bagby, George W., 119
Bailey, Robert, 138–40, 147
Barnard, Barbara Foster, 225, 227
Barnard, William, 113, 227
Barrow, Bennet (and wife), 107, 162
Baxter, Richard, 52
Bay, Elihu, 100
Beatitudes, 38–39
Becker, Ernest, 244
Behavior, rules of, 61–62. *See also*
    Ethics; Honor
Benevolent societies, 54, 55
Bennett, Thomas, 171–73, 177
Bernard, John, 127
Beverley, William, 80
Bishop, Joel P., 104
"Black sheep," 65–66, 77, 112–15, 130,
    225. *See also* Father-son relations;
    Oedipal conflict
Blacks, free, 155, 156, 172
Blair, Agan, 89
Blassingame, John (of Alabama), 64
Blassingame, John W., 160
Bloodlines, concepts of, 4, 31, 39, 41,
    64–70, 100. *See also* "Amalgama-
    tion"; Miscegenation; Mulattoes
Body, human, *see* Ascriptions
Boorstin, Daniel, 143, 147
Boredom, 88, 93, 120–21, 126, 152–53
The Bostonians, 43
"Boundary maintenance," 210. *See also*
    Conformity; Deviance

Brattle, William, 44
Bravery, *see* Courage; Masculinity;
    Valor; Women; as heroines
Breen, Timothy H., 133, 135
Bremer, Frederika, 127
Brooks, Preston, 27
Brother–brother-in-law, relations of,
    226–27
Brother-sister relations, *see* Incest;
    Siblings
Brown, Albert Gallatin, 29, 30–31
Brown, John, 159
Brown, John L., 98
Brown, William Garrott, 32, 122
Bruce, Dickson D., 131, 143, 145
Bruce, Philip, 60
Bruce, William Cabell, 34
Burke, Edmund, 48, 95
Burton, Hutchins, 110–11
Butt, Benjamin Jr., and Lydia
    (Bright), 109
Byrd, William, II, 40–41, 89, 156–57
Byrd, William, III, 141

Cabell, John C., 169
Calhoun, John C., 29, 37
Calvert, Cornelius, 180
Carlyle, Thomas, 95, 121
Carr, Frank, 161
Carr, Peter, 46, 51–52
Carter, Landon, 65, 90, 134, 140
Cartwright, Peter, 140
Cash, Wilbur J., 61
Catharsis (pity and terror), 8, 12, 150,
    210, 212, 241
Celts, 26, 33, 37, 193. *See also* Scots;
    Scots-Irish
Chalmers, Davidson, 64
Chaplin, Thomas B., 120, 130
Charivari (shivaree), 7–13, 17, and
    Africans, 196; and law, 194–95;
    and minor offenses, 203–5; and
    social order, 194; and unpopular
    ideas, 203–5; and wedding-day,
    197–98, 200; and youth, 197, 200–
    201, 402–4. *See also* Degradation
    ceremonies; Shamings; Saturnalia
Chastity: male, 9, 95–96. *See also*
    Honor: female
Chaucer, Geoffrey, 23
Chesnut, James, Sr., 94
Chesnut, Mary Boykin (Miller), 27,
    93–94, 105
Chew, Sarah R., 234
Childrearing: aggression encouraged
    in, 80–81; black families', 79;
    daughters in, 80, 88–91 (*see also*
    Father-daughter relations); decep-

tions in, 77; disciplining in, 81;
    evangelical Southerners and, 81;
    fathers in, 77–79, 80, 81, 82–84
    (*see also* Father-son relations);
    idiosyncratic character of, 81; ill-
    ness in, 80; Northern commercial
    style of, 79; Northern evangelical
    style of, 71–74; parental indul-
    gence in, 79, 80; poor whites', 80–
    81; and slavery, 84; traditionalism
    in, 80–84. *See also* Punishments
Chinn, Julia, 106
Chivalry, 23, 27, 44, 152, 245
Cicero, 45, 47, 134
Claiborne, Ferdinand L., 219
Classics, 44, 45–47
Clergy, 134, 208
Clingman, Thomas L., 150
Clinkscales, J. G., 71, 90
"Clothing stage," 70, 80
Cocke, John Hartwell, 54, 55, 169, 174
Cockfighting, 132, 133
Combat, *see* Duels; Homicide; Violence
Community, 4, 9, 10, 11–17, 26–27, 61,
    169, 184, 188, 192, 198–99, 204,
    205, 215, 241–42. *See also* Ascrip-
    tions, community evaluations of;
    Honor: and community
Condescension, 38
Condonation, 100
A Confederacy of Dunces, 189–90
Conformity, 14–15, 17, 26–27, 121, 134,
    174, 190, 198–200. *See also* Indi-
    vidualism; Privacy, Southern
    lack of
Conjuration, 108, 109, 176, 177
Conscience, 14, 22, 52–53, 71–74, 81–82.
    See also Guilt
Cornick, Jeremiah (slave), 179–83
Cornish, John, 128
Costuming, 6, 7, 8, 189–90, 195–96, 200,
    204. *See also* Charivari; Mardi
    Gras
Courage, 74, 211–12. *See also* Honor:
    as integrity; Masculinity; Valor;
    Women: as heroines
Courtesy, 23, 43
Cowardice, 28, 29. *See also* Crowd
    psychology
"Cowbellions," 195
Creecy, James, 238–41
Creoles, 200
Criminal conversation, 100
Crockett, David, 239
Crowd psychology, 12–13, 187–88, 211–
    13, 242–44
Cuckoldry, 35–38, 102–3, 105, 202, 241.
    See also Adultery; Fornication;
    Gallantry (sexual)

Cumming, William, 150
Curtis, Moses Ashley, 90–91, 160–61, 169–70, 196–97

Davis, Jefferson, 56, 58, 143
Davis, Reuben, 78
DeBow's Review, 32
Debts, 23, 137–38
Deference, 23, 74, 132, 161. *See also* Authority; Courtesy; Leadership
Degradation ceremonies, 158, 178, 189, 237, 238–45. *See also* Charivari; Shamings
DeMaret, Edgar, 230–31
Democracy, 20, 38–39 (*Herrenvolk*), 61, 149, 198
Dent, John Horry, 82–84
Dependency, despisement of, 125, 127–28. *See also* Kinlessness
Deviance, 111–12, 134, 158, 186. *See also* Charivari; Gossip; Lynch law
Dew, Thomas Roderick, 53, 86, 95
Dickens, Charles, 95–96, 214
Divorce, 100–105, 113–14
"Double standard" of sexuality, 37–38, 95
Douglas, Mary, 212
Drinking, 23, 46, 113, 121–22, 151, 163
Dudley, Theodore, 66
Duels, 120, 142–53
Dunn, Mary, 109

Education, 32; classical, 44–51. *See also* Learnedness
Elites, Southern, 43, 64–70, 103; Northern and Southern compared, 43–44, 122–23
Emerson, Ralph Waldo, 95–96
Entertainments. *See* Drinking; Gambling; Parties; Rituals: of speech
Entitlements, 4, 146–47, 171
Ethics: externality of, 26, 27; general, 18, 31; racial, 369, 183–86 (*see also* Racism); sacred rules of, 61–62, 188, 211–12; sexual, 85–115; Stoic-Christian, 25, 38, 51–61, 78, 245; work, 119–20, 126. *See also* Gentility; Honor
Evangelicalism: church discipline, 198–99; and dueling, 146; Northern, 71–72; Southern, 51–61, 134–35
Everett, Edward, 48
Evans, Hiram, 206

Falkner, William C., 143–44, 211
Family: defense of, 13, 14, 28, 35–38, 59–60, 75, 78, 188, 192, 198, 202, 206, 209, 220; loyalty to, 13, 14, 17, 28–29, 35–38, 65–67, 124–25, 220; and sibling exchange, 221
Farr, William, 107–8
Fatalism, 25
Father-daughter relations, 89–90, 225–26. *See also* Childrearing: daughters in
Father-son relations, 11, 63–70, 134, 141–42. *See also* "Black sheep"; Childrearing; Oedipal conflict
Faulkner, William, 21, 71, 86, 143, 180, 211, 223, 228, 245
Faust, Drew Gilpin, 50
Feminism, 85
Feuds, 143–44
Fithian, Philip Vickers, 141
Folk beliefs, *see* Conjuration; Oral traditions; Supernaturalism
Foote, Henry S., 33, 146, 191
Fornication, 95–96. *See also* Adultery; Cuckoldry; Gallantry (sexual)
Foster, Ellen, 225
Foster, Ephraim, 226
Foster, Isaac, 225
Foster, James, Jr., 113, 215–18, 226–28, 234, 237–39, 240–45
Foster, James, Sr., 221–22
Foster, John, 221–22, 234
Foster, Levi, 113–14, 218, 223, 225, 228–29, 242
Foster, Mary, 225–26
Foster, Mary, Sr., 221
Foster, Mary Carson, 226
Foster, Murphy, 242
Foster, Rachel, 223
Foster, Sarah, 225
Foster, Sarah Smith, 112, 216–21, 222–28
Foster, Susan Alpha, 214–17, 222, 225, 232–34, 240, 245
Foster, Susannah Carson, 112–14, 228
Foster, Thomas, Jr., 112–14, 216, 218, 222, 225, 228, 230, 241
Foster, Thomas, Sr., 112–14, 216–18, 221–24, 226, 228–30, 242
Foster, William, 217–20, 222–24, 229
Foster, Zeide DeMaret, 230
Foster family, 214–45
Frank, Leo, 191, 212
Freeman, Douglas Southall, 58, 60
Freud, Sigmund, 75, 112
Fuller, Corydon, 41, 121–22, 129, 215

Gabriel (Prosser) Insurrectionary Plot, 167, 168
Gallantry (sexual), 23, 201, 202

Gambling, 23, 131–42, 151, 228–29, 237.
    See also Debts
Garrison, William Lloyd, 205
Gavin, David, 181
Genovese, Eugene D., 123, 156, 160, 179
Gentility, 23, 27, 40–62, 245; Christian,
    53, 55; English influence on, 40–41;
    and piety, 51–61. *See also* Chiv-
    alry; Learnedness; *Megalopsychia*
Gentleman: concept of, 40, 41–43, 47,
    48, 55–60, 64–70, 94, 138, 243, 245;
    and gambling, 138–40; and golden
    mean, 48, 60–61; and learning,
    43–47
Gentry, 40–60
The Glass Menagerie, 125–26
Glory, military, 27–29, 30–31. *See also*
    Valor
Gossip, 36, 105–6, 139–40, 169, 198, 199
Gouge, William, 198
Grayson, Spence Monroe, 233–36, 239–
    40, 242–45
Grayson, William J., 23, 44–45, 48–49,
    54–55, 137, 147, 149
Greenleaf, Daniel, 220, 233–35, 239
Gregariousness, 121–22, 135
Gridley, Horace, 229, 238–40
Grigsby, Hugh, 54
Guilt, 3, 4, 52, 71–74, 76–77
Gutman, Herbert G., 201

Hall, Bolling, 66
Hall, Francis, 127
Hamilton, Alexander, 20
Hammond, James Henry, 53, 64–65, 88,
    96, 98, 100, 129–30
Hampton, Wade, 90
Harper, William, 97
Harvard College, 43, 44
Hawthorne, Nathaniel, 4–5, 9, 11–22,
    26, 37, 192, 207, 209, 212, 215, 237,
    242, 245
High-mindedness, *see* Megalopsychia
Holyoake, George J., 211
Homicide, 105, 155, 157, 175, 176, 214.
    See also Parricide; Wives, as vic-
    tims of abuse
Honor: and age, 7–8, 9; and atrocity,
    34–35; and bloodlines (*see* Blood-
    lines); and body (*see* Ascriptions);
    as Chivalry (*see* Chivalry); and
    Civil War causation, 24, 29, 245;
    colors of, 6, 7, 8, 206–7, 208; and
    commercial values, 29, 137; contra-
    dictions of, 4, 22, 23, 39; in decline
    21; definition of, vii–x, 4, 14, 26–27,
    60–61, 74, 104, 154; efficacy of, 60–
    61; exaggerations of, 22; and false

claims to, 28, 45; and fame, 27–28,
    45, 57; family, 12 (*see also* Family);
    female, 9, 91–94; and forbearance,
    60–61, 74; hierarchy, and *below
    under* status (*see also* Authority;
    Entitlements; Leadership) and im-
    mortality (*see above under* fame);
    and integrity, 31–32, 48, 58–60, 174,
    186; and kinship protection (*see*
    Family defense); lineage (*see* Blood-
    lines); and literature, 21–23; mis-
    interpreted, 3; and mistrust, 27,
    76, 131, 198; and patriotism, 59–
    61; primal, 3–39, 61–62; and pru-
    dence, 29–30, 245; and race (*see*
    Ethics: racial; Racism); and ration-
    ality, 22, 47; and self-dependence,
    75, 80–81 (*see also* Self-worth); and
    seniority, 7–8, 10, 46, 75; and sex-
    uality, 34–38, 95–113; and slavery,
    3–4, 15–17, 22, 29–31, 188; and
    status, 31, 41, 49, 77, 132, 136, 152–
    53; and thought process, 30–32,
    157–58; in titles (*see* Entitlement);
    and virilization, 95–98; vitality of,
    38, 60–61, 78; and wealth, 21
Hoole, Axalla, 66–67
Horse-racing, *see* Gambling; Sport
Hospitality, 42, 123–31. *See also* Largess;
    Magnanimity
Houston, Sam, 35, 148
Huger, Daniel, 101
Huizinga, Johann, 136
Humanism, *see* Ethics, Stoic-Christian
Hundley, Daniel R., 31, 33
Hunting, 120
Husband-wife relations, 35–36; oedipal
    feelings in, 112. *See also* Wives
Huston, Felix, 148–49, 220, 235–36,
    238–39, 242–44

Ibrahima, Abd-al-Rahman, 114, 216,
    224
Idleness, 31. *See also* Ethics, work;
    Leisure
Incest, 96, 107–8
Ingraham, Joseph H., 222
Insult, verbal, 36–37, 150, 152. *See also*
    Duels; Revenge
Insurrectionary scares: slaves, authentic
    revolts, 155, 167; and black crimes,
    175–76; and black leadership as-
    saulted, 163; and black reprisals
    in, 155; black response to, 165–68;
    black testimony in, 163–64, 166,
    168; and boatmen, 169; collective
    white involvement in, 166–67; and
    drinking customs, 163–64; and

economy, 159, 160; and everyday encroachments, 160–61, 167; free and skilled blacks in, 155, 156, 163, 164, 167, 172; lassitude about 156–57, 164; and "Maroons," 155, 156; militia in, 170–71; misinterpreted, 155, 156, 157; and poisonings, 175–76; politics in, 159–60; primal ethics in, 154, 155, 157–58; rumors in, 166, 169–70; scapegoating in, 157–58; and taxation, 170–72; and testimony, 154, 168, 172, 177–86; and West Indian, Latin Revolts, 156; and white insurrectionary participation, 154, 160; white officials in, 170, 171; and white skeptics, 168, 174, 179–83; and white supremacy, 154–56, 167
Intellectuals, Southern, 23, 50–51

Jackson, Andrew, 33, 42–43, 78, 135, 147–48, 236
James, Henry, 43
Jean, François, Marquis de Chastellux, 136
Jefferson, Thomas, 46, 51–52, 78, 129, 169, 171, 185, 214
Jefferson Academy, 221
Johnson, Richard Mentor, 106–7
Johnson, Samuel, 100
Johnson, William, 163–64, 172
Johnston, Albert Sidney, 148–49, 235
Jones, Bathurst, 168
Jones, Calvin, 163
Jones, Charles Colcock, Jr., 47–48
Jones, Charles Colcock, Sr., 55, 76
Jones, George Fenwick, 38
Justice, and mercy, *see* Pardoning, executive
Jones, Thomas, 80

Katzenmusik, 193
Kinship: and patronage, 5–6. *See also* Family
Ku Klux Klan, 192, 202, 206–7

Lacy, Daniel, 229
Lacy, Susan, 229, 231
Lamar, Lucius Quintus Cincinnatus, 28
Lane, Polly, 110–11
Largess, 38–39, 120–21, 128. *See also* Hospitality; Magnanimity
Latrobe, Charles, 127–28
Law: and finances, 73. *See also* Justice; *specific crimes, motions, suits, and terms*

Leadership: black, 164, 177, 184; white, 122–23, 148–49, 243–44
Learnedness, 43–47, 49, 50
Lee, William Henry Fitzhugh, 43–44
Lee, Mary Custis, 59, 81, 82
Lee, Richard Henry, 56
Lee, Robert E., Jr., 57
Lee, Robert E., Sr., 42, 55–60, 75, 81–82
Leisure, 119–21. *See also* Drinking; Ethics: work; Idleness; Sport
Lesesne, Thomas, 148
Leviticus, 193
Lewis, John, 146
Lewis, William B., 231
Lewis (slave), 178–79
Liberty, 60–61. *See also* Honor: and self-dependence
Lieber, Francis, 53–54
Ligon, Nancy, 216–19, 233
Lineage, *see* Bloodlines; Honor, and lineage
Lockett, Winfrey, 230, 232
Long, Edward, 109
Lord of Misrule, *see* Charivari; Saturnalia
Lovelace, Richard, 22
Luck, 136. *See also,* Providence
Luraghi, Raimondo, 123
Lynch law, 54, 140–41, 154, 160, 187–88, 191–93, 205–13
Lynn, Kenneth S., 28, 40

McClung, Alexander K., 151
McDuffie, George, 150
McGrath, John, 152
McIntosh, Caroline Foster, 217, 225
McIntosh, David Sinclair, 217–20, 227
McIntosh, George, 180–83, 186
MacMillan, Calvin and Daniel, 242
Madison, James, 135
Magnanimity, 38–39, 44, 60–61, 129. *See also* Largess; *Megalopsychia*
Males, in youth, 46, 63–70, 64–67, 202
Manning, John, 64
Mardi Gras, 190, 195–96. *See also* Costuming
"Maroons," 155
Marshall, John, 48, 55
Martineau, Harriet, 121, 127, 138, 149
Masculinity, 20, 27–29, 34, 35, 46, 78–79, 95–96, 105, 151
Masquerading, *see* Costuming
Megalopsychia (high-mindedness), 47, 75. *See also* Gentility
Merrick, Caroline, 88
Methodists, 53, 68
Middle class, 65, 134
Militia, 10, 27, 146–47, 170–71, 185

The Mind of the South, 66. *See also*
Cash, W. J.
Miscegenation, 94, 96–98, 105–15, 151,
201, 206
Missionaries, 54
Mobs, 169, 187, 188, 212–13. *See also*
Lynch law
Molineux, Major, 4–5, 7–8, 10–11, 13,
18, 25, 242
Molineux, Robin, 4–14, 21, 210, 215
Monogamy, 35
Monroe, James, 146, 165, 168, 170–72,
179, 181–82, 184, 186
Montaigne, 34, 47
Montgomery, Alexander, 235–36, 238–
39
Moore, John, 230, 232
Moralia (Plutarch's), 192
Morality, 15
Mortality, 30
Mosley, Betsy, 110
Mother-daughter relations, 88–92
Motherhood, 70–74, 91–92; ambivalence
toward, 70, 159
Mother-son relations, 35
Muhlenfeld, Elisabeth, 93
Mulattoes, 105–15, 156, 201. *See also*
Miscegenation
Murder, *see* Homicide; Parricide;
Wives: as killers, as victims of
abuse
Murrell, John A., 34, 167, 237
"My Kinsman, Major Molineux," 4–14
Myths, 8, 26; Southern, 91–92

Naming patterns, 65–70
Narrenschiff, 193
Neal, Claude, 34–35
Nerthus, 193
New Year's Day, 195
Newgate Prison, 211, 212
Nisbet, Eugenius A., 102
Noblesse oblige, *see* Condescension
Nonslaveholders, *see* Poor whites;
Yeomanry
Norcom, James, 87, 91
North-South comparison, 18, 20, 21, 24,
44, 47, 48, 67, 71–78, 95–96, 99,
156–57
Nouveaux-riches, 64, 147
Nullifiers, 29

Oaths, 207
O'Connor, Rachel (Weeks), 155, 203
Oedipal conflict, 13, 112–14, 141–42
O'Fallon, John, 197
Old Testament, 25, 193

Olmsted, Frederick Law, 128, 162
O'Neall, John Belton, 55, 98, 107–8
Onians, Richard Broxton, 26
Oral traditions, 22, 30–32, 78, 112–23,
245
Overseers, 98
Owsley, Frank L., 99

Page, Thomas Nelson, 90
Pardoning, executive, 168, 169, 183, 184
Parker, Theodore, 73
Parricide, 214
Parties, 121–22, 123–24, 129–30, 132
Patriarchy, 35–36, 39, 49, 57, 63–70, 74,
220–29
Patrols, slave, 163, 164, 185–86
Paulding, James K., 127
Pease, Jane H., 124
Percy, Walker, 26–27
Perry family, 98
Personal strategies, *see* Duels; Hospi-
tality; Gambling; Parties
Petigru, James Louis, 96–97, 146
Pettigrew, William S., 74
Pettus, Dabney and Elizabeth, 109
Pettus, John J., 90
Peyre, T. W., 120
Phillips, Ulrich B., 60
Poisoning, 175–76
Politeness, *see* Courtesy
Pollution, purifying effects of, 212
Poor whites, 31, 49, 68, 99, 102–3, 148,
186, 212. *See also* Yeomanry
Pope, William F., 152
Prentiss, Seargent S., 134, 145, 151, 235
Presbyterians, 53
Primogeniture, *see* Inheritance, prop-
erty
Privacy, Southern lack of, 26–27, 122,
157
Prostitution, 94, 98, 102, 110, 199
Protestantism, 19, 55
Providence, divine, 10, 12, 58. *See also*
Fatalism; Luck
Punishments, capital, 175, 210–12; in
school, 91. *See also* Charivari;
Lynch law

Quashing the venire, 235, 237, 238
Quincy, Josiah, Jr., 42–43
Quincy, Josiah, Sr., 30, 136
Quitman, John A., 114, 227
Quitman family, 239

Racism, 12; sacred rules of, 188; white
solidarity about, 154–55, 184

Ramsay, David, 67
Randolph, John, 28–29, 30, 34, 51, 65, 66, 140
Randolph, Vance, 86, 197, 200–201
Rape, 34–35, 36–37, 110–11, 160, 191–92, 242
Ravenel, Thomas, 120
Read, Thomas, 234
Reconstruction, 206–7, 210
Reeve, Tapping, 104–5
Respectability: Christian, 52–53; general, 23, 47, 51, 68–69, 102, 108. *See also* Honor: and status
Revenge, 25, 27–30, 37–39, 98, 104–5, 150–51
Revolution, American, 5, 19, 28, 29–30, 35, 50, 51, 204, 205
Richard II, 22
Rituals: of punishment, 158 (*see also* Charivari, Insurrectionary scares: slave); of speech, 45, 47, 122–23. *See also* Gambling; Hospitality
"Rogue's March," 193, 205, 240. *See also* Charivari
"Rough Music," 204, 240. *See also* Charivari
Royall, Anne, 41
Ruffin, Edmund, 28, 51, 124, 130, 157, 173, 174, 178
Ruffin, Thomas, 173
Runnels, Hiram G., 173

Saturnalia, 163, 185–86. *See also* Charivari; Mardi Gras
Scalping, 34, 212, 240
Scapegoating, 15, 152–53, 158, 186, 189, 192, 193, 203, 228, 237, 243–45
The Scarlet Letter, 13
Scots, 69
Scots-Irish, 16, 69, 131
Scott, Walter, 22–23
Scottsboro case (1931), 110
Secessionism, viii, 24, 27–30, 59–60, 115
Seduction, 37
Self-worth, concepts of, 4, 14, 27, 30–31, 47, 51, 52–53, 150–51
Semple, Emily Virginia, 89
Sewanee, Tennessee, 201
Sex: differentiation of, 35–38; and male misconduct, 94–98; and Quakers, 76
Sexton, John R. and Betsey, 103, 104
Shame, viii, 77, 83, 201; in childbearing, 151, 174; and family woes, 201, 204, 242–43; in military defeat, 81; in physique, 33–34
Shamelessness, vii, 25, 154

Shamings, 19, 22, 188, 200, 204, 212–13. *See also* Charivari
Sharkey, William L., 173
Shields, Joseph, 151
Sibling exchange, 221
Siblings, 80–81, 90
Simmons, James, 64
Simms, William Gilmore, 50
Skimmington, 193
Slander, *See* Gossip; Insult, verbal
Slaton, John, 191–92
Slaveholders: complacency of, 156–57. *See also* Insurrectionary scares: slave
Slaveholding; as moral evil, 58, 94
Slavery, 16, 17, 18, 22, 49–50; and nonviolent resistance to, 160–62
Smith, Daniel Scott, 67
Smylie, James, 218
Smyth, John F. D., 127
Sociability, *see* Affability
Solitariness, 13, 121–23, 152–53
Sorsby, Elizabeth Foster, 217, 225
Sorsby, Samuel K., 217
South, Old: regional identity of, 55, 60–61; uniqueness of, 31
South Carolina College, 53
Southern Literary Messenger, 45
Southern rights, *see* State rights
Sparks, W. H., 135
Speech, *see* Rituals: of speech
Speed, Cassandra Foster, 225–26, 245
Speed, John, 226–27, 235
Spencer, Cornelia A., 127
Spinsters, 125–26
Splane, Alexander, 230, 232
Sport, 33, 120, 133–34, 135. *See also* Hunting
Stang-riding, 193. *See also* Charivari
State rights, 59
Status, *see* Honor: and status
Stephens, Alexander H., 33
Stewart, Virgil A., 237
Stigma, 139–40, 158, 242–43. *See also* Shamings
Stoic-Christian tradition, *see* Ethics
Stokes, Montfort, 163
Storytelling, 32. *See also* Oral traditions
"Submissionists," 29
Sumner, Charles, 27, 28
Supernaturalism, 122, 206, 208. *See also* Conjuration
Susy (slave), 112–14, 225, 487
Suttle, Charles, 47

Tar-and-feathers, 7–9, 193, 204, 240. *See also* Charivari

Taylor, Nancy (Nuzum) and Thomas, 103–4
Thievery, 203, 209
"Thimblerig," 239–41
Thomas, Ella C. G., 106
Thomas, Keith, 111–12
Thought process, 31–32
Titles, *see* Entitlements
Toole, John Kennedy, 189–90
Townes, Samuel A., 64, 134, 147
Tradition, 19
Trotter, James, 104
Tucker, Beverley, 50, 51, 65
Tucker, George, 150, 152–53
Tucker, St. George, 139
Turnbull, Robert, 29
Turner, Jack, 160
Turner, Nat, 155, 160–61, 164, 167, 169, 173, 174, 184, 189, 204–5
Turner, Victor, 189
Twain, Mark, 187, 190, 204, 211–12
Tyburn, 211
Tyler, John, 163

Unionism, 20–21, 29–30, 59–60
University of the South, 49
The Unvanquished, 86, 144

Valor, 27–30, 45, 48, 57, 60–62. *See also* Courage; Masculinity
Vengeance, *see* Revenge
Vesey, Denmark, 159, 167
Vesey plot, 159, 161, 163, 164, 172, 177
Victorianism, 23, 86, 96, 115
Violence: continuity of, 27; in the culture, 144–53; and nuclear family, 214. *See also* Honor; Masculinity; *specific criminal offense*
Virtue, 22, 23
Voget, Fred W., 135

Walker, Robert J., 33
Washington, George, 48

Watson, Elkanah, 127
Watson, Thomas, 191–92
Wells, Frances Ann Foster, 217–18, 225, 233
White supremacy, *see* Ethics: racial; Racism
Wigfall, Louis T., 151
Wigglesworth, Michael, 52
Williams, Benjamin, 165, 171–72
Williams, John Sharp, 191
Williams, Sarah Hicks, 126, 157
Williams, Tennessee, 125
Wilson, Margaret, 87, 226
Witches, 11
Withers, Thomas Jefferson, 157
Wives: and barrenness, 93–94, 226; as killers, 33–34, 194–95; as victims of abuse, 99, 201, 202, 214–17, 222, 225, 226, 232–34, 240, 245. *See also* Childbearing; Divorce; Husband-wife relations; Motherhood; Women
Women, black: "shamelessness" of, 94, 113–14; mammies, 71. *See also* Miscegenation; Mulattoes
Women, white: careers for, 87–88; and chastity, 91, 200; enforced dependency of, 87–89; *see also* as heroines and arbiters of male honor, 27–28, 36–38, 89–93, 139–40; and lineage, 64–70; as ornaments, 85–86, role of, 17, 35–38, 91–93; and slavery, 114; and work, 126. *See also* Childrearing; Husband-wife relations; Motherhood; Spinsters; Wives
Wood, Nancy A., 216, 219, 225, 228, 233
Woodward, C. Vann, 93
Wren, Woodson, 219–20, 235

Yancey, William L., 29, 122, 150, 151
Yeomanry, 31, 68–70, 98, 103–4, 199. *See also* Poor whites
York, Brantley, 80–81
Youths, *see* Males, in youth